AMERICAN
WOMAN

AMERICAN WOMAN

—

The Transformation of the Modern First Lady, from Hillary Clinton to Jill Biden

—

KATIE ROGERS

CROWN
NEW YORK

Published in the United States by Crown,
an imprint of the Crown Publishing Group,
a division of Penguin Random House LLC, New York.

CROWN and the Crown colophon are registered
trademarks of Penguin Random House LLC.

Photograph credits appear on page 237.

Library of Congress Cataloging-in-Publication Data
Names: Rogers, Katie (Journalist), author.
Title: American woman / Katie Rogers.
Description: First edition. | New York : Crown, 2024. |
Includes bibliographical references and index.
Identifiers: LCCN 2023034122 (print) | LCCN 2023034123 (ebook) |
ISBN 9780593240564 (hardcover) | ISBN 9780593240571 (ebook)
Subjects: LCSH: Biden, Jill. | Presidents' spouses—United States—Biography. |
Presidents' spouses—United States—History. | Presidents' spouses—
United States—Conduct of life. Classification: LCC E918.B53 .R644 2024 (print) |
LCC E918.B53 (ebook) | DDC 973.934092 [B]—dc23/eng/20230824
LC record available at https://lccn.loc.gov/2023034122
LC ebook record available at https://lccn.loc.gov/2023034123

Printed in the United States of America on acid-free paper

crownpublishing.com

2 4 6 8 9 7 5 3 1

FIRST EDITION

Book design by Barbara M. Bachman

For my grandmothers
and for Lily, my mermaid

CONTENTS

INTRODUCTION

J ILL BIDEN IS AT PEACE NEAR THE OCEAN.

There are several long weekends during the year when the First Lady slips away from the White House and into a car bound for Rehoboth Beach, the Delaware town where her family has vacationed for decades. Rehoboth, 120 miles away from Washington, is the kind of place where wealthy families have a beach house, and where less wealthy families can afford to spend a week bunking in a place near the boardwalk, dipping their toes in the surf, and buying tickets for carnival rides that fling them high into the air. Unlike other presidential getaways, like the exclusive Martha's Vineyard, Rehoboth is easily accessible. The town is a perfect fit for the Bidens, a family that is not ordinary but loves the way ordinary sounds.

The beaches in Rehoboth are clean, and Jill can stroll and breathe in the fresh air a few paces from her ever-watchful Secret Service detail. On the boardwalk, tourists can buy a greasy bucket of fries, or a tray of Dolle's saltwater taffy, and follow it up with Biden's Summer White House Cherry ice cream at the nearby Ice Cream Store, a presidential favorite. The water is refreshing, with waves that deposit swimmers back on shore in a jumble of sand and swimsuits, along with hundreds of silver-dollar-sized jellyfish and sand crabs that clump along the shore in the evenings.

In the middle of town, there is a bookstore called Browseabout

Books, the kind of place where the owner picks her favorites and leaves little recommendation notes for shoppers. Jill, a teacher who is always reading—and when she is not reading, she is often grading papers—occasionally drops in to peruse the aisles. Despite her love of the beach, she is not a fan of beach reads, gravitating instead toward heftier works of fiction or volumes of poetry; she discovered Amanda Gorman, the young poet she chose to read at her husband's inauguration, at a poetry reading at the Library of Congress. She enjoys the grilled fish from DiFebo's on First Street and the eggs at a restaurant that is just called Egg.

The Bidens keep a home about a mile outside of town, in the North Shores neighborhood. Deer stroll along the streets, unafraid of the traffic, which now includes the regular appearance of the hulking SUVs that ferry Joe, Jill, and members of their extended family to their beach house. The house is near Cape Henlopen State Park and Gordons Pond, where the First Couple enjoys bike rides and strolls. The surrounding yellow-and-green grassland is wild until it reaches the blue ocean, which is visible from their back porch. In the evenings, Jill opens the windows to her bedroom so she can hear the waves. When she wants to open a window at the White House, Secret Service officers must first clear out the park below.

Years ago, Joe told Jill that he'd buy her a beach house whenever enough money materialized. An $8 million book deal for both Bidens, after they served as vice president and Second Lady in the Obama administration, finally provided the appropriate windfall for a $2.7 million home, a reward for a wife and partner who fervently campaigned alongside him as he ran for the presidency three separate times over their five decades together. Many of the homes out here have nicknames, but the Bidens are much too earnest to name their house after a beach pun. A PROMISE KEPT reads a sign hanging outside, echoing the title of Joe's first memoir.

The three-story house has been painted a color close to "Biden blue," a color unofficially adopted by the family, which is deep but not deep enough to be navy, and was the special color used for wooden eggs during the annual White House Easter Egg Roll. The blue home sits several doors down from a house stuffed with Secret Service agents. (The agency won't say if the home is a rental.) The agents take breaks in leather recliners when they are not out monitoring the neighborhood.

During an interview at her beach home in the fall of 2022 just before the midterm elections, the First Lady called out some advice: "Grab onto the stair railing. It's the mom in me." On this sunny day, she was taking a brief break from a busy schedule that required flying around the country to support Democrats in tight races. In between teaching English classes and visiting hurricane disaster zones with her husband, she had popped up at fundraisers in California and Florida as a much-requested campaigner for Democratic Senate, House, and gubernatorial candidates.

After I passed the threshold, a photo of Beau Biden was one of the first things I saw. Beau was Joe Biden's eldest son, who died of brain cancer at age forty-six in 2015, and had recently left his position as attorney general of Delaware when he died. (He was the one who was supposed to be president, as anyone in this orbit, and especially his father, will tell you.) Beau appeared in a poster-sized black-and-white photo that hangs along the staircase, the same image that used to hang in Joe's Senate office. In that photo, which the First Lady says was taken during one of Joe's many political campaigns, a young Jill stood between Beau and his younger brother, Hunter. Beau's death, and the profound, gutting effect it had on his family, is hard to over-state.

According to both Bidens, Jill first met the boys in early 1975, months after she began dating Joe. He had lost his first wife, Neilia, and his infant daughter, Naomi, in a car crash in December 1972, just weeks after winning his first Senate race. When Jill met him, she was twenty-three and recovering from the end of her first marriage, a youthful whirlwind she has called a "counterfeit love" and a relation-ship that left her scared to let her emotional guard down. The idea of marrying Joe, a thirty-two-year-old widower still knitting his family back together, was daunting. Which is why it took Joe five marriage proposals before she finally said yes.

Beau—a miniature version of his father, eyes always on the future—had pushed his father to marry her: "Dad, we think we should marry Jill," she says he declared on behalf of the family when he was seven years old. When Jill married Joe in June 1977, the boys came with them on a mini honeymoon, taking their own room in a hotel suite. Though Neilia would always be "Mommy," the boys began to call Jill "Mom."

And that's just the bit of history visible from the foyer. Under the photos, Commander, the family's German shepherd—a canine roughly the size of a miniature pony—lazed inside a massive crate at the bottom of the stairs. Commander was given to the Bidens after the death of Champ, the elderly dog that reminded Joe and Jill of an easier phase of their lives together, the one where Beau was still alive. After Major, a rescue dog and Champ's helpmate, bit at least one Secret Service agent, he was shipped off to live with family friends, according to the White House. (In this house, even the family dog has a backstory. Commander, like his predecessor Major, had his own problems with adjusting to White House life, which entailed biting several agents, according to reports.) In February 2023, the beach house itself was caught in the political maelstrom that is the modern presidency: When a cache of classified documents was found in the closet of a think tank office set up for Joe after his vice presidency, the Biden homes were swept by federal investigators. None were found in Rehoboth.

Upstairs, in the large kitchen and dining room, a welcoming amount of clutter bespoke a lived-in house. SUNNY DAYS AND STARLIT NIGHTS read a sign on the mantel, the sort of tchotchke you'd find in a HomeGoods store. The room was also filled with the trappings of a life in political office, including a life preserver that read, of course, BIDEN, hanging near a little bobblehead of Joe. There were bathing suits in frames on the wall. There was a stain of unknown provenance on the carpet.

Several White House aides were stationed throughout the house. Mala Adiga, the First Lady's longtime policy adviser, took a call on a porch overlooking the park. At the dining room table sat Anthony

Bernal, the First Lady's senior adviser, loyal enforcer, and one of the only people she really trusts. Her East Wing does not have a chief of staff. Bernal, her closest nonfamilial confidant, is the person in charge.

An Arizona native and onetime child actor, Bernal got his start in politics as an official for the Clinton White House, where he worked in trip planning and scheduling for Vice President Al Gore. Bernal's entry into the Biden orbit came during the 2008 presidential campaign, when Joe Biden was chosen as President Barack Obama's vice-presidential running mate and Bernal was hired as a scheduler for the spouse of the vice-presidential candidate. It was not a smooth transition: The Obama brain trust, having just sunk the powerful Clinton machine that everyone once thought was invincible, had no interest in taking strategic advice or additional requests from Joe, who'd served in the Senate for thirty-six years—and lost two prior presidential primary campaigns. Enter Bernal, who quickly won over Jill by bonding with her as she adjusted to seeing her husband treated as a sidekick rather than the north star of a campaign's orbit. It was the start of a loyal relationship that has lasted over fifteen years. When Obama won, the pair celebrated with French fries and champagne. (Christopher Freeman, a caterer who worked for the Bidens in the vice president's residence, said that Joe did not drink alcohol, but Jill enjoys a good glass of wine. She is, he said, "an oenophile of the first degree.")

With a perpetual half smile and darting eyes that never seem to stop assessing the room around him, Bernal is known for his ability to create the world Jill wants. In the Biden White House, he is powerful and adept at wrangling schedules and resources, but he has also been known to make life hell for junior aides who find him to be impatient, demanding, and overbearing. At times, people close to her question just how aware Jill is of her enforcer's abrupt nature, but she is not unaware. She has told people who have grown frustrated with him that they need to bring up their concerns with him directly.

Bernal proved his value to the Bidens years ago by fiercely guarding the family's privacy when Beau was sick. Now, he is the engine behind some of the First Lady's most publicized and popular decisions, including a secret trip to meet with the First Lady of war-torn

Ukraine in May 2022. He was also a driving force in helping her continue teaching as First Lady, working behind the scenes to make it happen even as Joe and his aides had expressed doubt. Bernal's power within the administration is derived from his unflinching devotion. The tight-knit Biden family prizes loyalty from their aides, and Bernal delivers: "The guy would walk in front of a speeding train for her," a person close to Jill told me.

Yards away from where Bernal sat in Rehoboth, a fireplace was lit in the living room. Willow, the family's gray cat and First Feline of the United States, was sunning herself in a reading nook. (A former barnyard fuzzball who caught Jill's eye on the campaign trail, Willow has improved her station in life: She now wakes the president up at night by walking on his head.) The First Lady spoke softly to the cat before she sat down on a vanilla-colored couch.

This home is Jill's happy place, her aides say, where she likes to relax and let her family parade through with sandy feet and wet beach towels. Her life is complicated and overscheduled, and she wants things here to feel easy. On this day, though, she was dressed for work, wearing a navy-colored shirtdress with matching booties. Her buttery blond hair had been curled into loose waves, and her makeup looked dewy. At seventy-two years old, she has maintained a rigorous fitness schedule that has kept her in athletic shape. The dress brought out her eyes, which are bright pools with a shade somewhere between cerulean and navy. Biden blue.

On the other side of the living room sat two of Jill's communications aides. One was Elizabeth Alexander, an inscrutable and practical force of nature who has been with the Bidens since Joe was in the Senate. A Texas-born attorney, she can take a litigator's approach to shielding the First Family from unflattering stories and headlines, and she is one of the few non-relatives in the Biden orbit who is known to deliver unvarnished advice about the most sensitive of matters, including Hunter Biden, the president's troubled son. Vanessa Valdivia, the First Lady's press secretary and a well-liked new addition to the close-knit team, sat nearby. Both held notepads, ready to capture snippets of conversation that might need to be walked back or clarified.

Over decades spent in the public eye, Jill has never particularly enjoyed the part of the job where she sits and talks about her life. ("Why do they think I'm interesting?" she has asked her aides when they come to her with yet another interview request.) She seems more at ease when she is talking about her husband's accomplishments, preferably on the stump, than answering questions that steer her toward introspection. I asked her if she felt it possible to keep anything about herself private when she has lived in the public eye ever since she was first introduced as Joe's new bride in a news article, all the way back in 1977.

"I don't think there's really much difference between my public persona and my private persona," she replied. "I mean—you wouldn't—but if you saw me in the classroom," she said, acknowledging that reporters have been forcefully walled off from this territory. "You've seen me out. I mean, do you think I'm much different in public and in private?"

She often answers a question with a question, which is either a way to keep the interviewer at arm's length or a tic developed after decades in a classroom. She used the same tactic when I asked her about her reputation in the White House for bluntly pointing out when she feels like an adviser has made a mistake: "I don't think that's a bad thing. Do you?" I didn't.

There are few parts of her life that she feels she has not offered up for public consumption. The rest of her private life—or the version of it meant for the public—is here, in her beach home, surrounded by aides and animals and artifacts and deep losses and sky-touching wins, sitting in front of a reporter.

"I don't feel like I'm this nebulous kind of woman, you know, that people don't know. I hope that they see me for who I am. I mean, I hope I'm just like your sister or your friend that you want to go have a glass of wine with. Because that's who I am. That's truly who I am."

Jill's allies, several of whom were preapproved by the White House to speak about her, and many others who were not, all describe a woman who is a more resilient and powerful force in her husband's life than many realize. Her friends, loved ones, and colleagues extol her commitment to her family but also to her career: She has taught at community colleges for thirty years, first at Delaware Tech and then at Northern Virginia Community College, just outside of Washington, D.C. Her legacy as First Lady was cemented before she ever moved into the White House: She is the first one in history to keep a day job.

"She's just grounded in her friends and her family," said Mary Doody, a former colleague and close friend. "It always did center her. She's not a creature of Washington. She was never, and neither was the president. She makes time for her family, exercise, reading, and teaching. And that's what grounds her."

Jill is the more disciplined communicator in her marriage. She rarely strays from talking points. A self-described introvert, she is a more opaque public figure than her husband, who is prone to over-sharing and off-the-cuff comments. Some polling suggests that Americans have a more favorable view of Jill than Joe—several modern First Ladies could say the same about their favorability compared with their husbands—but another swath of the public remains unsure of what to think about her, which some observers say could mean, at least in part, that her work as First Lady has not been as attention-grabbing as her initial decision to continue teaching was.

"The one area where I would say she is not doing as well as I had hoped is her media coverage," Myra Gutin, a historian who studies First Ladies, said in an interview. "The First Lady always has more difficulty getting coverage in Washington and does much better when she's out on the road. I think Jill Biden is going through the same thing."

As First Lady, Jill has continued a road-warrior streak developed over decades spent campaigning. She has evolved from a reluctant campaigner who was self-conscious about her Philly-regional accent to an adept messenger able to log fifteen-hour days on the road—*and* a spin class. ("She gets after it," Logan Coffey, a SoulCycle instructor in Los Angeles, told *Politico* of her vigorous approach to working out.) She likes being on the road, traveling the country, with weekends at home with the extended Biden clan—plus pets—in Delaware or at Camp David. This often seems to take precedence over her policy portfolio, which has included supporting military families, cancer research, and free community college—an initiative Democrats traded away in negotiations over a social spending package.

Though Jill has allowed glimpses into her internal life, like other modern First Ladies, her East Wing team forcefully pushes back against inquiries into sensitive parts of her life, including her family and—paradoxically—her day-to-day life as a teacher. Though she speaks often of her career and has made it the central focus of her public identity, the White House has walled off her teaching career, barring journalists from covering her work in the classroom and requesting that employees at a public community college immediately reroute media requests to them. Over time, Jill has become as adept as any other modern political figure at managing her reputation and public image.

When they got engaged all those years ago, Joe had promised her that her life would never change. Her life, of course, has changed dramatically, but she insists that she has not. Being First Lady, she says, is an honor, but it's also just another responsibility she has embraced. At her core, she still feels as though she is a working mother. She is still trying to balance it all.

"It's not really a job," she said of being First Lady, the most-scrutinized volunteer gig in American politics. "It's just another identity you have on."

OVER THE COURSE OF American history, over fifty women held the title of First Lady, but there is little consensus about what makes a First Lady "good" or "bad." As women in the public eye understand all too well, the same traits that earn them praise in one situation—independence, forthrightness, even loyalty—can be viewed as liabilities in another.

Americans expect a lot from our First Ladies. We want them to smilingly follow a rigid calendar that delivers a wholesome and dutiful slate of events, from the White House Easter Egg Roll to the annual Christmas tree unveiling. We expect them to give nice speeches, write nice letters, and adhere to protocol. We're riveted by their fashion choices, but also, do we *really* have to talk about what they wear? (For the last time: Yes, because these women have used fashion both as a tool for diplomacy and as a conduit to express their feelings. One prime example: Michelle Obama's no-frills ponytail and muted maroon coat accessorized the scowl she wore to President Donald J. Trump's inauguration.) We expect them to be the stoic and strong presence behind the man, the person who keeps a bird's-eye view of the staffing dramas and the influence peddling, the holder of the grudges. Their appearance and utterances are expected to appropriately fit every prism of our kaleidoscope of expectations of American womanhood. We believe they should weather partisan attacks and personal vitriol and still fulfill the role out of the kindness of their hearts. We project our raw, half-baked opinions about the duties of motherhood and the pitfalls of modern careerism onto them.

Yet we don't pay them, we don't give them a formal blueprint for how any of this is supposed to be done, and, until Jill Biden, we hadn't ever seen one of them demand to hold on to a day job. Nothing is too small to attract commentary: If the First Lady of the United States scrapes her hair into a scrunchie, as Jill did shortly after moving into the White House, the world has something to say. If the glassware runs out at an East Wing–organized state dinner and leaves invitees grumbling and starved for social lubricant, reporters like me will write a story about it. When Jill compared the diversity of the Hispanic community to breakfast tacos and mispronounced the word "bodega," the misstep ended up as a demerit on the First Lady's Wikipedia page.

And yet every First Lady, in her own way, has challenged what is expected of her. Jill's predecessor, Melania Trump, is the most notorious modern example of bucking expectations, but an earlier one is Louisa Adams, an English-born First Lady and an adept hostess, who walked away from the limelight once her husband, John Quincy Adams, won the presidency. Adams had not won the popular vote, and the news coverage of his British wife often raised unfair questions about her loyalty to her adopted country. According to accounts, the bitter election season took its toll, sending the once lively hostess into a depression. She spent much of her time in the White House eating chocolate, playing the harp, and writing plays about a repressed woman, a character she based on her life. One such play was titled *Suspicion, or Persecuted Innocence.*

I've been fascinated with First Ladies since college, when I visited an exhibit called *Jacqueline Kennedy: The White House Years* at the Field Museum in Chicago. The exhibition was curated by the Metropolitan Museum of Art and the John F. Kennedy Library and Museum, with assistance from the longtime *Vogue* editor Hamish Bowles. I loved how the curators deftly meshed the idea of substance and style—there is always such a fine line between the two—and made the subtle point that Jacqueline Kennedy's power as a diplomacy builder on behalf of the American people was one of the most overlooked of her public achievements.

Her trip to Paris in 1961 was a memorable part of her legacy. Jacqueline, who had studied abroad in Paris in college, charmed French officials and artists with her knowledge of the French language and culture. ("I am the man who accompanied Jacqueline Kennedy to Paris, and I have enjoyed it," her proud, if slightly upstaged, husband quipped at one point during that state visit.) During her final dinner, she remarked to one of her companions that it would be a dream to host the *Mona Lisa,* one of the country's most valuable national treasures, in the United States. A year later, the *Mona Lisa* was shipped across the Atlantic Ocean so that millions of Americans could see Da Vinci's masterpiece for themselves. I was born and raised in a small town in the Midwest. When I saw the Jacqueline Kennedy exhibit, I was only beginning to understand just how deeply the East Coast, male-dominated worlds of politics and media had shaped my understanding of influence and power. But I didn't enjoy the exhibit because it was about a woman and her fashion choices. I enjoyed the exhibit because it was about how an intelligent woman had figured out a way to start a conversation between Americans and the rest of the world—during the height of the Cold War, no less. To me, that looked a lot like power.

Years later, I began covering the White House during the first months of the Trump administration, and the lessons of that exhibit I first saw all those years ago held true: First Ladies are at their most successful when they trust their instincts and draw from their own experiences when they communicate with the public. Melania Trump's humanity—and her identity as a mother—was visible when she used her platform to raise awareness for children born with opioid addiction or visited with mothers who had been affected by the country's opioid epidemic. Every First Lady, no matter how controversial, can start important conversations and hold up issues that can fall between the cracks while the daily drama of governing plays out in Washington. But Melania Trump would end up teaching Americans her own crucial lesson about the role: There are no formal requirements attached to it, just expectations. A First Lady can do as little or as much in response to those expectations as she pleases.

When Jill Biden took over, she, like her husband, embraced the chance to reset the relationship between the White House and the American public. Neither Biden wanted to be at the center of a 24/7 reality television show, and both wanted to represent what Joe Biden was promising: stable governing.

I saw her story as modern. She came of age during the 1960s, when young women were starting to wrangle with the idea that they did not necessarily need to be wives and mothers to be successful or happy. She married young and divorced young, married again and then went on to become the matriarch of a complicated blended family. She has struggled with balancing her own ambitions with her identity as a political spouse. She is educated. She is influential with her husband and his advisers in ways the public does not often see. But on the other hand, she's got her own schedule to handle, because she works full-time. She is present for every major political discussion involving her husband and sits in during the interview process on most major Biden staff hires, from cabinet secretaries to spokespeople. Sometimes, she gets her own separate audience with a new hire.

The more I learned about her, the more I began to see that her experience is the culmination of a run of several modern First Ladies who have held the position since the turn of the century, beginning with Hillary Clinton. To be sure, there have been other influential First Ladies throughout American history, but only members of this group have had to contend with rapid changes in technology, the calcification of our tribal politics, and an ever-evolving debate about what (or how much) American women can want for themselves, whether it is simply to be paid the same amount as men or to be elected president. So I set out to write the first definitive exploration of the role of the twenty-first-century First Lady, painting a comprehensive portrait of Jill Biden and tracing the evolution of the First Lady's role from ceremonial figurehead to political operative.

After taking a jaunt through First-Lady history, this book starts with Hillary Clinton, the first of this modern and millennial crop of First Women, and explores how she learned—the hard way, and more than once—that the position is still surrounded by guardrails, some visible and others hidden in the political underbrush. The book travels forward and, with fresh reporting, tells the stories of the women who've held the position since: Laura Bush became a wartime First Lady after the September 11 attacks; Michelle Obama, whose identity as the first Black woman to hold the role was celebrated but was a source of immense pressure; Melania Trump, whose sporadic attempts at traditionalism devolved into absenteeism by the end of her tenure; and Jill, who is balancing her career with her unpaid job as the Biden family's only effective political surrogate.

As the president and his last surviving son, Hunter, have become targets for conservatives in a rapidly toxifying political landscape, Jill has emerged as the powerful guardian of the Biden inner circle, defining herself as a "Philly girl" who is not to be crossed. She is powerful within the Biden White House and was an enthusiastic supporter of her husband's decision to announce a run for reelection at age eighty. But she has struggled with low approval ratings, critical headlines, and a more volatile Washington than the one she first encountered as a young political spouse in the 1970s. Her decision to keep teaching as First Lady also took more internal lobbying than is publicly known—it is a previously untold story that shows just how much power she wields in the Biden orbit.

She and her immediate predecessors have all struggled with questions about their personal influence on the most politically powerful person on the planet. They all have struggled with defining their legacies. They all have faced criticism for the personal choices they've made in the interest of protecting their professional identities or shielding their families from scrutiny. They of course live singularly privileged lives, but, like many American women, they struggle with issues surrounding identity, ambition, and the expectations of others.

Something else makes these women unique compared with others who held the role earlier in history: Not only is their every move captured, but more people exist on more platforms to vocally criticize everything they say or do. With the country essentially polarized into swaths of deep red and blue, this means that intense coverage of every misstep is virtually assured. When Jill invited both the losers and the winners of the NCAA women's championship game to visit the White House in the spring of 2023, she found herself at the center of a white-hot debate about sportsmanship, competition, and race. All her office could say was that she meant no harm.

There is immense pressure to perform: "It's a role that I think has become one of the most important in the White House," said Lauren Wright, a professor at Princeton University who studies the evolution of First Ladies, "I could even argue, from a messaging standpoint, the most important one."

This book is based on previously unreported correspondence, firsthand recordings and notes, documents from Freedom of Information Act requests, and interviews with more than 125 people. The interviews include two with Jill Biden and one with Hillary Clinton, whose time in the White House illuminated all of the role's thorny, invisible boundaries for the women who came after her. I thank both First Ladies for their time and their candor, and Jill Biden for inviting me into her home in Rehoboth. Many interviews were conducted on background—which means people spoke, at least initially, without wanting to be quoted—so that those close to the First Lady, her office, and the Biden family could speak freely.

Only a small group of women can understand just how unforgiving the public's expectations can be, but this modern group of First Ladies is not exactly a sisterhood. The role has been complicated by increasingly tribal politics.

"Until relatively recently, it was a safe place. I felt like I could ask questions or raise concerns, and somebody would be willing to engage with you," said Hillary Clinton.

Jill, who watched Michelle Obama at close range for eight years, arrived in the East Wing with a more refined understanding of the pitfalls and potential of the role than almost anyone. Her predecessor, Melania Trump, was a newcomer to politics who had to learn those obstacles in real time, but her sporadic efforts at traditional duties were overshadowed by a husband who was impeached twice and refused to concede his election loss. Melania's former aides argue that her tumultuous experience with the role created a clear runway for Jill Biden.

"We really reminded people that there is no defined role for the First Lady," said Stephanie Grisham, who served as Melania's spokeswoman, chief of staff, and communications director, roles she punctuated with a stint as White House press secretary. "We went to the extreme, but we reminded people you should be able to do it the way you want to do it."

The growing pains that each of these women have experienced in the role reflect larger conversations about gender, race, and culture that many Americans have at their kitchen tables before they ever set foot inside a voting booth. First Ladies are not perfect avatars for American womanhood, given the fact that they live in a protective bubble, but they are often looked to as nurturers and mediators in times of tumult—this is a gendered expectation, and one that falls upon women from all walks of life. They are expected to rise above the fray without becoming enmeshed in the bare-knuckle world of political debate—a lot like that elusive "suburban woman" slice of the electorate that tends to decide presidential elections.

At work and at home, women and girls are told they can do and be anything. First Ladies are imperfect models of that promise; they must acknowledge that theirs is still a supporting role, and their existence implies that there is a ceiling still to be broken. But those conversations have become franker—and more raw—than ever before.

As First Lady, Jill Biden has been willing to address those disappointments when she hosts equal-pay events at the White House. After *Roe v. Wade*, which had granted women a constitutional right to abortion, was overturned in June 2022, she spoke plainly about what was at stake for women and girls if reproductive freedoms continued to be restricted. Jill and her predecessors have shown American women what is possible, but they remain reminders of the uncomfortable double standards that still exist for women who dare to push boundaries.

AMERICAN
WOMAN

CHAPTER ONE

MERMAIDS

IN JUNE 1990, BARBARA BUSH VISITED THE CAMPUS OF Wellesley College to perform the routine duty of delivering a commencement speech to that year's graduating class. She was roughly eighteen months into her tenure as First Lady and was in the midst of a busy graduation season; she had already delivered remarks to graduates at the University of Pennsylvania and St. Louis University. Her appearance at Wellesley, an elite all-female school in the woods of eastern Massachusetts, was supposed to be the sort of choreographed assignment that she could carry out in between fundraising trips to Texas and White House events in Washington.

But Barbara had known that her Wellesley visit would be different. The students hadn't wanted her to come.

The year had marked the dawn of a new decade, and a generation of young American women had been raised on the promise that they would benefit from the landmark political and cultural changes that had occurred during their lifetimes. The Equal Pay Act of 1963 had prohibited workplace and pay discrimination on the basis of sex. In 1973, *Roe v. Wade* established a constitutional right to abortion. The 1980s saw women enter the workforce at unprecedented levels, prompting new discussions about how to balance having a family and a career—and whether it was at all possible. So the First Lady's trip to Massachusetts was overshadowed by a roiling debate over whether Barbara—then the sixty-four-year-old wife of a Republican president and a woman whose primary life achievements included supporting her family—deserved to deliver the Wellesley commencement address.

"Wellesley teaches that we will be rewarded on the basis of our own merit, not on that of a spouse," read a petition that circulated among students protesting the First Lady's speech. "To honor Barbara Bush as a commencement speaker is to honor a woman who has gained recognition through the achievements of her husband, which contravenes what we have been taught over the last four years at Wellesley."

Barbara had not been their first choice. That privilege had gone to the Black novelist Alice Walker, who won the 1983 Pulitzer Prize for *The Color Purple,* an exploration of Black womanhood, gender roles, sexual discovery, and resilience. American feminism was slowly beginning to expand its gaze from the white middle class to include women of color, but Walker was vocal in her belief that feminism—at least as it was understood, discussed, and marketed—had not been inclusive enough. She had coined the term "womanist" to make the point that feminism—at least as far as a generation of white women had defined it—largely excluded the experiences of women of color. Walker was a provocative and accomplished author who could challenge a graduating class primarily composed of middle-class white women, but she declined the invitation.

The invitation was repurposed and sent to the Bush White House, where it promptly sparked a debate about modern feminism that drew national attention. The graduates were trying to understand, really, the limits of what they were allowed to want. Was it a career? Was it a career and a marriage? Was it a career, a marriage, and children? This was the first generation to be introduced to the idea of "having it all," a phrase that has, for decades, prompted endless searching discussions but no universal answer. (If you ask Jill Biden, a working mother and grandmother with a demanding schedule, what "having it all" means, she will look at you quizzically before answering, "I don't think you can really have it all. You know, at least not at the same time. And I think I would never say that for myself.")

The criticism over the invitation to Barbara was so widespread that even the president got involved. President George H. W. Bush could not resist defending his wife: "I think these young women can have a lot to learn from Barbara Bush and from her unselfishness and from her advocacy of literacy and of being a good mother and a lot of other things," the president said, according to a front-page story in *The New York Times* that appeared in May 1990.

On graduation day, the First Lady appeared onstage at Wellesley with Raisa Gorbacheva, the wife of the Soviet leader Mikhail Gorbachev, who at the time was overseeing the dissolution of the Soviet Union. Their appearance was meant to telegraph a new sense of optimism that the Cold War would finally end.

Barbara wore a robe, her trademark string of pearls, and brick-red lipstick. Her white hair was rolled into a tuft of snowy curls. She understood that she wasn't exactly the picture of modernity. She had dropped out of school after two years at Smith College to marry George Bush, a handsome navy warplane pilot who had narrowly survived a combat mission in September 1944. (They married in January 1945.) The couple moved to Texas and had six children, with Barbara watching over the brood as her husband built an oil business and, later, a career in politics.

Forty-five years later, she found herself speaking to a crop of young and idealistic graduates who had been conditioned to question the offerings of domesticity. Instead of trying to assure the young women that she was one of them, and instead of being defensive about her background and her decisions to marry rather than pursue a career, she honestly and elegantly drew contrasts between her generation and theirs.

"Now, I know your first choice for today was Alice Walker—guess how I know—known for *The Color Purple*," she told the crowd. "Instead you got me, known for the color of my hair."

The speech that followed was earthy and full of humor, delivered with the sly smiles and in-on-the-joke grimaces of a woman who understood what the crowd expected from her and who was intent on delivering something else.

She recounted a story by the author Robert Fulghum about a young pastor who created a game called Giants, Wizards, and Dwarfs for a group of unruly children. "You have to decide now," the pastor instructed the children, "which you are . . . a giant, a wizard or a dwarf."

As the children rushed to sort themselves into categories, the pastor felt a small girl tugging at his pants leg: "But where do the mermaids stand?" she asked. The pastor told her that mermaids didn't exist, but the little girl protested, insisting that she was, indeed, a mermaid.

"She intended to take her place wherever mermaids fit in the scheme of things," the First Lady told the graduates in the crowd. "Where do mermaids stand, all of those who are different, those who do not fit the boxes and the pigeonholes?"

There had been so much controversy surrounding the event that three major networks aired it live, an unusual occurrence for a First Lady's speech. She urged the women in the crowd to embrace their passions, nurture their relationships, and prioritize their time with their families.

"At the end of your life, you will never regret not having passed one more test, winning one more verdict, or closing one more deal," she told them. "You will regret time not spent with a husband, a child, a friend, or a parent."

Americans who observed the speech that day saw a First Lady who used grit and grace to nod to a new generation and acknowledge that times were changing: "Somewhere out in this audience may even be someone who will one day follow in my footsteps and preside over the White House as the president's spouse," she said. "And I wish him well."

When she was finished, the graduates got to their feet and cheered. The stakes had been high and the margin for error was slim, but it only took eleven minutes for the First Lady, whose very presence had been the subject of protest and ridicule, to disarm her audience. When

Barbara arrived back at the White House, aides had strung up a banner to greet her home: A JOB WELLESLEY DONE.

"You can see the winds of change in that crowd of women," said Anita McBride, who served as chief of staff to Laura Bush and now studies the history of First Ladies. "That, for me, is really a signal for the modern age of the First Lady. Society was changing, the generations were changing, and they had different expectations for women's roles."

THE ROLE OF FIRST LADY is an unpaid position that bestows upon its holder no formal responsibilities, only the pressure of meeting the ever-shifting expectations of the president, his aides and allies, the American people, and a restive press corps. In biographies and memoirs, the women who have served the American people alongside their husbands have grappled with the responsibility and difficulty of occupying this rare space in government.

This singular dynamic means that First Ladies have always struggled to balance who they are expected to be as First Lady with the person they were before. Attorneys, teachers, housewives, mothers, grandmothers, activists, models, economists, actresses, librarians, and former congressional aides have all served in the role. Some struggled with addiction, illness, infidelity, and, in a handful of high-profile, supremely unlucky cases, the deaths of their husbands or children.

All of them, at one point or another, have found the experience stifling. The loss of a basic feeling of freedom has been a perennial concern since the dawn of the republic when Martha Washington wrote to her niece and described feeling as though she were a "state prisoner" in her role.

"I live a very dull life hear and know nothing that passes in the town—I never goe to the publick place—indeed I think I am more like a state prisoner than anything else, there is certain bounds set for me which I must not depart from—and as I can not doe as I like I am obstinate and stay at home a great deal," she wrote in the letter from Mount Vernon, dated October 23, 1789.

The nebulous nature of the role means that each woman who has held it has had a chance to define it. American history has been punctuated by women who have used their time in office to broaden the role's influence—a move that is generally popular with the public, but only to a point.

Eleanor Roosevelt is perhaps the most enduring example of a First Lady who readjusted the public's expectations about how much a president's spouse could be integrated into his political life. Franklin Delano Roosevelt's expansion of his West Wing staff, deft use of the media, and increased number of government plans ushered the presidency into the modern era. Eleanor had a similarly expansive vision. In 1933, she delivered her first news conference, and since women were traditionally barred from the president's news conferences, she permitted only women to attend. (She also issued the invitation to women, in part, because she believed male reporters would "encroach on my husband's side of the news.") Called "the president's eyes, ears, and legs" by observers, she traveled throughout the United States and brought stories back to her husband, whose bout with polio earlier in life had left him confined to a wheelchair. During World War II, she traveled to England and the South Pacific to visit with American troops stationed overseas. She was active in politics after she left the White House, authoring a syndicated column until shortly before her death in 1962.

Through her efforts to bolster the morale of the military, her interest in soft diplomacy, and her willingness to serve as an emissary for her husband, Eleanor was influential in shaping the public's current understanding of what First Ladies should do and how they can best use their platform. Her work would be a blueprint for the generations of women who would follow.

But she had given up her own ambitions to help her husband win. She left her teaching job three days before her husband was inaugurated, according to Lorena A. Hickok, an Associated Press reporter who wrote a book about her friendship with Eleanor.

"I hate to do it," she told Hickok, according to the book. "I wonder if you have any idea how I hate to do it." During one of her last days with a group of high-school-aged students at the Todhunter School for Girls in New York, Eleanor, who had taught American history and who was now about to become part of it, asked her students to visit her in Washington.

"I've liked teaching more than anything else I've ever done," she told Hickok sadly. "But it's got to go."

Eleanor found ways to keep working and earning her own income, which was important to her. During her first months in the White House, she was contracted as an editor of a parenting magazine called *Babies Just Babies* and took on numerous columnist and magazine-writing jobs. But it would take almost another ninety years for another teacher—Jill Biden—to demand that her husband, his advisers, her advisers, the Secret Service, and a phalanx of attorneys figure out how she would be able to keep her career.

It is difficult to assess what, exactly, makes a First Lady effective. Is it loyalty? Intelligence? Ambition? Even researchers seem unable to ascertain what Americans want from them.

The amount of available research pales in comparison to the work that has been done to identify the qualities that make a president good at the job. Broadly, researchers have found that some of history's most revered commanders in chief have generally been highly ambitious, assertive, and stubborn. They also possess a certain willingness to manipulate the truth to fit their political aims.

One of the few institutions that attempts to measure the effectiveness of First Ladies is the Siena College Research Institute in Loudonville, New York, which periodically publishes a survey of historians that ranks American First Ladies. The respondents, a group of academics and historians, rate each woman on the following metrics: background, value to country, integrity, leadership, White House stewardship, being her "own woman," accomplishments, courage, public image, value to president. (What a dizzying variety of factors! None of which, notably, is ambition.) Over the five times Siena has conducted the poll, Eleanor Roosevelt has been a consistent front-runner. The last one came out in 2014, and the breathless, horserace-style coverage previewed in the press release is entertaining:

> Eleanor Roosevelt Retains Top Spot as America's Best
>   First Lady
> Michelle Obama Enters Study as 5th, Hillary Clinton
>   Drops to 6th
> Clinton Seen First Lady Most as Presidential Material;
>   Laura Bush, Pat Nixon, Mamie Eisenhower, Bess
>   Truman Could Have Done More in Office
> Eleanor & FDR Top Power Couple;
> Mary Drags Lincolns Down in the Ratings

(Poor Mary.)

So much has happened since the poll was last conducted, but at least one portion of the survey was prescient: Hillary Clinton did, indeed, enter the presidential race.

The poll is unforgiving to other First Ladies who spent large stretches of time out of the public eye, often citing illness or tragedy. Eliza Johnson, the wife of President Andrew Johnson, became the First Lady after Abraham Lincoln was assassinated. She suffered from tuberculosis and made only two public appearances during the Johnson presidency. Jane Pierce, the wife of President Franklin Pierce, is a tragic example: Her first son, Franklin, died within days of birth. Her second son, Frank Robert, died from typhus when he was four. The third, eleven-year-old Benjamin, was killed in a train accident during the period between her husband's election and the beginning of his presidency in 1853. Jane occupies last place in the latest Siena survey, though she deserves extra points for courage.

"Each one's had her own adjustment period," said Lisa Kathleen Graddy, an author and curator of an exhibition on First Ladies at the Smithsonian National Museum of American History, "and some never really adjusted at all."

Several First Women were influential with their husbands but had very little interest in the public-facing expectations of the role. Bess Truman, the wife of President Harry S. Truman, never adjusted to her time in the White House and instead preferred frequent visits to her hometown (and her bridge club) in Independence, Missouri. She grudgingly performed the necessary functions but did not enjoy life in Washington, despite helping to oversee a renovation of the White House in the early 1950s. She was also focused on protecting the privacy of her daughter, Margaret, who had spent much of her childhood and all her teenage years as the daughter of an elected official.

The Siena survey suggests that Bess Truman and other contemporaries, including Mamie Eisenhower, could have done more to expand their role. But Bess's theory was that "she was not the one that had been elected," Graddy said. "Therefore, the public only had a certain amount of time that they could expect from her." Privately, like so many First Ladies, she was happy to be a trusted confidante to her husband rather than focus on building out her public profile.

Expectations for politicians—and their wives—had abruptly changed by 1960, when televisions were ubiquitous in American homes. The option to see leaders live and in Technicolor forever altered how the public engaged with political news and evaluated potential leaders. The presidential debate between Richard M. Nixon, the Republican vice president, and John F. Kennedy, then a Democratic senator from Massachusetts, would become infamous partly because of Kennedy's ease with the camera and Nixon's unwillingness to wear makeup, a decision that made his stubble and sweatiness under the lights more visible.

With his ascension to the White House in 1961, President Kennedy promised a more youthful and more worldly approach to the presidency, but his wife, the glamorous thirty-one-year-old Jacqueline Kennedy, would be instrumental in fulfilling his pledge. A college graduate who attended Vassar and George Washington University and had lived in France, she enchanted the news media and the American public with her fashionable style, international trips, and televised renovation of the White House. Shortly after her husband won the presidency, she gave birth to a son, John Fitzgerald Kennedy, Jr., who became the first infant to live at the White House since the beginning of the twentieth century.

Born Jacqueline Lee Bouvier on July 28, 1929, in Southampton, New York, she was elegant and even-keeled, but she had her limits with the public. As a mother, she had endured a miscarriage; the birth of a stillborn child, Arabella; and, in 1963, the loss of a son, Patrick, within days of his birth. She was fiercely protective of her family's privacy. She said she was most proud of her work as a wife and mother and defined her major role as "to take care of the President," according to her White House biography, adding that "if you bungle raising your children, I don't think whatever else you do well matters very much." (She also never much cared for the term "First Lady"—she thought it sounded too much like the name of a racehorse, according to the historian Carl Anthony.)

After the assassination of President Kennedy on November 22, 1963, President Lyndon B. Johnson and Claudia Alta Taylor Johnson, called Lady Bird, moved into the White House. Born on December 22, 1912, in a mansion near Karnack, Texas, Lady Bird was a more politically inclined spouse than her predecessor had been but wielded her influence quietly. Only since her death, in 2007, has the full extent of her support for her husband come into view, thanks to the research of intrepid biographers.

In 1964, when her husband was paralyzed with uncertainty over whether he should run for a full term, he asked Lady Bird to draft a memo exploring her worries, which included concerns over his health and their desire to return home to Texas. She was pragmatic and strategic in presenting a set of options to him—including the idea of dropping out as the first option. She even drafted a resignation statement for him. But despite concerns over his health and the toll the presidency would take on it, she concluded her memo by suggesting he do the best he could for one term, then announce his decision to step aside.

"My conclusion: Stay in," she wrote to him. "Realize it's going to be rough—but remember we worry much in advance about troubles that never happen! Pace yourself, within the limits of your personality. If you lose in November—it's all settled anyway!"

Her plan was prescient: In 1968, at a point of intense, fast-moving cultural change, Johnson announced, during a speech that was ostensibly about the war in Vietnam, that he would not run for reelection.

American failures in Vietnam, largely attributed to missteps taken during the Johnson administration, had prompted widespread protests across the world and in Washington. The civil rights leader Martin Luther King, Jr., was assassinated that spring, triggering riots in dozens of cities across the United States. Two months later, Robert Kennedy, the Democratic presidential candidate and younger brother of President Kennedy, was shot and killed during an event with supporters in Los Angeles.

That November, Richard Nixon won the presidential election by a slim margin and promised he would work to unite the divided country. Though his career would go on to be plagued by the Watergate scandal that eventually forced his resignation, his wife, Pat, stood by him—though always quietly. Born Thelma Catherine Ryan on March 16, 1912, in Ely, Nevada, Pat took pleasure in making her husband's life easier, whether that meant ensuring that his suits were pressed in the morning or standing beside him in endless receiving lines. She disliked life on the campaign trail.

"Even people who can recall the Nixon presidency probably can't remember the sound of her voice," said Katherine Jellison, a professor at Ohio University who studies First Ladies. "She would have preferred a very different kind of life."

The trio of successors who followed—Betty Ford, Rosalynn Carter, and Nancy Reagan—began steadily reasserting the role's public-facing powers, though each of them took a radically different approach.

Born Elizabeth Anne Bloomer on April 8, 1918, in Chicago, Betty was an outspoken former model who had few qualms about disagreeing with her husband or speaking with the press. In September 1974, she hosted a news conference and spoke passionately about her support of the Equal Rights Amendment, which sought equal rights for both sexes. She made phone calls in support of the amendment, whipping up votes and lending her credibility to the uphill fight for its passage. (The ERA later fell short of the thirty-eight states needed for it to be ratified.) Unafraid to discuss issues that were previously seen as taboo, she went public after she was diagnosed with breast cancer and downplayed the idea that she should be embarrassed after undergoing a mastectomy.

"No! Oh, no—heavens, no," she replied. "I've heard women say they'd rather lose their right arm, and I can't imagine it. It's so stupid. I can even wear my evening clothes."

She spoke frankly about sex—it was considered risqué when she announced that she intended to share a bed with her husband, President Gerald Ford, in the White House—and endorsed legalized abortion. (Her husband was against the procedure but did not agree with a national ban.)

"I do not believe that being First Lady should prevent me from expressing my views," she said at a conference in 1975. "Why should my husband's job or yours prevent us from being ourselves? Being ladylike does not require silence." Later in life, she was open about her struggles with addiction and alcoholism and opened the Betty Ford Center in California in 1982.

Then came president Jimmy Carter and his wife, Rosalynn. The daughter of a dressmaker from Plains, Georgia, Eleanor Rosalynn Smith, born on August 18, 1927, earned the nickname "Steel Magnolia" from journalists on the campaign trail. They believed her unassuming exterior masked a tough, influential behind-the-scenes operator. She and her husband publicly maintained that they were equals in their marriage—which, in the 1970s political realm, was still a relatively radical proclamation. Like Betty Ford, she jumped into an area that was frequently seen as taboo for public discussion when she began lobbying for better care for the mentally ill, including advocating for better insurance, care, and research funding. While in office, she became a member of the president's Commission on Mental Health, which made recommendations for improving care for the mentally ill. Those contributions became the basis for the Mental Health Systems Act of 1980, which provided grant funding for community centers. The law was signed just before her husband lost his reelection effort to Ronald Reagan, whose administration quickly dismantled many of the law's provisions.

Rosalynn also became the first to establish a dedicated office space in the East Wing. In 1979, she appointed Edith J. Dobelle as the first chief of staff of the East Wing. Compared with the cramped bustle of the James S. Brady Press Briefing Room and the fabled frenetic pace of the West Wing, the East Wing of the White House can appear unnervingly quiet. Considering all that happens just a hundred feet away, and given how the West Wing captures the public's attention in movies and television shows, the East Wing can feel like a cross between the reading room of a library and one of those fancy sitting rooms where no one is allowed to relax.

In the East Wing, the wood-paneled walls seem to absorb sound—and, with it, the energy that emanates from the other side of the Executive Mansion. In a reception room, oil portraits of mothers and children and grassy landscapes seem resigned to the quiet. The offices are small. The place smells old: It's a slightly musty scent, one of un-cracked books and carpeting unbothered by foot traffic. The lives of the most known (and often least understood) women in American life are guarded here. It makes sense that the place is arranged to feel politely unyielding to visitors.

The East Wing, which was added to the White House in 1942, houses the presidential movie theater, the East Colonnade—known to much of the American public as that window-filled hallway where they put the Christmas trees—and the visitors' entrance. Rosalynn was the first to establish an official office there, and since then, the East Wing has become a formalized arm of the White House where modern First Ladies have worked alongside their chiefs of staff, policy advisers, social secretaries, press aides, and schedulers. While First Ladies since the Carter era have approached their time in the East Wing in different ways—Hillary Clinton opted to spend the bulk of hers in an office in the West Wing—only Melania Trump would choose to avoid it altogether.

Rosalynn Carter's successor, Nancy Reagan, would focus her platform as First Lady on drug awareness, creating the "Just Say No" program that was a hallmark of her time in office. Born Anne Frances Robbins on July 6, 1921, in Manhattan, Nancy was a fledgling film actress when she met Ronald Reagan in November 1949. Their romance evolved into a bond that observers called both passionate and codependent.

While most First Ladies before her had been publicly protective of their families and privately influential with their husbands, Nancy had little interest in downplaying her power. From the moment she and her husband—Ronnie, as she called him—moved into the White House in January 1981, Nancy made no qualms about her place in the administration or in her husband's life. In their romantic and political pursuits, Nancy and Ronnie saw each other not as two individuals but as two pieces that, when fit together, made a whole person. Throughout their lives together, they would say as much in their own words.

Nancy was the child of an unhappy marriage between a struggling actress named Edith Luckett and an insurance agent named Kenneth Robbins. Her parents split up when Nancy was a toddler, and Edie, seeking a career on the road, deposited her daughter in the care of an aunt and uncle who lived in a suburb of Washington, D.C. Years later, Nancy would persuade her mother's second husband, a physician, whom she adored, to adopt her. Dr. Loyal Davis eventually acquiesced, and Nancy eagerly assumed his last name and an identity as his daughter, all but striking any memory of her biological father from the record.

"I'm not a psychologist," her son, Ron Reagan, told the journalist Karen Tumulty for her expansive biography, *The Triumph of Nancy Reagan,* which traces Nancy's life, "but I think she suffered from a kind of separation anxiety ever since and was very concerned about being left—abandoned—her whole life."

When Nancy first met Ronnie, he was a bankable actor and she was making a living playing secretaries and docile wives. Nancy had been swept into a growing investigation by House lawmakers into Hollywood actors and actresses thought to be communist sympathizers, and she thought a meeting with Ronald, then the president of the Screen Actors Guild, could help her. Their first date lasted until 3:30 the next morning.

The pair went on a flurry of dates, but she was not the only person he was taking out on the town. Ronald was in the midst of a separation from his first wife, the actress Jane Wyman. He was hoping for a reconciliation, but he was also spending $750 a month on nightclubs. It was a period of his life he described as an emotional "deep freeze." The child of an alcoholic salesman who moved the Reagan family from one ramshackle apartment to the next in search of a payday, Ron had only known upheaval at home. He took after his mother, Nelle, whom he believed was hardwired to see the good in people. He outran a rough childhood by living in constant motion, until Nancy caught up with him.

The two had a connection that was so strong that it had the tendency to shut everyone else out—aides, children, critics—and the two were still exchanging love letters well into their marriage, including while they pondered a run for the White House in the late 1970s. In a letter dated January 10, 1978, that Tumulty unearthed at the Reagan Library, Nancy revealed her advice on a successful marriage to a young woman named Adrienne Bassuk:

> I've been very lucky—however, I don't ever remember once sitting down and mapping out a blueprint. It just became "we" instead of "I" very naturally and easily. And you live as you never have before despite problems, separation, and conflicts. I suppose mainly you have to be willing—and want—to give. It's not always 50-50. Sometimes one partner gives 90% but then sometimes the other one does—so it all evens out. It's not always easy, and it's something you have to work at, which is what I don't think many young people realize today.
>
> But the rewards are so great. I can't remember what my life was like before, and can't imagine not being married to Ronnie. When two people really love each other, they help each other stay alive and grow. There's nothing more fulfilling, and you become a complete person for the first time.

Her husband, who was sixty-nine when he was elected, was the oldest person to hold the office of the presidency (until President

Donald Trump and, later, President Joe Biden). Nancy had always been intently focused on his health, his free time, and his schedule, but her attention grew more intense after a gunman shot her husband outside the Washington Hilton on March 30, 1981.

"Nothing can happen to my Ronnie," she wrote in her diary that night. "My life would be over." After the assassination attempt, Nancy, who had been a longtime follower of astrology, began regularly consulting well-known astrologists, including Joan Quigley, a San Francisco astrologer, for advice on how to best construct her husband's schedule. After the assassination attempt, the First Lady began reordering events on the president's calendar to make sure the timing was right with the stars. The astrological guidance was among the more fascinating, and more closely guarded, secrets in the Reagan White House.

Nancy's star-guided reordering of the commander in chief's calendar gave her an unusual level of control over her husband's movements. Her close watch led to a notable conflict with White House chief of staff Donald Regan, who served in that role from 1985 to 1987.

By the beginning of 1987, the First Lady and the chief of staff were openly fighting in the pages of *The New York Times:* "Two of President Reagan's closest advisers, Nancy Reagan and Donald T. Regan, have apparently reached the point where they cannot stand each other," read the beginning of the story by Gerald M. Boyd, which went on to detail squabbles between the First Lady and the chief of staff over how much to pack the president's schedule during his recuperation from prostate surgery. White House aides also told Boyd that the president had chosen a draft of the State of the Union address favored by Nancy, overriding Regan's opposition to the draft. After this report hit the press, Nancy, who had long been gunning for Regan's resignation in the wake of the Iran-Contra disclosures, did not have long to wait. Regan was gone by March 1987.

Two months after Regan's resignation, Nancy worked with a White House speechwriter, Landon Parvin, to deliver a defiant and lengthy speech to a group of journalists at an Associated Press luncheon in New York City.

In spite of everything I've learned these past six years, there's one thing on which I'm inflexible. The First Lady is, first of all, a wife. That's the reason she's there. A president has advisers to counsel him on foreign affairs, on defense, on the economy, on politics, on any number of matters. But no one among those experts is there to look after him as an individual with human needs, as a flesh-and-blood person who must deal with the pressures of holding the most powerful position on earth . . . I see the First Lady as another means to keep a president from becoming isolated. I talk to people. They tell me things. They pass along ideas. And, sure, I tell my husband. And if something is about to become a problem or fall between the cracks, I'm not above calling a person and asking about it.

She also famously thought little of associating with Barbara Bush, who was Second Lady at the time: "She really hated us," Barbara told the journalist Susan Page for her biography. "I don't know why, but she really hated us."

Barbara, Nancy's successor, was a woman so powerful within her family that her nickname was "the Enforcer." Born Barbara Pierce on June 8, 1925, in Manhattan, she was a First Lady different in both disposition and style. She spent much of her time in office lending her platform to raise awareness around adult literacy. Her efforts led to the National Literacy Act of 1991, which authorized the Department of Education to give grants to establish literacy resource centers and provided funding for workplace literacy. The Bushes were elected during the AIDS epidemic, and though the virus had terrorized several American communities, including gay men and African Americans, since the first months of the Reagan administration, both Ronald and Nancy had stayed quiet about the virus. In 1989, Barbara's literal embrace of a child did more to raise awareness around the AIDS virus than anything the Reagans had done.

"You can hug and pick up AIDS babies and people who have the HIV virus," she said during that visit, in which she cradled a toddler suffering from the virus. "There is a need for compassion."

While Nancy saw fit to be defensive about her place in the White House and the broader political firmament, Barbara led by instinct, offering compassion and comfort during a time of distress. This is the same fearless style she showcased at Wellesley, when she acknowledged that cultural and political forces were rapidly changing how women saw themselves: "Well, the controversy ends here," she told the Wellesley graduates as she closed her speech in 1990. "But our conversation is only beginning."

She was only half right. Two years after Barbara Bush took the stage at Wellesley, William Jefferson Clinton was elected to the presidency. His wife, Hillary Rodham Clinton, was a Wellesley girl—class of 1969—and a woman who had embraced the ideals of second-wave feminism but who was still a wife and mother. She didn't see the concept of "having it all" in the abstract; she had been trying to live out that concept all her life. The Clintons were the first baby boomers to occupy the White House: youthful enough to understand that technology, politics, and media were changing. Intelligent and ambitious, Hillary held a law degree—another first for a steward of the East Wing. Even during Bill Clinton's presidential campaign, Hillary seemed ready to turn her new role into a more ambitious, more politically involved version of a First Lady than Americans were used to seeing.

To the Clintons, America seemed ready. And besides: Hillary was one of those mermaids Barbara Bush was talking about. Wasn't she?

CHAPTER TWO

AMBITION

EVEN THOUGH SHE INSISTS THAT NEARLY EVERYONE SHE meets call her Jill, the First Lady is formally called Dr. Biden. Her doctorate in educational leadership, which she received in 2007 from the University of Delaware, is central to her identity, and her life as a teacher is something she has clung to as a respite from her public life.

"I'm a working woman," she said in the fall of 2022, adding that she had no current plans to retire. (At the time, she was seventy-one, years past the typical retirement age in the United States.)

She and her faithful East Wing staffers treat the division between teaching and politics as sacred. In January 2021, when officials at Northern Virginia Community College asked to put her name on promotional materials, she declined.

"I am an English teacher at NOVA—not First Lady," she wrote to a member of the marketing team and other colleagues shortly after her husband took office. "I am trying to keep my roles separate as I did as Second Lady. I appreciate your enthusiasm, but I want students to see me as their English teacher. I am not mentioning it in my classes AT ALL. Thanks for honoring my teacher identity. Jill."

If Joe had won the presidency the first time he ran, Jill Biden might have been the first working First Lady in history several decades earlier: In an interview with the *Los Angeles Times* in July 1987, she said that she had no plans to step away from her job if her husband was elected: "It's my profession," she said at the time, "and I don't think Joe would expect me to give it up." That year, polling showed that the majority of Americans supported the idea of a First Lady keeping her own career while in the White House.

Though she has not encountered much pushback about working as First Lady, Jill's doctorate in educational leadership has been a lightning rod for critics who have said she does not deserve to tout her academic credentials, in part, because being First Lady is more than enough. In December 2020, the writer Joseph Epstein published an op-ed in *The Wall Street Journal* suggesting that only people who had delivered a child should call themselves a doctor.

"Forget the small thrill of being Dr. Jill," Epstein wrote, "and settle for the larger thrill of living for the next four years in the best public housing in the world as First Lady Jill Biden."

The suggestion that the First Lady should strip the honorific from her name is part of a larger, often willful tendency of Americans to address high-achieving women informally: In the 2008 presidential race, Hillary Clinton and Barack Obama had both been senators, but Clinton's title was left out more often than Obama's was, and she was called by her first name much more often.

Another Biden-era example includes Tucker Carlson, the former Fox News host, mispronouncing Kamala Harris's first name on purpose. "So what?" he has said. The white television talking head doubled down, dismissing any anger over his truculent behavior as liberal angst. In fact, it is the willful distortion of the name of a woman with a Jamaican father and an Indian mother. Her name, she has written, means "lotus flower"—a plant that blooms above the surface of the water but has deep roots underneath. To Tucker Carlson, it appeared to be a chance to underscore for his followers how different this vice president—a mixed-race woman—was from the men who came before. Grade-school bullies have been doing this since time immemorial, but they often grow out of it. (In 2023, Tucker shocked the media world by leaving Fox days after the network reached a $787.5 million defamation settlement with Dominion Voting Systems, whose company he had repeatedly disparaged.)

After the Epstein piece, the response from the Bidens was measured—in part because Joe had privately encouraged Jill not to respond to the criticism, lest she give it any more air. But in a December 2020 interview with Stephen Colbert, she admitted to being taken aback by the piece.

"It was really the tone of it that I think—he called me 'kiddo,'" she said.

Still, there was an ensuing firestorm, of course; Northwestern University, where Epstein once taught, went to great lengths to emphasize that he was no longer affiliated with the school, and high-octane Twitter commentators, from the writer Charlotte Clymer to Mark Pitcavage of the Anti-Defamation League, eviscerated Epstein for what they said was a misogynistic piece. Doug Emhoff, the Second Gentleman, took to his Twitter account and pointed out the obvious: "This story would never have been written about a man."

Epstein's implication seemed to be that Jill, who had spent decades working toward her degree, should trade in the right to reference her doctorate of education, or EdD, and relish the trappings of her new life in the White House. Several of her defenders echoed what the Second Gentleman had written on Twitter.

"What was at the root of this unmerited attack?" Eleanor Herman, author of *Off with Her Head: Three Thousand Years of Demonizing Women in Public Power,* wrote in her book. "On the personal level, probably sour grapes. Epstein, it should be noted, had only a bachelor's degree. And people like Jill Biden—female people, that is—don't deserve to have a higher educational degree than a man."

Another one of her defenders, the writer Virginia Heffernan, speaking directly to Epstein on Twitter, noted that she used her own PhD title because she and women like Jill are "mistaken for housewives." Indeed, Jill decided to use the honorific, in part, because she wanted people to understand that she is her own person, with her own list of accomplishments—and because the title of "Mrs. Biden," she has told people, had been used by her husband's first wife, according to someone who has heard her explain her reasoning directly. Whatever her motivation for using her title, it is her choice. She earned the degrees.

Jill is only the fourth First Lady in history to come to the office with an advanced degree. Hillary Clinton and Michelle Obama came to the role with law degrees, and Laura Bush with a master's in library science. The doctorate debacle illustrated the degree to which swaths of the American public still treat a First Lady with an advanced degree as a novelty, or even an oddity. First Ladies are held up to be the picture of strong motherhood and stoic femininity, or whatever other virtue is needed from them at any given time. The role is hailed as powerful, and it certainly does have the potential to be. But ambition can be a third rail for First Ladies, just as it is for women who are not in the public eye.

When Hillary Clinton referenced her legal career or her past work, she was called the Antichrist—literally—and was broadly accused of demeaning American mothers. Michelle Obama seemed wary of the scar tissue, and in 2008, she denied that giving up her career was hard for her. Motherhood, she said, was enough—though she has since been more open about the emotional toll of the decision to leave her job. By 2020 it had become possible for Jill Biden to keep her teaching job, but she has emphasized how much her family has meant to her life. (She is also not an attorney.)

Hillary said in an interview that she briefly considered trying to keep working but knew it would be impossible to avoid questions of conflicts of interest.

"Even though I considered it in passing," she said. "I couldn't in any way figure out how that could possibly work. I quickly set it aside."

REALLY, HILLARY RODHAM CLINTON's journey to the East Wing makes the controversy surrounding Jill Biden's doctorate look quaint.

In the late 1970s, after Hillary met and married a fellow Yale law student named William Jefferson Clinton, and when he successfully ran for attorney general, then governor, of Arkansas, it was not her law degree that raised eyebrows. It was the fact that she wanted to be called by her name: Hillary Rodham.

Hillary met Bill among the library stacks in New Haven in 1971. Bill, a floppy-haired charmer—and so unapologetically a smooth-talking boy from Arkansas in a sea of bluebloods—kept glancing at Hillary, who was blond-haired and bookish, with blue eyes framed by large glasses. Finally, after he shot her one glance too many, Hillary strode over and fixed her gaze on him. "Look, if you're going to keep staring at me, and now I'm staring back, we at least ought to know each other's names. I'm Hillary Rodham. Who are you?" Her direct-ness, and the sure-footed way she carried herself, Bill has said, left him speechless. Almost from the beginning, the über-ambitious cou-ple began careening around the country in hot pursuit of their future.

In the summer of 1971, they drove to Berkeley, California, where Hillary had a temporary job at a law firm. She spent much of her free time cocooned in that cloying haze of early love, baking peach pies and taking long walks with Bill. After graduation in 1973, Hillary worked as a researcher for Marian Wright Edelman, the civil rights activist who founded the organization that would later become the Children's Defense Fund. Part of Hillary's work for Edelman included investigating several Southern private schools that had popped up after a 1969 decision by the Supreme Court forced schools to inte-grate. At one so-called segregation academy in Dothan, Alabama, Hillary, a prim-looking white woman, posed as a mother who was new to the area and looking for educational opportunities for her son. She asked detailed questions about the school's enrollment and de-mographics. She was assured that no Black students would be en-rolled.

Her research was funneled into a larger project that gathered evi-dence that the Nixon administration was failing to enforce provisions of the segregation ban, including a rule that prohibited granting tax-exempt status to the private schools that catered only to white stu-dents. More than forty years later, as the first female Democratic presidential nominee, her studied approach to social justice and civil rights, formed during that summer in Alabama, was on display when she was confronted by a group of Black Lives Matter activists.

"I don't believe you change hearts," she told the activists in a rare candid moment caught on tape in 2015. "I believe you change laws, you change allocation of resources, you change the way systems operate." It was a clear-eyed and direct response to heightened emotions, an approach that tends to reassure her supporters and incense her critics.

At Yale, Hillary's blossoming relationship with Bill, and her belief in him, would push her away from the policy work she loved and toward campaign-trail life. A dizzying series of events followed. In 1972, she joined Bill in Texas to work on George McGovern's campaign for the Democratic presidential nomination, registering voters while Bill worked as the Texas point man for McGovern. After McGovern won the nomination but lost to President Richard Nixon, Hillary spent a year working for the Children's Defense Fund, later joining the House Judiciary Committee's impeachment inquiry into Nixon. ("You cannot make my life up. Really," she has said.)

Rather than continue in Washington, she joined Bill in Arkansas in 1974, taking a position teaching criminal and constitutional law at the University of Arkansas School of Law. Bill, who was then a twenty-eight-year-old law professor at the same school, decided to run for Congress against John Paul Hammerschmidt, the Republican incumbent. Bill lost with 48 percent of the vote, but his interest in pursuing public office was ignited. Hillary accepted his marriage proposal on the third try, only after he had found a home for them, and they married in their living room on October 11, 1975. It was just in time for Bill's successful campaign for attorney general in 1976, and he went on to win the governorship in 1978.

In 1976, Hillary had signed on with the white-shoe Rose Law Firm, a move that made her the first-ever female partner. At company events, where she would wear her name tag, people would point to the offending RODHAM written on it and demand that she assume her married name.

The Clintons covered an extraordinary amount of ground before the end of their first decade together. Their daughter, Chelsea, was born in 1980. From the beginning, they regarded each other as partners and intellectual equals, a dynamic that has enriched them and served as the basis for many of the conflicts and conspiracy theories that have followed.

Of the two of them, Bill has always been the natural retail politician. He is as at home on a debate stage as he is celebrating Dyngus Day at a diner in rural America—as a cub reporter, I saw him do just that in the spring of 2008 as he worked to support his wife's presidential run. Hillary believes she is most comfortable on the other side of that coin: She is a good listener and policy wonk who would much rather spend time quietly taking apart a problem and rebuilding it with a solution attached. Bill became a politician, and Hillary tried to fix the problems, which included making money for her family and building a nest egg that could withstand the volatility of a life in politics—such as when Bill lost his gubernatorial reelection campaign. "It was up to her to just keep holding things up," Nancy Pietrafesa, a college friend, told Amy Chozick of *The New York Times*. By the time Bill ran for election a third time, successfully, in 1982, she had quietly started going by Hillary Rodham Clinton. Adding his name, she was told by Vernon Jordan, a trusted adviser, could help his political chances. Later, during Bill's campaign for the presidency, campaign officials would not even allow her to have stationery that read "Hillary Rodham Clinton" until she demanded for the letterhead to be reprinted with the reference to her maiden name.

The financial decisions the Clintons made during their early years have haunted them in the decades since and become grist for critics who see their pursuit of money as evidence of deep-rooted corruption. In 1978 and 1979, Hillary, then the First Lady of Arkansas, was scrutinized for investing $1,000 in cattle futures that returned nearly $100,000 in less than a year. In 1978, the Clintons, during Bill's first campaign for governor, struck a deal with Jim McDougal, a real estate developer, to borrow $183,000 and put that toward buying 230 acres of land in the Ozarks. They hoped the land had the potential to become prime vacationing property. They called it the Whitewater Development Corporation.

In the background of all of this, threatening to break into the fore, was her husband's extramarital behavior with women, which had reached open-secret status well before Bill announced a bid for the presidency. In 1992, the grocery-store tabloid *Star* published an account by a woman named Gennifer Flowers—a former reporter, Arkansas state employee, and burlesque dancer—who alleged a long-term affair with Bill.

Her story forced the Clintons to make a joint appearance on *60 Minutes* in which they downplayed Flowers as nothing more than an acquaintance. As the Clintons told it, Flowers had occasionally called one or both of them to lament that her life had been "rooned" by rumors, Hillary said, her words laced with a pronounced Southern twang, but the relationship had gone no further. There they sat, with Hillary's arm slung along the back of a couch and protectively around her husband, as Steve Kroft quizzed them on Bill's extramarital activities. Kroft suggested to the couple that they had developed an "arrangement" for the good of their relationship *and* their political fortunes—a comment that stung both of them.

"Wait a minute," Bill replied. "You're looking at two people who love each other. This is not an arrangement or an understanding. This is a marriage. That's a very different thing."

Hillary has regretted what she said next—in fact, she has regretted that she spoke at all—because she delivered an infamous sound bite that was foundational in shaping her relationship with the public.

"I'm not sittin' here as some little woman standing by my man like Tammy Wynette," she said, the adopted Arkansas drawl overshadowing the flat-voweled Chicago accent she was born with. "I'm sitting here because I love him and I respect him and I honor what he's been through and what we've been through together. And, you know, if that's not enough for people, then, heck, don't vote for him."

Both had emphasized that voters could understand what they

were willing to disclose about their marriage, without either of them saying explicitly whether Bill had engaged in an affair. They were also betting that Americans would ultimately be more responsive to the Clinton campaign's promises to vanquish rapidly rising inflation and high unemployment than a tabloid story about an extramarital dalliance. Two weeks later, Bill christened himself "the Comeback Kid" when he placed second in the New Hampshire primary.

Still, the 60 *Minutes* interview had shaken Hillary, and it only fueled criticism that she was somehow unable to do what the situation required of her—even though, really, she had. But she was constantly trying to overcome the suggestion that she was just too *much* of a certain something: too eager, too ambitious, too willing to tout her own credentials. When Bill suggested that Americans would be getting two politicians for the price of one—"buy one, get one free"—if he was elected, it was his honest assessment of the partnership that existed, and still exists, between them: He was the politician, and she was the one he turned to on policy matters.

"It wasn't a shallow kind of thing," said Melanne Verveer, who served as deputy chief of staff to the president and, later, as chief of staff to the First Lady. "It was a deep respect between them. He would often talk about how smart she was."

Still, his two-for-one comment drew several detractors, including former president Richard Nixon—a target of impeachment proceedings that Hillary had worked on. Nixon weighed in: "If the wife comes through as being too strong and too intelligent," he said, "it makes the husband look like a wimp."

Two months later, shaken from the Flowers report and the reaction from 60 *Minutes,* Hillary was facing accusations by Jerry Brown, the governor of California and a Democratic candidate, of taking state business to her law firm. She and Bill were answering questions from reporters in Chicago when one of them asked her whether she could have worked harder as First Lady of Arkansas to avoid perceived conflicts of interest. She was visibly frustrated as she spoke to the pack of journalists on behalf of "those of us who tried" to have an independent career. The twang in her voice was gone, replaced with a steeliness that has lingered in her throat ever since.

"You know, I suppose I could have stayed home and baked cookies and had teas, but what I decided to do was fulfill my profession, which I entered before my husband was in public life," she told them that day. "And I've worked very, very hard to be as careful as possible, and that's all I can tell you."

When Bill defeated President George H. W. Bush and Hillary finally became the First Lady, she found she could do very little—not even change her hair—without observers trying to figure out whether a headband or fresh-cut bangs in her sandy-blond hair represented a deep-rooted personality flaw. She began to feel that there was nothing she could do to be understood.

"While Bill talked about social change, I embodied it," she wrote in her 2004 memoir, *Living History*. "I had my own opinions, interests and profession. For better or worse, I was outspoken. I represented a fundamental change in the way women functioned in our society. And if my husband won, I would be fulfilling a position in which the duties were not spelled out, but the performance was judged by everybody."

When Bill won the election, he entrusted Hillary with reforming the healthcare system, based on his belief that curbing healthcare costs was a crucial way to fix the American economy. Looking back, after the elections and the battles, Hillary said that being First Lady gave her the opportunity to immerse herself once again in her first love: policy.

"I found an incredible opportunity to understand much better the full landscape of what was possible," she said in an interview reflecting on her ascension to the East Wing—where one of her first orders of business was to set up a West Wing office. "It was an extraordinary experience for somebody like me, who's primarily interested in the policy and the impact that you can achieve through politics that will actually make a positive difference in people's lives." But, as she pointed out, there were both successes and setbacks.

———

SINCE THE EARLIEST YEARS of her life, Hillary has been described as being ambitious and intelligent in a way that people find intimidating.

Hillary Diane Rodham was born on October 26, 1947, and she was raised in Park Ridge, a northwest suburb of Chicago. She was the only daughter and the eldest of three children born to parents who were profoundly shaped by Great Depression–era childhoods.

Her mother, Dorothy Howell Rodham, had survived a difficult childhood in which her neglectful parents had sent her away to live with her paternal grandparents in California. Dorothy began living on her own at age fourteen, as a mother's helper for a family that paid her three dollars a week plus room and board. She would tell her daughter that this was her first experience of a strong family, and it taught her how to raise Hillary and her two younger brothers, Hugh and Tony.

After high school, Dorothy traveled to Chicago, hoping to reconcile with her mother, who had promised to help pay for her education if she moved to the Midwest. Instead, Dorothy was again forced to move out and provide for herself. She was applying for a job when she met Hugh Rodham, a traveling salesman who had arrived in Chicago after hopping a freight train from his hometown of Scranton, Pennsylvania.

Her parents wanted to foster a sense of independence in their children and prized the opportunities that came along with education. Hillary's father was the stricter of the two; Hugh had received a degree in physical education from Penn State, and often woke a fourth-grade Hillary up before school to practice multiplication tables before her weekly math tests. Dorothy, who amassed college credits as an adult but never obtained a college degree, took a more free-range approach to educating her daughter: She took Hillary on regular trips to the local library, where Hillary tunneled her way through the offerings in the children's section.

While Dorothy's political leanings were Democratic, Hugh Rodham was an opinionated conservative who often shared his thoughts with his children. "We all accommodated his pronouncements, mostly about communists, shady businessmen or crooked politicians, the three lowest forms of life in his eyes," Hillary wrote in *Living History*. She described her upbringing as *Father Knows Best*, with an emphasis on avoiding the kind of peer pressure that could steer her away from her education and toward pursuits like boys, fashion, and gossip.

The combination of a secure upbringing and conditioned respect for her parents' authority created a child who began to actively seek out the respect of other adults and her classmates. She won her first election when she was elected co-captain of her elementary school's security patrol. She was in sixth grade. She described the victory as her first real lesson in the ways people react to election outcomes. She had won, and people treated her like she was special.

In the fall of 1960, Hillary was in eighth grade. Her father was a fervent supporter of Vice President Richard Nixon's campaign for the presidency. So was her eighth-grade social studies teacher, who told his students that he had been roughly treated when he tried to confront Democratic poll watchers in Chicago on Election Day. After calling Mayor Richard Daley's office to complain, young Hillary set out on a mission to the city's South Side, where she tried to interview people and compare names with those listed on voter registration lists—anything to find proof of voter fraud that had led to President John F. Kennedy's victory. (She did find a vacant lot that was listed as the address for several Kennedy voters, but, of course, Kennedy prevailed.) She has said Kennedy's assassination in 1963 made her realize that she wanted to help her country in some way.

In high school, Hillary honed her debate skills and prioritized debate practice and homework over chasing boys. She had a nickname—Sister Frigidaire—and was not exactly popular. She didn't date anyone seriously and was puzzled when she noticed her girlfriends drop out of advanced courses or downplay their good grades, all to avoid alienating their boyfriends: "I simply could not imagine giving up a college education or a career to get married, as some of my girlfriends were planning to do."

Instead, she began to dabble in a more personally expressive form
of Republicanism. She ran for student council and class vice president and was active in a Young Republicans club, where she supported Barry Goldwater, "right down to my cowgirl outfit and straw
cowboy hat emblazoned with the slogan 'AuH$_2$O.'" She credits one
of her high school teachers with reinforcing her burgeoning conservatism.

But she also sought the guidance of a local Methodist youth min-
ister, Donald Jones, who gave her a firsthand view into the civil rights
movement, taking her to see Dr. Martin Luther King, Jr., speak at
Orchestra Hall. Her childhood, she has said, is what gave her the
ability to reconcile different belief systems and to live within the
push-and-pull of different influences, from her father's conservative
beliefs to her youth pastor's attempts to bring her into contact with
people from different racial and ideological backgrounds.

She entered Wellesley College as a member of the class of 1969
and was elected president of the campus Republicans her freshman
year. It was not long until outside forces, which included the roiling
civil rights movement and the Vietnam War, began to change the
trajectory of her political evolution. Some of the more transformative
moments of the decade—including the assassinations of Martin Luther King, Jr., and Robert Kennedy—happened within the space of
her junior year. After King was killed, she wrote that she "returned to
campus wearing a black armband and agonizing about the kind of
future America faced." She made it a point to begin getting to know
her Black classmates and worked with an organization called Ethos,
an activist group that pressured the school's administration to diver-
sify the student body and change its recruiting methods.

She traveled to Washington, D.C., for the first time that summer
as part of a college internship program and worked for the House
Republican Conference. She and several other interns were asked to
travel to the Republican National Convention in Miami, where they
worked on behalf of Governor Nelson Rockefeller, who was running
for his party's nomination against Nixon. His loss signaled to Hillary
that a staunchly conservative brand of politics was prevailing over a

more moderate approach within the Republican Party. (As history shows, she was not wrong.) She began to drift away from an ideology that had been a part of her life since her childhood, but one she had never fully interrogated until she had arrived at Wellesley.

During her senior year, she resisted entreaties to head directly into the world of grassroots organizing and instead chose to attend law school. She was elected president of the student body, and she was admitted to law programs at Harvard and Yale. That development that led her to New Haven—and to Bill—was because a Harvard law professor looked at her at a cocktail party and sneered, "We don't need any more women at Harvard."

But Hillary had no intention to leave Wellesley quietly. One of her friends on campus, Eleanor "Eldie" Acheson, whose grandfather, Dean Acheson, had served as secretary of state, led a campus effort to appoint a student commencement speaker. Ruth Adams, the school's president, had invited Senator Edward Brooke of Massachusetts to deliver a speech. There had never been a student-body graduation speaker at Wellesley before, but the women of 1969 were part of a generation that was not interested in adhering to precedent. Just a decade earlier, legions of young women passed through campuses like Wellesley with the intention of snagging a respectable husband and a comfortable home life. The world had opened a crack and they wanted to commemorate the moment.

Ambitious young women were starting to understand that they could live on their own, follow their own desires, and—just maybe—circle around to getting married when and if they felt like it. This feeling was not confined to the elite Wellesley campus: Across the country that year, a young teacher named Laura Welch had set out on her own to teach at a school in Houston. In Delaware, Jill Jacobs was enrolled at junior college, but she was also about to get married, a decision that would put her on a long path to accomplishing her personal dreams while juggling a family life.

In her memoir, Hillary wrote that she suggested to Adams, the president of the college, that her class could use a student commencement speaker, and then she put herself up for the job. After getting Adams's grudging approval, she began to survey her classmates to reach a consensus about what, exactly, the four-hundred-strong, all-female graduating class of 1969, who had watched the civil rights movement unfurl and participated in demonstrations against the Vietnam War, wanted out of their lives.

Senator Brooke spoke first, criticizing what he called "coercive protest" and making no mention of the war or of the assassinations that had taken place a year before. He cited declining poverty numbers as a sign that society was making progress. Brooke, the first Black man to be elected a state attorney general and the first Black man to be elected to the Senate, had broken his own series of glass ceilings. But his remarks seemed out of touch with the fiery mood on college campuses across the United States.

In her former life as a campus Republican, Hillary had once campaigned for Brooke. But on May 31, 1969, she took the microphone and talked back.

"We're not in the positions yet of leadership and power," she told him. "But we do have that indispensable element of criticizing and constructive protest."

Her speech received a standing ovation but dropped the jaws of the more conservative, older adults in her midst. "Courtesy is not one of the stronger virtues of the young," Adams, the president of the school, wrote to Brooke a week after the commencement, apologizing for the unruly commencement speaker. "Scoring debater's points seems, on occasion, to have higher standing."

Hillary was an instant star, hailed as one of the ambitious young voices of a generation stunned by war, civic violence, and social uproar. In June, *Life* magazine featured her remarks alongside several other speeches under an article titled "The Class of '69." During a photo session taken a week after she left Wellesley, she wore striped trousers and a white oxford shirt. Her octagonal eyeglass frames were either in her lap or in her hand or on her face. Her hair was long. She was looking directly back into the camera, undaunted.

———

TWENTY-FOUR YEARS LATER, SHE became First Lady. Five days after his first inauguration, President Bill Clinton delivered a news conference at the White House and announced that Hillary would lead a task force that would examine ways to reform healthcare in the United States. He had campaigned on a promise that he would bring healthcare costs under control, which in turn could help reduce the national deficit. Speaking to reporters, the president said that he expected a plan on his desk within one hundred days.

The undertaking was ambitious, and the work was complex. Officials on the Clinton campaign had not articulated a plan for how such a monumental overhaul would be paid for or how it would be done, but now they were the first Democratic administration in over a decade. An anxious American middle class, Clinton aides assumed, was ready to embrace the idea of sweeping change to an industry that amounted to one-seventh of the country's economy. Even though Bill Clinton had only won 43 percent of the vote. Even though he and his most senior advisers, including the new First Lady, were untested by Washington. The public wanted change, right? Hillary was perfect.

"I am grateful that Hillary has agreed to chair this task force, and not only because it means she'll be sharing some of the heat I expect to generate," the president joked before ticking off a list of Hillary's accomplishments as First Lady of Arkansas. "I think that in the coming months the American people will learn, as the people of our state did, that we have a First Lady of many talents, who most of all can bring people together around complex and difficult issues to hammer out consensus and get things done."

The planning took longer than one hundred days. The early efforts appeared promising as Hillary met with influential lawmakers on both sides of the aisle. But the task force quickly devolved into an unwieldy group of hundreds of staff members, with the First Lady and an inexperienced aide, Ira Magaziner, a campaign-era loyalist, in the driver's seat. In October 1993, the Clinton White House unveiled a 240,000-word document that outlined a plan for universal health insurance—a gargantuan effort, the particulars of which Hillary quickly cautioned could be negotiable. "This will be an opportunity for all of us to work together, to go beyond politics as usual, to make it clear to the American people that this president and this Congress hear them and are committed to solving their problems in a very real way," she told members of Congress in a question-and-answer session after the unveiling.

The provisions of the bill, introduced as the Health Security Act a month later, required Americans to enroll in the new healthcare system, and employers would have to pay the lion's share of their employee's health plans. Small businesses and unemployed or underemployed people would receive government subsidies, but everyone would be covered. Despite flashes of bipartisanship earlier in the process, Republicans assailed the plan and its ambitions, equating the potential outcome to government-run medicine. Critics also were suspicious of what they said was a secretive planning process by the White House, and some medical groups filed lawsuits against the administration, demanding that the task force's meetings be publicized.

The healthcare effort was unfolding amid burgeoning staffing and financial scandals that threatened to divert attention away from policy and toward the Clintons. In the spring of 1993, several career officials were fired from the White House travel office and replaced with Clinton loyalists. By the summer, Vince Foster, the White House deputy counsel, was found dead in a Washington park, a month after filing several years of delinquent tax returns on the Whitewater Development Corporation to the Internal Revenue Service. Though an independent counsel investigation found that Foster's death was a suicide, the report did little to stop conspiracy theorists from spreading rumors that his death was the result of foul play.

An investigation into the Whitewater controversy, led by the independent counsel Kenneth Starr, would continue for the next four years and cost some $52 million, after his inquiry expanded to include a scandal surrounding the president's behavior toward Monica Lewinsky, a White House intern.

Over the course of the investigation, former Clinton associates, including Jim McDougal and his wife, Susan, were convicted of bank fraud related to questionable loans. Starr's effort ensnared Bill's successor, Governor Jim Tucker of Arkansas, who was convicted of mail fraud related to the real estate development plan. The Clintons were never charged, but since that period, they have never been able to fully shake the conspiracy theorists who believe they are part of a sinister cabal designed to protect their business and political interests.

Well before the Lewinsky revelations, the First Lady was grappling with a politically lethal cocktail: complicated policy, secretive meetings, murky financial dealings, a confidant's death, a White House in which the crew from Arkansas didn't quite seem to know how the rules were followed in Washington, and a Republican party foaming at the mouth for any evidence of malfeasance.

By the spring of 1994, public interest in the healthcare effort was flagging, and by the summer, there were swaths of voters who began to attack the plan—and its authors—on personal terms. In a field in Kentucky, farmers doused an effigy of Hillary in gasoline and lit it on fire. During a trip to Seattle in August, Verveer, Hillary's former chief of staff, remembers the First Lady being quickly ushered into a motorcade after delivering a speech. When they arrived back at her hotel garage, people were pressed up against the car, yelling and banging on the windows. Hillary had been asked to wear a bulletproof vest for the earlier event.

"I don't know how they got so close, but they were there screaming," Verveer said in an interview, "all white men in a rage. And it was, you know, this very personal attack on her."

The bill was declared dead in late September. In November, Democrats lost fifty-four House seats, and the Senate and House majorities in the midterm elections. It was the First Lady who eventually publicly offered her regrets, stopping short of a full apology. "I regret very much the efforts on healthcare reform were badly misunderstood," she told a group of journalists. "So I take responsibility for that, and I am very sorry about that."

No First Lady had ever tried to push the boundaries of her role so far and so fast. The speed and aggression of the effort, combined with the Clintons' closed-off approach to their work behind the scenes, was too much for Americans, who showed their displeasure at the midterm ballot box. Other First Ladies had advocated for policy, but none had testified before the Senate, or traveled the country, or been burned in effigy. None had been told by Secret Service agents to wear a bulletproof vest while making a reasoned case, even if it was for a policy deemed unreasonable. The historian Allida Black said the problem was a version of what Hillary first encountered on the campaign trail: Her mistake had been her belief that she had the right to fight at all.

"The issue is that Hillary really pushed in public," said Black. She got "whipsawed and stereotyped to hell and back. That didn't mean she stopped. That meant she learned how to advocate in different ways."

Looking back decades later, Hillary says she would approach healthcare differently if she could do it over, and said she would not have led the task force: "If I had known that being a First Lady and doing this would cause so much cognitive dissonance, I certainly would have been very publicly supportive," she said in an interview; "I would have shown up in meetings, I would have traveled the country, but I wouldn't have taken on a formal role."

She believes that it was never about her—or, at least, it shouldn't have been. Putting someone else in charge and having an ultimately successful healthcare law would have been, she said, "a dream for me."

THE SECOND TERM OF the Clinton presidency saw a chastened First Lady, who found a way to advocate for the things she believed in while trying to float above the bare-knuckle politics of Washington. Bruised from the battles of the first term, she searched for a way to differentiate herself from her husband without drawing a horde of pitchfork-wielding detractors.

"I started doing things that, you know, didn't have highly organized interests—ideological, partisan, financial interests against me," she said in an interview.

On September 5, 1995, Hillary traveled to Beijing and spoke about the importance of women's rights at the United Nations Fourth World Congress on Women. The East Wing was met with some pushback from the State Department, where officials feared she would cause a diplomatic rift with the Chinese. Conservatives found something to dislike about the trip, accusing her of traveling overseas to promote a "radical feminist" agenda. A wary West Wing downplayed her trip, promising reporters that she was not going to Beijing to make news. She did anyway.

"Human rights are women's rights, and women's rights are human rights," Hillary said from the dais. It earned her positive headlines, and back in Washington, aides in the East Wing were ready to deploy a preplanned domestic tour and a slate of talk show appearances to make sure her pivot was well received by the American public. "Not only would this serve as a way to immediately bring your trip to Beijing back home, but it will also give fresh domestic B-roll footage to tie in with the footage from Beijing," Lisa Caputo, who served as Hillary's press secretary, wrote in a memo the week before Hillary delivered her speech.

Hillary's critics said her statement had been modest and the sentiment behind it obvious, but East Wing officials found themselves diligently explaining the concept on the media tour that followed. Verveer still remembers an appearance the First Lady made at Voice of America after returning from Beijing.

"It was a call-in show she was doing, and a male from the Middle East actually asked her, 'Mrs. Clinton, what did you mean when you said women's rights are human rights?' And I still remember this answer, because she said, 'Sir, just close your eyes and think of all the rights men have. Well, women are human beings and deserve all of the same rights.'"

The First Lady who had been put in charge of a major West Wing policy effort just two years earlier was now having to explain to callers that women were indeed human beings. As she quietly rehabilitated her image, she also began a syndicated newspaper column, called Talking It Over, in the model of the column Eleanor Roosevelt wrote for years. The Hillary of Talking It Over had very little of the steeliness of the Wellesley Hillary, Campaign Hillary, or Healthcare Hillary that had earned her accolades and attention and derision. In her first column, she said that a woman approached her at a Washington art museum and said she looked familiar.

"'You sure look like Hillary Clinton,' she said," the First Lady wrote. "'So I'm told,' I answered. The truth is that sometimes it is hard even for me to recognize the Hillary Clinton that other people see. Like millions of women across our country, I find that my life consists of different, sometimes paradoxical parts."

DURING BOTH OF HER husband's presidential terms, Hillary's influence was felt throughout the White House, thanks to what Verveer calls an integrated mix of East Wing staffers throughout the West Wing. And Hillary held significant sway with the president, weighing in on key nominees—she recommended to her husband that he pick Madeleine Albright, whom she called "the best communicator in his administration," to become the first female secretary of state, Verveer said.

"As time evolved, it became very clear that when the president said, 'You know, Hillary and I did talk about it,' that the influence was there."

Hillary's East Wing was family friendly: Verveer recalled that at least one staffer had an infant when she was hired, and was encouraged to bring the baby in on days she had childcare problems. On one memorable occasion, the First Lady picked up and held a crying baby while she and her aides were working through a list of calls to lawmakers on the healthcare bill. The maternal picture Verveer paints is at odds with how the First Lady was viewed publicly—in part, because Hillary came across as sharp and serious when she was on the defensive, which was pretty much all the time. As the Whitewater investigation continued, Hillary played a key role in keeping key documents out of the hands of the press and the public—a decision former advisers of the Clintons now view as a grave mistake that ultimately caused the inquiry to drag out and create a permanent shadow over the First Couple. She was ultimately called before a grand jury to deliver four hours of testimony about the documents.

"Hillary Clinton is a woman of many strengths and virtues, but like all of us, she also has some blind spots," David Gergen, a former Clinton adviser, told *The Washington Post* in 2016. "She does not see the world in the same way that others do when it comes to transparency and accountability."

But, given the constant churn of scandal surrounding the Clinton White House, Verveer pointed out that there were so few leaks from the East Wing because people enjoyed working for the First Lady, and felt protective of her. This was true in 1994, when a woman named Paula Jones filed a lawsuit accusing Bill of accosting her in a hotel room while he was serving as governor of Arkansas, and alleging that she suffered professionally when she turned him down. And it was especially true in January 1998, when Kenneth Starr announced that he would be investigating the president's relationship with Monica Lewinsky.

At first, it was the assertive and direct Hillary Clinton who emerged to defend her husband that month, after the president issued an initial denial about having a sexual relationship with Lewinsky. The First Lady gave an interview with Matt Lauer in which she decried a "vast right-wing conspiracy" against her husband. She believed that Starr was working in direct alliance with the Republicans opposed to her husband's presidency, and she believed that her husband should "absolutely not" have to admit, as he did during the 1992 campaign, that he had caused pain in their marriage. The "right-wing conspiracy" comment would follow her for decades and into her presidential campaign.

It was not until August of that year that Bill, who had tried to keep the truth from everyone, including his attorneys and advisers, told Hillary that he had engaged in "inappropriate intimacy" with the young intern. She has called his admission "the most devastating, shocking and hurtful experience of my life," one that required her to retreat into herself, and her faith, to work toward forgiveness. This would be hard to do given the firestorm that followed. The president's denials to a grand jury that he had behaved improperly with Lewinsky triggered a House impeachment effort on the grounds that he had obstructed justice.

Hillary, who was on the impeachment staff that investigated Nixon—and who, as she pointed out in an interview, actually wrote a guiding memo outlining what constitutes an impeachable offense—dismissed the impeachment process, led by former House Speaker Newt Gingrich, as "nothing but a crass political stunt."

During that period, she later said, she was given an up-close view of the fomenting of some of the populist forces that have driven the Republican party she knew in her youth to the far-right side of the political spectrum. "Gingrich had a big role in shaping the modern Republican Party," she said. "And, you know, it culminated in someone as totally unfit to serve as the president," she said, a reference to Trump.

By the time Bill was acquitted by the Senate on February 12, 1999, Hillary's image had undergone a fundamental transformation. She was no longer a two-for-one political adviser and keeper of the Clinton family secrets. She was the wife who had stood by her husband and had endured public pain. She began to quietly consider her future. Eight months after Bill was acquitted, she filed a statement of candidacy with the Federal Election Commission, laying the groundwork for a campaign for retiring senator Daniel Patrick Moynihan's seat in New York. Her victory on November 8, 2000, over Rick Lazio, a forty-two-year-old four-term congressman from Long Island, was the first time in the history of the United States that the nation's First Lady had been elected to public office. And so on. She left office with approval ratings at 65 percent, according to Gallup—proof, she wrote in *Living History*, that "Americans are fundamentally fair and sympathetic."

People who are loyal to Hillary point out that the First Ladies who have followed her have done things that she never could have gotten away with during her eight years at the White House. The examples are so small—Laura Bush got to wear pantsuits, no problem!—that they seem illustrative of the thousand small cuts, and some very big ones, either self-inflicted or unfairly administered, that shaped her into the guarded political figure she is today.

"When the Taliban were overthrown in Afghanistan, it was Laura Bush who gave the president's radio address," Verveer said. "I can remember being in Berlin at that moment, when women in Germany were saying, 'Oh, my gosh, your First Lady did the president's radio address.' Now, if Hillary Clinton had done that, you know, she'd probably be hung in effigy the third or fourth time around."

As for Jill Biden working?

"There is no way in God's green earth that Hillary Clinton could have had that kind of work outside of her role as First Lady," Verveer added. "I think that's progress, that Jill can make that choice."

Anita McBride said the story of Hillary Clinton became a cautionary tale for the women who have held the role since. Hillary's experience, she said, also highlighted a tension between a First Lady whose life experiences, from early campus activism on civil rights to working on education reform in Little Rock, led her to believe that America was ready for someone like her and the discomfort legions of voters had with a woman who wanted to help her husband lead.

"I think it was a classic sort of example of wanting and expecting First Ladies to be activists but not crossing the line and threshold of policy maker," McBride said. "The country maybe was not quite ready for that sort of very activist model."

Americans have not seen another First Lady quite like her since, but Hillary's time in office permanently and fundamentally shifted how Americans view the role. Each woman who has come after her has faced perennial questions about what she might do with the platform she has been given—and, of course, how far she might try to go.

CHAPTER THREE

TRADITION

J OE BIDEN HAS BEEN FOCUSED ON HIS PRESIDENTIAL LEGACY for so long that he wasted no time ushering a group of historians into the White House once he finally got the job. Six weeks after taking office, he met with presidential scholars in the East Room to discuss what sort of president he could be, should ambitious plans for social spending and infrastructure bear fruit.

The listening session was organized by Jon Meacham, a Pulitzer Prize–winning biographer and historian who moonlights as a Biden speechwriter. Other attendees included the author Michael Eric Dyson and a selection of historians from Ivy League universities. (Though Joe has emphasized his lack of Ivy credentials, in practice he is happy to be surrounded by advisers who have them.) Meacham was the person the president looked to when he wanted to muse about what the Biden presidency could mean when viewed against the long scope of history—a favorite topic for the politician who, when he was elected at seventy-seven, was the oldest commander in chief the country had ever seen.

It would not be the president's last check-in with historians, but his first meeting with them in office was notable because very few meetings like this were being held at the White House at that time. On March 2, 2021, the day of the meeting, the coronavirus vaccine was still not widely available. Masking mandates and public health guidelines on social distancing were still strict. Very few people were authorized to be in the same room with the president, lest they be unwitting vectors for disease. In the meeting with historians, the paper covering their water glasses was embossed with a golden presidential seal.

The sit-down occurred as the Biden administration was working to contain a wily virus; put checks on an aggressive authoritarian, Vladimir Putin of Russia; and craft a sizable social spending plan to sell to the American public. Given the hectic backdrop, a meeting with historians sounded like Joe's idea of a good time. It was one of very few in-person pandemic visitations he had been allowed to enjoy with people outside of his tight circle of aides and family members.

As he eyed social spending and infrastructure legislation that, together, could add up to more than $3 trillion, he was curious to know what some of his most admired predecessors had done to secure their transformative legacies: How much change, he wondered, could the United States tolerate at once?

"I'm no FDR, but . . ." Biden said to the historian Doris Kearns Goodwin at one point, a reference to one of his heroes, the news site *Axios* reported. Michael Beschloss, the presidential historian, compared what the president was trying to accomplish to the New Deal, the Great Depression–era relief plan Franklin Delano Roosevelt championed in 1933 to help stabilize the American economy.

By the end of the meeting, Biden felt satisfied with the comparisons to historical giants. He told an aide that he could have gone another two hours listening about presidential history and scribbling notes in his little black notebook.

The invitees to that meeting recalled a West Wing so quiet that it felt like a snow day. Across the White House, the East Wing was similarly calm, mostly because March 2, 2021, was a Tuesday. This meant that Jill was scheduled to teach. While the president picked the brains of historians in the chandelier-studded opulence of the East Room, the First Lady was in her office, teaching English over Zoom to community college students.

Unlike her husband, who has been ruminating over his presidential legacy since the Carter era, Jill Biden has not spent an inordinate amount of time thinking about what her own impact on history might look like. But over a year after Jill's husband first summoned historians to the White House, she invited a group of them to the East Wing.

A year into the presidency, the sense among people close to Jill was that she was not doing enough to shape her legacy as First Lady. Several people, including Cathy Russell, Jill's former chief of staff and a close friend, had urged her to make the most of her time in office—whether that was four or eight years. Russell had left Biden world to become the executive director of UNICEF, but she was still an occasional presence around the East Wing, taking walks with Jill on the South Lawn out of earshot of her deeply curious aides. Privately, Russell had encouraged her to think about streamlining the many trips she was taking in the service of her husband's policy goals into one cohesive initiative that fit more into the grand tradition of modern First Ladies who focused on a single issue, according to people familiar with their discussions.

Jill was bucking modern tradition: Hillary Clinton maintained an office in the West Wing and used her platform to champion healthcare—for which she would pay the political price—and do what she could to bolster women's rights around the world. Laura Bush, who was more of an activist and steadying force as First Lady than much of the coverage at the time gave her credit for, became an advocate for Afghan women and girls. Michelle Obama launched the fitness- and nutrition-focused Let's Move campaign. Melania Trump had funneled her efforts into a child-focused platform called Be Best—not that anyone in Jill's orbit would ever say she was an example worth emulating. Jill had followed her own instinct to keep a broad profile while maintaining her teaching career, but she took Russell's private advice to heart.

IN JANUARY 2022, JILL gathered her staff for a weekend retreat at Camp David to discuss a way forward. What could she be doing better? Did she need a single issue? Even if she only had one term, what should her legacy be?

Jill knew that Laura Bush, who was concerned about shaping her identity for the press and for the history books, had once organized a panel of historians and East Wing experts to share their insights, so she asked her staff to arrange the same thing. She wanted to quiz them on how she was perceived, and what she should do with her role, yes, but she also wanted to explain herself and her choices. The event, she told her staff, was to be no longer than ninety minutes—and nothing so formal as a lunch. The event would be a simple coffee in the Blue Room, the oval-shaped parlor in the middle of the state floor of the White House.

The guest list, according to several people who attended, included Allida Black, a preeminent scholar on Eleanor Roosevelt who had been an adviser to Hillary Clinton, and Susan Page, the author of a biography on Barbara Bush. Anita McBride, a former chief of staff to Laura Bush, was also invited, as was Karen Tumulty, an opinion columnist from *The Washington Post* and author of a biography on Nancy Reagan. Authors Carl Anthony and Diana Carlin rounded out the guest list.

The timing of the event immediately struck at least one of the invitees as odd. Laura Bush had held her own historian summit toward the end of her second term as First Lady. Jill Biden was in a trickier part of her tenure: She was *only* a year in—and yet, she was *already* a year in.

"A year plus into this and only now are they trying to figure out what she is going to do with it?" one invitee, who spoke anonymously to preserve relationships, recalled thinking. "It isn't like she didn't spend eight years watching a First Lady at close range. So, what takes a year and a half?"

The group gathered in the Blue Room in April 2022, a week after the Gridiron Dinner. Under the watchful eyes of portraits of William Taft, James Monroe, and John Tyler, the First Lady opened the discussion by explaining that she had been unable to think about her role in traditional terms. The political violence of the January 6 attack on the United States Capitol Building, coupled with the coronavirus pandemic, she said, had rerouted her ambitions. She told the group that what she saw during her campaign travel was "a nation that needed to heal" from the shock of a pandemic and the rawness of a divisive political season.

She had wanted to position herself as a healer for the nation: someone who could travel to any community, liberal or conservative, and listen to the concerns of American citizens. She had prized her willingness to shake hands and give hugs and pep talks as a special kind of political talent. After all, she was just about the only person in her husband's orbit who saw outside of the administration's bubble, not only in her First Lady role but also as part of her day job. But she was beginning to wonder if it was all enough.

"What interests me is how you see the role," she told the historians, according to a recording of the meeting. "I don't want to focus on the pandemic but how you see the role evolving, changing. How you define it. What kind of things are you looking at? What interests you?"

She offered up an idea of her own first: As part of her work in education, she had become interested in meeting with young women and young mothers and found it so rewarding that she had started a mentoring program at NOVA. It had pained her to step away from the program to help Joe campaign. Perhaps she could help staff members on Capitol Hill.

"You know what? Maybe I should go up to the Senate, talking about mentoring. Just talking to the women who are up there who are young moms, maybe single moms. Just women who are starting their careers and finding their own paths, and just having a dialogue with them, and how interesting it would be to mentor, to carry on this theme of mentoring. I'm just thinking about that in different ways."

Then she stopped and beckoned the historians to weigh in. "Just jump in," she said. "I don't know. Maybe this would be easier if we had wine."

What followed was a free-for-all from a group of historians whose feedback suggested that her interests were not expansive enough.

"I'm not saying you have to be Hillary, you have to be Hillary, you have to be Nancy," Allida Black said. "But for example, community colleges or second-chance programs: Testify on the Hill." That suggestion drew a wry smile from the First Lady, who, at this point in her tenure, had little faith in the functional capacity of a Biden-era Congress.

She was unmoved as the historians, one after another, regaled her with the work previous First Ladies, including Lady Bird Johnson, had done to discreetly tie their trips and visits to their husbands' legislative agendas.

"Congress is different now," Jill told them bluntly at one point.

As the conversation continued, members of the East Wing staff, who were sitting coiled and had grown increasingly defensive, jumped into the discussion. Mala Adiga, Jill's policy director, interjected to defend their work, rattling off a list of initiatives that Jill had participated in as Second Lady, from highlighting the importance of community college to supporting military families. Their struggle, Adiga said, was "sort of reconciling what we know she does versus what the public knows."

But at different moments throughout the meeting—which, true to the directive, ran about ninety minutes—the First Lady was either unable or unwilling to share the particulars of what she wanted to achieve, which of her predecessors she wanted to emulate, or what she wanted her legacy to be.

When one historian asked her what her overall goal was, she seemed puzzled. "What is my *goal*?" she repeated back, as if she had never pondered such a question. Such a question sounded silly to her. Hadn't she always been clear? She had wanted her husband to *win*, and she wanted to keep her career. She had worked alongside Joe for decades to make his goals happen, overcoming her own sense of discomfort with politics and the isolation she felt raising their family while Joe toiled away in the Senate. Her family had been scrutinized, the closets thrown open and the skeletons dragged out. She had lost a son, Beau, to cancer, and another, Hunter, had been battling a devastating addiction to crack cocaine. And all of that had been open for public consumption. Now a group of people she'd invited into the White House were sitting in front of her and asking, *Okay, but what else?*

Another historian tried the same question in a different way: At the end of eight years, what would she most like to say she had done with the role?

"I can't really choose just one," she replied. She listed free community college and "changing cancer as we know it" before quickly switching back to a topic she was more comfortable with: her husband's record on civil rights and education reform. The interactions illustrated the limits of her patience with being asked for more and moving beyond what she felt she had already given.

The feedback from the group was a franker assessment than she had expected. Allida Black suggested that she branch out from the issues that Americans saw her as personally involved with, which included military families and cancer research—both issues that had emotional ties to Beau.

"The meeting that I was in was not a fluff meeting," Black said in a later interview regarding the meeting in the Blue Room. She declined to describe the meeting at length, except to confirm that it had happened.

Still, after spending ninety minutes with a First Lady and an East Wing staff that seemed more interested in continuing as usual than developing another formal initiative, several attendees left feeling unsure about which of their suggestions, if any, had made a lasting impression.

Afterward, alone with her staff, Jill winced at the idea that the historians thought she was only doing what was personally important to her, despite the element of truth to that feedback. The Bidens have been safely ensconced among their loyalists for decades but have often publicly said that they wanted to hear from people outside of their established bubbles. The feedback, at least momentarily, jarred Jill, who had come into the White House set on managing her routine as a working educator and juggling the neatly organized policy items her staff had laid out for her. The suggestion that she was only undertaking those causes because she was personally attracted to them was not something she was used to hearing.

But Jill had decided long ago that the best use of her skills was not lobbying lawmakers or testifying on Capitol Hill. After almost half a century in public life, and with the last fifteen years spent watching the state of American politics go from partisan to polarized and tribal, she believed that she was at her best when she was speaking to and hearing directly from the people her husband was hoping to reach.

In October 2022, I asked her if she had given any more thought to how she wanted to be remembered beyond being a wife, a mother, and a First Lady who did not give up her independence and her career. After nearly two years in the role, after all the questions about portfolios and issues and messaging, she seemed unconcerned with the idea that she should do more to define herself. She seemed in no rush.

"Well, not really. I mean, it's also—it feels so new, actually," she said. "You know, even with eight years as Second Lady, this is a whole different thing, just a whole different responsibility. The platform is so much bigger. So, not yet, but stay tuned."

In the years since Hillary Clinton blazed into the White House and left as a senator-elect, modern First Ladies have struggled with the idea that they should leave a substantial lasting legacy, something that could signal to generations far from now that they existed and that they had tried. They all struggle with feeling understood.

TWENTY YEARS BEFORE JILL was answering questions about portfolios and policy, Laura Bush was also grappling with the question of her legacy as First Lady. A Texas-born teacher turned librarian, Laura shares several of the qualities that have made Jill a formidable political spouse. Both are introverts by nature who have discovered that their inner resolve can temper their more gregarious and at times gaffe-prone husbands. Both share a love of reading, and both light up when they have the chance to discuss teaching and working with students. And both have privately questioned how they might be remembered or understood.

Presidents like to wish for the best at the beginning. In their Inauguration Day speeches, they all enjoy playing with poetic imagery meant to soothe supporters, reassure critics, and motivate a public that has been completely exhausted by the ugly relentlessness of a two-year (longer, really) presidential election season.

President Bill Clinton likened his election to "a spring reborn in the world's oldest democracy that brings forth the vision and courage to reinvent America." President George W. Bush quoted the Virginia statesman John Page when he told the crowd on his first day in office that an "an angel still rides in the whirlwind and directs this storm." President Barack Obama encouraged progress and promised that Americans were "made for this moment, and we will seize it—so long as we seize it together." President Donald J. Trump, reliably the outlier, was less sanguine but similarly determined: "This American carnage stops right here and stops right now."

And President Joe Biden, the man elected to put the brakes on the dark carnival ride, used his speech to return to traditional form. "We shall write an American story of hope, not fear. Of unity, not division. Of light, not darkness," he told the country.

The rhetoric is sweeping, but in reality, presidents don't have all that much control over how the next chapter of this sprawling democratic experiment unfolds. Each president is subject to forces, whether external or of their own making, that will shape their legacy. War especially rewrites the story of a presidency in ways that are unpredictable and permanent. Joe Biden will be remembered as the president who ended a two-decades-long war in Afghanistan, but his presidency was marred by a botched and bloody withdrawal of American forces from the country. More than twenty years after September 11, 2001, Americans are still evaluating the legacy of President George W. Bush, the commander in chief who first approved the Afghan invasion as retaliation for the worst terror attack on American soil in the country's history.

In the brief eight-month period between George W. Bush's inauguration and September 11, George and Laura Bush were still adjusting to the White House after winning a controversial election. George's win hinged on 537 votes in the state of Florida, a margin so slim that it triggered a legal battle over a manual recount and introduced the unfortunate phrase "hanging chad" into American political discourse. After the Bush legal team challenged the timeframe of the recount under the state's election laws, the process was ultimately halted by the Supreme Court, and Bush was declared the forty-third president of the United States. The episode produced the first presidential win without the popular vote since 1888. George won Florida's crucial 25 electoral votes, putting him just over the line of the 270 votes he needed to win.

It was a rocky start for a man who had not been driven to the presidency by ambition so much as nudged toward it because he was part of an American political dynasty.

Since Prescott Bush—the father of President George H. W. Bush, George W.'s father—was elected a senator from Connecticut in 1952 (on his second try), members of the family have pursued and won some of the highest offices in the land, including two presidencies: the forty-first and the forty-third. Other victories in the family trophy case include one vice presidency, two governorships, and a House seat. According to the political scholar Stephen Hess, who wrote *America's Political Dynasties: From Adams to Clinton,* the Bush family ranks sixth among the ten most influential American dynasties, behind the Kennedys, the Roosevelts, the Rockefellers, the Harrisons, and the Adamses. The Bushes have tended to reject the idea that they are part of a dynastic structure. "I wouldn't call it a dynasty," George the younger told the author Susan Page. "I'd call it a tradition." Which, of course, is something only a person born into an incredibly privileged family can say.

TO UNDERSTAND JUST HOW quickly the Republican Party has veered to the conservative right since the 2000 election, look no further than the tale of George P. Bush. Handsome and bilingual, he is the former land commissioner of Texas and the son of Jeb Bush, the former governor of Florida, and his wife, Columba, who was born and raised in Mexico. In other words, he was supposed to be the latest fruit from a family tree that bore men destined for higher office.

In the spring of 2022, the young George lost an attorney general primary challenge against Ken Paxton—a beleaguered two-term incumbent facing a litany of legal and personal problems, including a federal indictment for securities fraud charges and reports of an extramarital affair. His loss to Paxton signaled that Republican voters were more interested in a candidate who would assail Democratic leaders than one who had name recognition but had been rebuffed by Donald Trump, the new party kingmaker.

There were no such signs of trouble a generation earlier, when George W. Bush's own ascent was largely unobstructed—the only thing that had ever threatened his rise was his own sense of listlessness and a period of heavy drinking—and he would remain untested until after he'd already won the presidency.

His father had moved to Texas after graduating from Yale University and serving in the military. He had taken his family, which included his eldest son, George, born on July 6, 1946, with him. In the 1950s, George senior began running the Zapata Petroleum Corporation, and the family's wealth, boosted by success in the oil business, gave the younger George the freedom to indulge in an extended Peter Pan era.

Like his father, George attended Yale as a legacy, the latest in a line of men in his family who had tooled around the leafy campus in New Haven. At Yale, he joined the secretive Skull and Bones society that his Ohio-born grandfather, Prescott, had once used as an entrée into the world of the East Coast business elite. In 1968, at the height of the Vietnam War, George signed up for pilot training with the Texas Air National Guard, despite only achieving a 25 percent—the lowest acceptable grade—on a pilot aptitude test. He had no interest in going overseas, and his involvement with the branch, then a well-known venue for well-connected young men to maneuver around the draft, was called into question during his presidential campaigns.

In 1973, after a suspension from the National Guard for missing an annual medical exam, George was discharged so that he could enter Harvard Business School—a development that seemed to please his parents. George was twenty-seven. People in Cambridge didn't quite know what to make of the young political scion who made middle-of-the-road grades and demonstrated little interest in the rigors of academia.

"One of my first recollections of him," Marty Kahn, a Harvard classmate, told *The Washington Post*, "was sitting in class and hearing the unmistakable sound of someone spitting tobacco." Kahn turned around and saw George W. Bush, then the son of the chairman of the Republican National Committee, spitting into a cup. Yosemite Sam among the pearl clutchers.

He continued to drift. In 1976, at age thirty, he was arrested for drunk driving near the family home in Kennebunkport, Maine. Years later, as Texas governor and a presidential candidate, George, under fire about his past partying, would later recall 1974 as the year when he stopped taking illicit drugs. Perhaps it was the specter of turning thirty that made him straighten up. Maybe it was the fact that his father had been a war hero, a husband, and a father with a bustling business by that age. Whatever it was, George returned to Midland, Texas, where he would try to see about striking out on his own in the oil business. Just like dad.

LAURA WELCH WAS A Midland girl. Born on November 4, 1946, to Harold, a home builder, and Jenna Welch, who handled his accounting, Laura lived out a comfortable childhood in a West Texas city that was built to do business. The streets arranged themselves in a sensible grid, making it impossible to get lost. Laura spent her teenage years living with her parents in a three-bedroom brick home on Humble Avenue, a street named not for virtue but for the oil company. In her bedroom, she would sit and read at a broad desk with bookshelves that reached to the ceiling.

With glossy brown hair, wide-set blue eyes, and a voice with a syrupy twang, young Laura was raised an only child, though her childhood was punctuated by miscarriages her mother suffered. In 1948, her mother gave birth prematurely to a baby boy who died days after he was born. Laura had wanted those siblings, and her parents had wanted those babies. Laura and her mother found peace in the moments when they could slip outside into the yard in the evenings, spreading out blankets and looking up into the vastness of a West Texas sky sprinkled with stars. The place where she is from is a city surrounded by nothing and everything. She would tell you that this does something to a person.

"Any sort of pretensions look especially ridiculous when you're there in such a hard West Texas landscape," she said in 2010. She was indeed unpretentious, a good girl, who, for the most part, was raised with everything in its right place. She was seventeen when she made the sort of mistake that makes it impossible to know if she was always going to grow into the kind of woman she became—one who is quietly and wholly protective of her internal life—or if she was broken that way.

Laura was driving too fast one evening in November 1963, chatting with her friend Judy, who sat in the passenger's seat, when she blew through a stop sign. She was driving her father's Chevy Impala when she plowed into a 1962 Corvair driven by Michael Douglas, one of her classmates at Robert E. Lee High School. At school, he had a gaggle of friends and had been voted most popular his junior year. In the cold shock of those first moments after the crash, before she knew who the other driver was and before she had learned that he had died, Laura found herself searching for God. She prayed. Then she begged.

"It was the first time that I had prayed to God for something, begged him for something, not the simple childhood wishing on a star but humbly begging for another human life. And it was as if no one heard," she wrote in her 2010 memoir, *Spoken from the Heart*, which was published forty-seven years after the crash and contains the most expansive thoughts she has ever shared about the accident.

"I think that she is an empathetic person by nature, and it probably made her less judgmental about other people, in a way we don't often see in Washington," said Ann Gerhart, who wrote *The Perfect Wife: The Life and Choices of Laura Bush,* a lyrical accounting of Laura's life. "She is more given to thinking people may have interior backgrounds and things that shaped them that we don't know."

In those first moments, she had prayed, but Mike, who had been a close friend of hers, was gone. He had suffered a broken neck. He was seventeen. No charges were filed and the crash was deemed an accident, but news of his death, and who had caused it, spread quickly through Midland. Rumors have surrounded the circumstances of the crash ever since; the gossip was that Mike and Laura had dated— a claim she has denied—and some said that she had not been headed to a drive-in theater, as she has said, but had been on her way from a party.

Laura, who was fearful of what the Douglases or anyone else in town might feel or say about her, did not show up to the funeral. Her guilt about the crash and her decisions in its aftermath, she has said, will haunt her for the rest of her life.

After a senior year spent turned inward, Laura enrolled at Southern Methodist University, declaring education as her major and joining the Kappa Alpha Theta sorority. Though many college-bound members of her generation came of age raging against the Vietnam War and fighting for civil rights, Laura was uninterested. In 1966, when Martin Luther King, Jr., gave a speech on the SMU campus to condemn the war, she did not attend.

Laura spent her time at school smoking, practicing a mechanical Miss America wave of her hand—"You just never know when it will come in handy," she told her friends—and honing her skills as a Midland debutante. But somehow she absorbed some of the teachings of second-wave feminism: When she accused her father, Harold, of "programming" her to be a teacher, he pulled out his wallet and declared that he would send her to law school.

"I had to admit, when he did that," she recalled to the journalist Frank Bruni in 2000, "that I didn't want to be a lawyer. I wanted to be a teacher." After graduating in 1968, she took a whirlwind tour of Europe before eventually settling into a job teaching third grade in Dallas. She was only there for a year before she hopped to Houston, where she taught at a majority-Black school, following a group of students from second to third grade during the two years she spent there. (In Houston, she lived at the Chateaux Dijon, the same memorably named apartment complex as her future husband, though their paths never crossed.) By the time she enrolled in graduate school at the University of Texas in Austin for a degree in library science, her parents were worried that she would end up an unmarried librarian.

Really, she was restless. After graduating, she went back to Houston, where she took a job as a children's librarian, but boomeranged back to Austin for better job and dating prospects. She joined the staff at Mollie Dawson Elementary School as a librarian in 1974. She was working there when she went home to Midland for a backyard barbecue, where she met George, a fellow drifter who was trying hard to tether himself to solid ground. Instead, he found—and fell for—the placid Laura.

On paper, the two of them didn't make much sense: George was a rambunctious jock from a complicated, powerful family. Laura was a public-school librarian with an independent streak. More than that, she was aware of his reputation. But she thought he was cute, and he made her laugh. (Bigger empires have been built with less.) It was only a bit of kindling, but it sparked an intense whirlwind of a courtship. George, his mother said, regarded Laura as "a lovely creature," and he liked that she was self-possessed and independent. She also did not seem to fear his family—Marvin Bush, George's brother, once described the dynamic as "Audrey Hepburn walking into the Animal House." They were bluebloods, but if she was intimidated by them, she did not let it show. In one Bush-lore scene from Kennebunkport, Laura was undaunted when the family matriarch, Dorothy Walker Bush, asked her what she did.

"I read, I smoke, and I admire," came the answer from the blue-eyed Texas wallflower, according to Barbara Bush. In a routine that was emblematic of their relationship, the two would go back and forth, publicly and in the press, about what Laura said in that interaction. (Laura is very sure she did not say "admire.") Barbara contended that the elder Mrs. Bush was shocked. When she married into the family, Laura would have to grapple with a mother-in-law who tended to take control, but Barbara praised Laura for her mediating influence on her son. Privately, Barbara said that of all her daughters-in-law, Laura was the one with First Lady potential.

Six weeks after their first date, George proposed—without a ring and without dropping down on his knee. Six weeks after that, they were married. There was an urgency to their courtship, perhaps to escape the existential morass that comes with starting a new decade: Their wedding date—November 5, 1977, at the United Methodist Church in Midland—was the day after Laura's thirty-first birthday, and a day before the fourteenth anniversary of the car crash. But, by all accounts, it was George who pushed the timetable. He, too, was in his early thirties, but more important, he was running for Congress.

"It wasn't like other couples who might let a relationship drag out because they had time to," said Laura in one unromantic recollection. "If we were going to be together, we needed to get married, and I needed to move to Midland."

If one or both of them rushed the engagement out of an urgency to start a family or to run for public office, the Bushes have never felt a need to explain themselves further. "Part of what is unique about both George and Laura is they hate to be 'interpreted,'" said Mark McKinnon, a former Bush adviser.

Laura resigned from her job and, after they married, joined George on the campaign trail. On that campaign, he made the vow to her that she would never have to deliver a political speech. George's promise echoes the one made by Joe Biden when Jill finally agreed to marry him: "I promise you, your life will never change." The Bidens and the Bushes were married within months of each other in 1977. Soon after she married Joe, Jill was brought before Democratic supporters in Delaware so they could get a good look at the woman who had taken Neilia Biden's place. And within three months of George's promise, Laura uneasily delivered her first speech, at a courthouse in a tiny town outside of Lubbock, Texas.

"If I'd have said, 'Honey, you'll be the kickoff speaker at the Republican convention in the year 2000,' she would have said, 'You've totally lost your mind, and I'm not marrying you,'" he told reporters during his first presidential campaign.

Laura's born-and-bred Texas twang could not save George's 1978 campaign for Texas's nineteenth congressional district. Under fire for his Connecticut roots and accused of being a carpetbagger, he lost the race. Still, by then, Laura had proven that she was steady, strong, and invested in whatever was best for George, even it required her to leave her comfort zone. She was the introverted teacher who became a haven for an extroverted and ambitious husband who seemed to need her to steady him. The Bidens share a similar dynamic.

In the years that followed George's congressional loss, the younger Bushes focused on establishing a family and a comfortable life that could function outside of his powerful family's long shadow. After years spent trying to conceive, and enduring a difficult pregnancy, Laura gave birth to twins, Barbara and Jenna, in November 1981. At that point, George was still trying to strike oil, trying to make money, and trying to establish himself as his own person. Somewhere in that whirlwind, he began drinking heavily, imbibing too much at functions and, at least once, accosting a reporter on behalf of his father. "This is a guy who's got problems," recalled Al Hunt, a journalist who had been on the receiving end of an expletive-laced tirade.

In Bush lore, this is the point where Laura threatened to leave him and is credited with delivering the hard line "It's either Jim Beam or me." She has denied ever saying it, instead choosing to credit her husband for a decision to go cold turkey after a drunken fortieth-birthday weekend in 1986. George also credited recommitting to his Christian faith—with an assist from the Reverend Billy Graham—as part of the reason he found the strength to quit.

"Our marriage was enduring, we loved each other, and we were two people who did not have divorce in our DNA," she wrote in her memoir, again putting a more demure spin on what had been reported. "But I was disappointed, and I let him know that I thought he could be a better man."

As George cleaned up, a whirlwind of self-actualization activities followed. He used his charisma and smooth-talking business skills to sell off his fledgling oil company, took a salary as a consultant, and moved his family to Washington, where they could advise the elder Bush's 1988 presidential campaign. It was during this period that observers say he became enchanted with the idea of national politics, even if he didn't so much care for substance or policy. "My motivation was, he's been a great dad," he told reporters about why he worked so feverishly on his father's presidential campaigns.

As a campaign adviser with a $5,000-a-month salary, he was devoted to his father—traveling on his behalf, meeting with supporters, and getting a firsthand lesson in what it might take to be a candidate. He also kept the blinders on when faced with the sort of temptation that had derailed him earlier in his life. When a young campaign aide became overly flirty with him, he told her off, and when it was suggested he apologize, he was indignant.

"I'm a married man," he said, his feathers ruffled. "I'm glad she got the signal." When there were rumors that his father, the vice president, had engaged in an affair with an assistant, George single-handedly worked to kill the story, ensuring that aides leaked a conversation he'd had with his father—and his father's denial—to the press.

After the election, George and Laura and the kids loaded up and went back to Texas, because it had become clear to George that he needed, again, to become his own person if he was going to succeed in business or politics. Using his gift of gab, he leveraged the sale of his oil company and pooled money with a roster of well-to-do buddies to buy the Houston Astros. But he kept a close eye on his father's orbit—Bush 41 officials were never completely free of the son who could be confrontational with his father's aides and made sure powerful friends back in Texas received the occasional autographed trinket from the president.

After his father lost his reelection bid, George and a team of ad-

visers, including Karl Rove and Joe Allbaugh, began preparing for the
1994 Texas gubernatorial race. He defeated Ann Richards, a popular
Democratic incumbent, by targeting her liberal policies, promoting
the idea that encouraging personal responsibility was at the root of
his self-described compassionate brand of conservatism. Texans responded to his pitch by voting him into office.

The Bushes were on the move again, this time to Austin. There,
the Bush administration created an accountability system for public
schools—the precursor to the No Child Left Behind Act—and pre-
sided over a historic increase in executions. He won reelection in a
landslide. In the six years he served as governor, he allowed 152 executions to go forward and granted a single stay. His critics saw his politics not as compassionate but as a merciless and extreme application
of the law.

Still, the Bushes were popular in Texas, and Laura was a well-liked
First Lady. In 1995, she created the Texas Book Festival, which is now
one of the most popular of its kind in the United States. She had arrived in Austin with trepidation about what—and how much—she
might be required to do. In the end, she stuck to what she knew.

"I finally said, 'Well, if I'm going to be a public figure, I might as
well do what I've always liked doing'"—which, to her, meant "acting
like a librarian and getting people interested in reading."

Championing literacy was about as uncontroversial a topic as one
could choose, but critics were hoping that Laura was secretly a mod-
erating force behind her husband as he hewed to his conservative
agenda. There were public and private suggestions among people in
her orbit that she supported abortion, and gun control, and protecting
the environment. ("She's a Republican by marriage," a former Bush
White House official told me.) Like so many women before and
since, she became the person people expected to drag her husband
toward the middle, but this was never really their dynamic. In Austin
and in Washington, she was not there to push George toward policy
or to mediate some of the more conservative voices in his ear. She was
there to remind him where he came from.

"I think she was good at helping George W. maintain perspective among all the pomp and circumstance," Mark McKinnon said. Laura was, he added, "always ready to give her husband a gentle yank on the leash to remind him that West Texas wasn't that far back in the rear-view mirror."

In the days after her husband was declared the winner of the 2000 presidential election, she sidestepped requests for interviews about how she intended to use her new platform. Instead, she issued a brief statement, pledging to stay in the modest lane she'd established for herself in Austin. She had no interest in trying to push the role forward, at least not in the way that Hillary Clinton had tried. There were no plans to keep an office in the West Wing. She came to the White House as the second First Lady in history with a postgraduate degree, but was not going to use her credentials to launch a hefty new policy initiative. She was going to be, in her own words, traditional.

"I have a lifelong passion for introducing children to the magic of words. I was a public school teacher and I know what a difficult and rewarding job teaching is. I am proud of my efforts on behalf of the children of Texas and I look forward to building those efforts on behalf of all American schoolchildren."

It was a plainspoken and vague statement, free of the sort of lofty language that an incoming president brings to work on the first day in office. There was wiggle room inside that statement, and it didn't overpromise. Always the steady girl from Midland, Laura Welch Bush had learned long ago that even the best-laid plans could unravel in the space of an instant. Her hard-won respect for fate would serve her well in the months and years to come.

ON THE EVENING BEFORE her husband was inaugurated, Laura approached James Billington, then the librarian of Congress, and told him she had an idea: She had organized the Texas Book Festival as First Lady back in Austin, and that had been a hit. Could the same sort of thing work in Washington?

For the first several months she was in office, it seemed that Laura was hitting her stride early. She hosted the first White House state dinner for the president of Mexico, and the East Wing worked with the Library of Congress to organize the first book festival held on a national scale. Sixty authors, including Richard Peck and Nathaniel Philbrick, agreed to appear on Capitol Hill for the event, held on September 8, 2001. The festival drew thousands of book lovers from across the country. Olympians and NBA stars signed up to read children's books at a specially designed young-adult reader's pavilion. Attendees recalled beautiful weather, and some lazed under trees as they listened to storytellers.

Three days later, the sky was still strikingly cloudless and blue. Hurricane Erin was churning off the East Coast of the United States, but a cold front was pushing her farther out to sea. It was one of those late-summer days in Washington that felt like a reward after a soupy, hot August spent in the capital.

That morning, Laura saw her visiting in-laws off and was preparing to appear before the Senate Education Committee, which at the time was chaired by Senator Edward M. Kennedy, Democrat from Massachusetts. The introverted Laura was anxious about delivering a speech on early childhood education and was rehearsing as she got ready. She was so distracted by the appearance that she did not turn on the television and did not learn that a plane had hit the North Tower of the World Trade Center in New York City until she was in the car on the way to the Capitol. A second plane, one of four hijacked by terrorists from the radical Islamist group al-Qaeda, hit the South Tower as she was en route to deliver her speech.

In Senator Kennedy's office, the stunned First Lady went through the motions as Kennedy gave her a tour, presented her with a gift, and tried continuing genial small talk without acknowledging that the planes had hit the towers. The two were joined by Senator Judd Gregg, a Republican from New Hampshire and an ally of the Bush White House. In the haze of shock and confusion, they told reporters that the hearing had been postponed. As Laura was escorted out of Kennedy's office and toward a safe part of the Capitol, she answered a question from a reporter asking for a message to the country's children: "Well, parents need to reassure their children everywhere in our country that they're safe," the First Lady said.

As she walked away from reporters, one of her staffers told her that a plane had hit the Pentagon. She was moved to a secure office, where she began trying to reach her daughters. Both were safe in their college dorms: Jenna at the University of Texas at Austin, Barbara at Yale. Laura was evacuated from the Capitol and taken to the Secret Service headquarters. On the way, United Airlines flight 93 plunged into a field in Shanksville, Pennsylvania, forced down by passengers. She could not reach George, who was flying aboard Air Force One, until noon that day. The Bushes were safe, but after that, nothing was the same.

"From the way he spoke, I could hear how starkly his presidency had been transformed," she wrote in her memoir.

The attacks killed 2,977 people. In the days and weeks afterward, the names of the dead ran on a ticker at the bottom of newscasts across the country, a slow-motion accounting of the attack's breathtakingly ferocious scale. Without Twitter or Facebook or widely available cellphones, Americans watched television—imbibing the coverage of people dropping out of buildings, the first responders who died in the rubble, the rescue dogs, the farewell voicemails, the men and women still searching for loved ones, New York City's mayor at Ground Zero, the president in Washington promising vengeance.

On his inauguration day, George W. Bush had spoken about an angel guiding America, but there was no room for grace, no collective interest in litigating democratic ideals, in the aftermath of the attacks. Americans were united in their need for revenge, and George's approval rating soared to 86 percent as he sent American troops into Afghanistan to topple the Taliban and hunt for Osama bin Laden, the architect of the attack. The rally-around-the-flag effect was short-lived: His approval ratings cratered as the public's trust in the American military response plunged. The mishandled federal response to Hurricane Katrina sank his popularity even further.

The attack redefined George's presidency, but it also gave Laura a new focus as First Lady. She quickly had to learn to become the healer-in-chief alongside her husband. In November 2001, Laura, the woman who had married George under the expectation that she would never have to make a political speech, took over the president's weekly radio address, making her the first of any First Lady to do so. The Taliban was in retreat, and American officials were beginning to envision a country that embraced Western ideals. Bush administration officials, including Karen P. Hughes, had launched a public campaign to push for increased freedoms for women and girls, and Laura was brought in as an uncontroversial voice who could circulate the administration's message.

"Civilized people throughout the world are speaking out in horror—not only because our hearts break for the women and children in Afghanistan but also because, in Afghanistan, we see the world the terrorists would like to impose on the rest of us," she said in her first address.

Laura's communication style as First Lady is what Lauren Wright, a Princeton University professor who studies how these women are deployed on behalf of their administrations, calls "covert, not overt." By taking on a specific chunk of the larger 9/11 response, she was able to put herself at arm's length from the politicized and controversial actions taken by her husband's administration. Wright said that Laura did the same with her so-called pet projects, which included the literacy festival, an effort that paired with the administration's No Child Left Behind policy but did not directly involve her in the politicking. In her book *On Behalf of the President: Presidential Spouses and White House Communications Strategy Today,* Wright argues that Laura's strategy was "perhaps a reaction to the unsuccessful attempts of the Clinton administration to place the first lady at the center of the public policymaking process." A former official who worked in Laura's East Wing told me this was exactly the strategy.

Laura responded to the demands of being a wartime First Lady with characteristic resignation, but she also did something she had never done before: She started revealing more of herself. In a question-and-answer discussion she held after a speech in Washington in November 2001, she showcased a dry and sometimes irreverent sense of humor when she was asked if she'd consider writing a book about her time at the White House: "I guess it'll be whether or not I can get that $8 million advance," she said, referencing Hillary Clinton's recent book deal.

During that same session, she also said she handled the stress of her life by reading, before adding, "I'm also working out. Can y'all tell?" Laura's East Wing always deployed her allies to talk to reporters about how tough she was, how grounded and witty she could be. But she was best when she stepped onto the stage and spoke for herself.

As the rebuilding of Afghanistan continued and American troops entered Iraq, Laura continued her work to support Afghan women and girls. In 2005, she made a secret trip there, visiting the country before her husband did and spending six hours on the ground with young teachers, students, and President Hamid Karzai. She returned in 2006 with her husband, and again in 2008, amid surging violence and appeals for billions of dollars more in American assistance toward building the fledgling democracy.

"Everybody knew that whatever Laura Bush was doing was not for her own sake; it was for his," said Anita McBride, the First Lady's former chief of staff, as she recalled the planning process for the Afghanistan trips, which required significant resources to pull off under the cover of secrecy. "In my interview with her, to be her chief of staff, one of the first things she said to me was 'I'm not here for me, I'm here for George.' I knew instinctively, that opened up every possible opportunity that I needed to utilize the West Wing to help her help him."

Laura had little interest in wading into domestic matters and, true to form, preferred to stay neutral amid cultural battles, including the debate over same-sex marriage. Her White House Easter Egg Roll became a hotbed of controversy when same-sex couples were vowing to attend the event, despite the objection of religious conservatives. The East Wing sidestepped the opportunity to stake a position, but it did declare that "all families" were welcome, no matter their composition. While George publicly tied himself into knots trying to explain his stance on whether gay and lesbian couples should marry, Laura was almost casual in her acknowledgment that the Bushes had gay friends. "Sure, of course, everyone does," she said.

Something happens when a First Lady begins to speak up more and show up more. Observers begin to wonder how much talking she does with her husband, and how much influence she might have over him. Reporters began to file stories about Laura's influence over West Wing staffing (an idea she downplayed) and her interest in George replacing Justice Sandra Day O'Connor, the first female justice to serve on the Supreme Court, with another woman. (Bush allies scrambled to say that she was just reflecting her husband's thinking.) The push-and-pull of her taking a step forward only to have her allies or administration officials walk her statements back became common enough that the people who tried to assess her legacy often ended up back where they started: She was there for George.

"First ladies are stereotyped as either the powerhouse or the woman behind the man, baking the cookies, and for some reason my mom got that stereotype, and she is nothing like that," her daughter, Jenna Bush Hager, told *The Washington Post* in 2014. "Throughout my dad's presidency and afterward, she's been this sort of quiet force."

Still, there is some evidence to suggest that Laura was curious about how her work as First Lady would be viewed against the scope of history, especially since her husband's presidency was overshadowed by a terror attack and two wars.

In the fall of 2008, months before the Bushes were due to leave the White House, Laura invited a group of journalists and historians to spend the day with her—just like Jill would do years later.

The historian Myra Gutin attended and said that it was clear that Laura and East Wing officials wanted to understand how she might be viewed by history. The group was treated to morning coffee, a private lunch, and an afternoon tour of the White House, including when she showed them an unrestored spot that was still scorched from 1814, when British troops burned down the building. (After spending several hours with her, one attendee was surprised to find out that Laura had an impressive recall for names, faces, and the finer points of the Bush administration's foreign policy doctrine. "I did not think she was that sharp.")

When it came to her press coverage and how she would be seen after leaving the White House, said Gutin, Laura was circumspect and careful in her remarks and questions with the group.

"I'd been studying First Ladies for a long time, and it was the first time I had been invited to the White House as a guest with an incumbent First Lady," Gutin said. "No historians or scholars had been given that opportunity previously. It was a big deal."

In the meeting, Laura emphasized that she had taken over her husband's radio address to further the White House message on Afghan women and girls and told the group that she hoped to keep working with them in the future. When she and her husband left the White House, she had an approval rating among American adults of 76 percent, according to Gallup, compared with her husband's, which hovered around 34 percent.

In the years since leaving the White House, the Bushes have largely retreated into private life, but she has given periodic speeches about the need for progress for Afghanistan's women. In December 2022, when an ascendant Taliban government took away the right of young women to study at university, the Bushes released a joint statement condemning the government for taking away "universal human rights."

President George W. Bush's decisions in the wake of the September 11, 2001, attacks, and their effect on American life, will continue to be explored by a fleet of historians and journalists. People who know Laura well say her legacy is one of more depth than she was initially given credit for, and that it should include an assessment of her work on Afghanistan. She also took several trips to Africa to promote the U.S. President's Emergency Plan for AIDS Relief, or PEPFAR—an enduring global funding program that began with the Bush administration. But it is her steadfast defense of her husband and sense of self-direction that most stands out.

"I used to say to her, 'Mrs. Bush, how do you handle this criticism of your husband all the time? It's the person you love the most,'"

McBride recalled. This is when she saw the steelier side of the First Lady.

"'You don't get into this world if you can't take it,'" she said Laura once replied. "'Do I like it? Of course not. But I know who George is. This is a part of politics.'

"That grounding really allows you to not curl up in a ball, and you just keep going," McBride added.

CHAPTER FOUR

EXPECTATION

I N RICHARD BEN CRAMER'S OPUS RETELLING OF THE 1988 PRES-
idential campaign, *What It Takes: The Way to the White House,* Jill Biden
appears as the wife who gamely went along for the ride, even if she
was not always enthusiastic. Cramer also noticed something important about her: Jill was not the political "infant" her husband's advisers had assumed she would be.

She had good instincts, and she was concerned about Joe's ability
to break ahead in a crowded field of potential candidates. As the campaign continued, she had become disillusioned at different points on
the trail, largely because the "family time" with Jill and the children
that Joe had promised was whittled down and then stripped away
altogether in favor of dinners with bigwigs and other must-do glad-
hand events. She wanted her husband to win, but she did not enjoy
watching their old life recede by the minute. Ironically, back then,
what bothered her most was the idea that Joe would lose and keep
trying to win indefinitely.

Solidifying the family unit was so crucial to Jill that she had included Beau and Hunter in the announcement when she became
pregnant with Ashley, the daughter who came along in 1980. To stave
off any concern that the boys might feel left out, Jill ferried them to
the drugstore to buy the pregnancy test. Then she let them announce
to their father that a new baby was coming.

"The boys actually knew we were going to have a baby before I did," Joe wrote in his memoir *Promises to Keep*, "and Jill never forgot how excited they were that day. She told them they could pick the baby's name, and Beau and Hunter named their sister Ashley."

But keeping the family stable would be more challenging now that Joe's first presidential race required more time and energy. There is a scene in *What It Takes* that Cramer captures, a private moment between Jill and Ruth Berry, a Senate aide who had begun traveling with the Bidens when the campaigning started in earnest.

The two women were sitting on a plane and, as Joe napped, quietly discussing what Jill might do if everything worked out. Jill wanted to know: What might be expected of her if she became First Lady? Then, the slumbering candidate woke up and turned to his wife.

"Honey, don't listen to anyone," he told his wife. "You just do what you're comfortable with."

He was hardly as chivalrous to Berry, a hired hand. "Goddammit!" he said to her, per Cramer's retelling. "Don't you *ever* tell Jill what she's got to do."

Though Jill would apologize on her husband's behalf ("He just gets that way sometimes"), the exchange was a lesson for staffers on how to interact with Jill. She was not the one who'd been elected and therefore was not to be pushed into doing anything that she did not want to do. This has been the operational guidance for all Biden aides for the past four decades.

Still, Jill has been undoubtedly shaped by her efforts to live up to the expectations of the family she married into. At points throughout her life, she has pushed herself out of her comfort zone and polished her presence as a public figure, because it was what was necessary to help her husband win. That does not mean she has been comfortable with the idea that she is expected to look or act like a capital-P Political Spouse. As Second Lady, she spent eight years watching Michelle Obama wrangle with the role and its expectations—both external and internal, both reasonable and unreasonable. Neither of them had wanted their lives to change as much as they did, and both have had to shape their identities in real time as they went.

———

A LIFE IN POLITICS is not something Michelle Obama ever wanted. She only reluctantly agreed to let her husband run for the presidency, and once he won, she carried the responsibility of being the first Black First Lady in the country's history. She raised two young girls while she did all of this. So her post–White House life is, comparatively, all about Michelle.

During the winter of 2022, at book tour appearances for *The Light We Carry: Overcoming in Uncertain Times,* Michelle's memoir with a self-help spin, she strode onstage to an introduction from Oprah Winfrey, with Beyoncé thumping through the venue speakers. Statuesque, Michelle glided across stages toward tycoons and talk show hosts, dressed in citron-hued Proenza Schouler suits, all-denim Ganni ensembles, or a fire-engine red Versace tunic—all curated by her longtime stylist, Meredith Koop. Her hair, twisted into tree braids by a traveling hairstylist, was either worn down, swept into a chignon, or styled half up and half down with a topknot.

She is so popular within the Democratic Party that she is still sometimes asked about running for the presidency—a question she detests, because the answer is no. Michelle is enjoying the post–East Wing phase of her life, which involves watching her daughters furnish their shared Los Angeles apartment with Ikea finds and mastering the art of knitting. On her book tour, sharing her insights on overcoming adversity in front of a rapturous audience, she appears less like a political spouse and much more like a blossoming lifestyle mogul.

Like any other woman who has held the role of First Lady since the turn of the century, Michelle defined herself and her legacy in real time. She faced the same questions the others did: Would she work? Was she *just* going to be a mom? What would her platform be? For Jill and Melania and Laura and Hillary, the questions stopped there. Only Michelle carried the extra weight of being the first Black woman in the role, which meant she spent eight years grappling with an additional set of queries directly and indirectly about the color of her skin.

If she expressed an opinion, did that make her an angry Black woman? Was she showing sufficient gratitude for her life in the White House? And why were her arms so toned and strong-looking? Suddenly it seems like no coincidence that Michelle, who was criticized for appearing in a sleeveless sheath dress in her official White House portrait in 2009, looked so visibly happy—and free—to be wearing a Fila jacket and braids, entirely celebrating her identity and her heritage.

From the very beginning of her time in the public eye, which has been for a shorter period than any of her recent counterparts, Michelle has presented herself as a political spouse who has little patience for politics. According to her newest memoir, when Barack, then a Senator from Illinois, came to her in late 2006 and shared that he was interested in a presidential run, he ultimately told her that the decision to move forward was hers. She wanted to say no. They had two young daughters. She loved her job. And she wanted to avoid facing the scrutiny and judgment that would come with campaigning at the highest level of politics. But she said yes, she wrote, because "I didn't want to live with the alternative version of that story. I didn't want to be a family that sat around the dinner table, talking about the paths not taken or what might have been." She did not want to tell her children or grandchildren that her husband had once had the potential to be president.

After a period spent hashing out a path forward with his advisers—and after Michelle had personally approved the plans—Barack announced his campaign on February 10, 2007, entering a race that already had a perceived front-runner: Hillary Clinton. For a spouse with little interest in politics, Michelle worked hard campaigning for her husband. In her earliest appearances, Michelle, a Harvard-educated lawyer from the South Side of Chicago, traveled to crucial primary states, including New Hampshire, and told the story of her biracial, Hawaiian-born husband—whom she had expected to be "weird" before she met him—with a particular emphasis on their love story. She cultivated a reputation as the blunter of the two Obamas, most notably beginning in February 2008, when she declined to say if she would support Hillary Clinton as the Democratic nominee. "I'd have to think about—policies, her approach, her tone," she said in an interview on *Good Morning America*. She was much more cynical than her husband about the very nature of politics and had been that way long before she appeared on the national stage.

"I didn't come to politics with a lot of faith in the process," Michelle said in 2004. "I didn't believe that politics was structured in a way that could solve real problems for people, so you can imagine how I felt when Barack approached me to run for state senate. I said, 'I married you because you're cute and you're smart, but this is the dumbest thing you could have ever asked me to do.'" Different versions of that conversation would continue to creep into the dynamic of their marriage as Barack's star continued to rise.

She brought a dry wit and a straightforward speaking style with her to the trail, qualities that she quickly sanded down when she made a well-documented misstep, telling voters in Wisconsin in February 2008 that her husband's campaign had ushered in an era of hope: "For the first time in my adult lifetime, I am really proud of my country," she said.

That was the end of the honeymoon phase. After a spring and summer spent weathering headlines accusing her of hating her country and enduring racist nicknames—one that particularly stung her was being called "Obama's baby mama"—she became a more polished and more guarded campaign wife. She responded to some attacks, like when she was accused of delivering a speech criticizing "whitey"—"That's something that George Jefferson would say," she quipped, a sign that her sense of humor was still alive—and she passed on others, including when a congressman from Georgia called the Obamas "uppity."

Contrasting himself with Hillary Clinton, an establishment figure with baggage, the forty-seven-year-old Barack campaigned on change. He promised to end the Iraq War—which Hillary had initially supported—and to overhaul healthcare, an effort Clinton had started fifteen years earlier. The Obama campaign was powered by grassroots supporters who harnessed social media and the internet to reach small-dollar donors, raising $656 million from individual contributions. Compared with Hillary, who could come across as stiff during her campaign appearances, Barack was a charismatic and gifted orator. And he was a Black candidate who appealed to blue-collar and rural voters. Lightning in a bottle.

By the time Barack was declared the nominee, Michelle had begun to take an almost academic approach to her role. She practiced her speech for the 2008 Democratic National Convention in Denver so many times that she spoke from memory when the teleprompter broke. "Through weeks of careful and slightly anxious preparation, I had managed to armor myself against panic," she wrote in *The Light We Carry*. "I knew it inside and out." In her memoir, she said her sense of preparation resulted from her brother, Craig, coaching her family through regular fire drills as a child. Her childhood had taught her to plan for the worst and look for the exit routes. In a sixteen-minute speech delivered at the convention, Michelle painted a portrait of her husband as the embodiment of what America could be if it just tried.

Her speech hit all the marks. She portrayed her husband as a doting father who had cautiously driven home from the hospital after his first daughter was born, and how becoming a parent had allowed him to give his children what he had never had: "the affirming embrace of a father's love." He was the candidate whose campaign was built on hope—she used the word eight times. But her remarks also seemed designed to reintroduce her after a campaign season in which she'd been criticized for not sufficiently praising her country and other candidates. In a graceful moment, she also praised Hillary Clinton, "who put those eighteen million cracks in the glass ceiling, so that our daughters—and sons—can dream a little bigger and aim a little higher." She ticked through the people she said were threads of the American story, from Joe Biden to teachers to America's caregivers.

"That is why," she said, "I love this country."

Barack was elected with 53 percent of the popular vote, trouncing

John McCain, a senator from Arizona, whose campaign had been beset with problems—most memorably the selection of Sarah Palin, the firebrand governor of Alaska, as his running mate. The Obama victory demolished a significant racial barrier, but there were signs of trouble during the campaign. A month before the election, McCain defended his opponent when a woman at a campaign event remarked that she had been doing some reading on Obama and that he was "an Arab." With a "No, ma'am," McCain immediately defended Barack as a "decent family man," stressing that the campaign was about their differences over issues ranging from the military to the economy. Later at the same event, McCain was booed for saying he respected his opponent. Barack may have won states that had not voted Democratic in decades, but the angry, nationalistic reaction from the conservative right was making its way from the fringes to the political mainstream.

Just before Barack's presidential run, Michelle had made $273,618 a year as vice president of community external affairs at the University of Chicago Medical Center, then gradually reduced her hours to a part-time role. Her decision as First Lady to leave her job prompted a widespread debate over whether the most visible woman in American politics had given up the chance to be a pioneer for working women. Even Cherie Blair, the wife of Tony Blair, the former British prime minister, weighed in from across the Atlantic.

"It is something of an irony that in these days of pushing for equality those of us married to our political leaders have to put their own ambitions on hold while their spouses are in office and keep their views to themselves," wrote Blair, an attorney and mother of four. "I, at least, had my career. That is not an option for Michelle Obama."

Years later, Michelle is still explaining that initial decision: "I know how to work, I know how to be a professional. I knew, you know, but I thought it was an important thing to say, 'I have to control what I can,'" she told the talk show host Conan O'Brien in 2022. Making sure her daughters were settled was such a priority to her that she considered delaying her move to Washington, an idea she ultimately abandoned. A First Lady not accompanying her husband to Washington was simply unheard of, and after years of commuting back and forth between Washington and Illinois, Barack wanted everyone under one roof.

MICHELLE LAVAUGHN ROBINSON WAS born in Chicago on January 17, 1964, the second child of Fraser Robinson III, who worked at one of the city's water treatment plants, and Marian Robinson, a homemaker. Michelle and her brother were raised in a second-floor apartment in a house on leafy Euclid Avenue on the city's South Side. She has called her upbringing traditional, and she and her older brother, Craig, interacted with a rotating cast of extended family members, including a great-aunt, Robbie, a piano teacher who owned the building and occupied the apartment on the home's first floor. Michelle grew up listening to the sounds of plinking piano keys and the voices of local church ladies loudly practicing their hymns. The struggles of the late 1960s, even the nearby riots during the 1968 Democratic National Convention in Grant Park, were mostly lost on Michelle, who enjoyed a peaceful existence with her attentive parents and her protective brother.

She was only glancingly aware of the prejudices her family members had faced, including the prim Robbie, who had once sued Northwestern University for discrimination when she was denied a dorm room after registering to attend a music workshop on campus in the 1940s. Robbie's husband, Terry, had been a porter on an overnight train line, a job that Black men almost exclusively staffed. Her maternal grandfather, a man the family called "Southside"—his birth name was Purnell Shields—had moved to Chicago in the 1920s from Alabama to escape the Jim Crow South. The descendant of a woman named Melvinia Shields McGruder who had grown up in slavery in Georgia, Southside "didn't trust the police, and he didn't always trust white people, either," Michelle wrote. She grew up celebrating her birthdays and listening to music at her grandfather's house, playing Stevie Wonder and Ella Fitzgerald and Miles Davis on the turntable.

Michelle was a diligent student, whether the assignment involved earning her strict aunt's praise at the piano or learning to read before she started kindergarten at Bryn Mawr Elementary. She was reserved compared with other kids at school, preferring to stay home and play with her dolls rather than join the pack of youngsters who played outside after school in the afternoons. Meanwhile, the neighborhood outside was changing as white residents rapidly moved away, seeking sameness in the suburbs or in more affluent areas of the city. The changes began to manifest at Bryn Mawr, where Michelle's mother quietly negotiated for her daughter to be tested and moved into a gifted third-grade class—away from an unruly group of classmates in a basement classroom. She has called her mother's advocacy a small move that changed her life. Her father, who suffered from multiple sclerosis, coached her in the ways of neighborhood survival, including how to throw a punch at a neighborhood bully.

As they grew, Michelle and Craig, who were born less than two years apart, began to stand out from the other neighborhood kids, who asked pointed questions. "How come you talk like a white girl?" a neighbor once asked ten-year-old Michelle, which gave the future First Lady the distinct impression that she didn't quite fit in anywhere. At Bryn Mawr, Michelle and other students in the gifted program took field trips to local colleges and dissected rodents in a biology lab. Her mother was in the PTA, and was a constant presence in her children's lives, serving as a sounding board and confessor.

As she prepared for high school, Michelle took another round of tests and was admitted to Whitney M. Young, the first magnet school in the city of Chicago. In her 2018 memoir, *Becoming*, Michelle called the place "a kind of equal-opportunity nirvana, meant to draw high-performing students of all colors." Her commute from her South Side neighborhood to the school's modern campus outside of the Loop could take her ninety minutes by city bus each way. The nineteen-hundred-strong student population intimidated Michelle, who had been raised in a relative cocoon on the South Side. For the first time in her life, she was around Black students from affluent families—kids who talked about fancy vacations and summer internships and that final frontier: college.

"At Whitney Young," she wrote in *Becoming*, "it was safe to be smart. The assumption was that everyone was working toward college, which meant that you never hid your intelligence for fear of someone saying you talked like a white girl." Her parents, who had never been to Europe, scraped together money for Michelle to attend a trip to Paris with her classmates. She made friends with Santita Jackson, the eldest child of the Reverend Jesse Jackson, which gave her a first brush with political activism. She attended a local march with the Jackson family and felt distinctly uncomfortable with being on display. "The fanfare was fun and even intoxicating, but there was something about it, and about politics in general, that made me queasy."

Michelle followed her brother to Princeton University and was one of 94 Black students out of 1,100 students who enrolled in the fall of 1981. She and her brother, who was a basketball star, became adept at navigating all-white spaces, but they did not escape comments about their race from classmates and, in Michelle's case, from the mother of one of her freshman-year roommates, who lobbied the school for her to be replaced with a white student.

"If you're young and black and from the South Side, there are always going to be people who feel you should not be there," Craig Robinson told reporters Michael Powell and Jodi Kantor of the experience in 2008. "You build up a thick skin." In Michelle's senior-year thesis, titled "Princeton-Educated Blacks and the Black Community," she explored how attending a majority-white institution had made her more aware of her Blackness than ever before. "The path I have chosen to follow by attending Princeton," she wrote in the introduction, "will likely lead to my further integration and/or assimilation into a white cultural and social structure that will only allow me to remain on the periphery of society, never becoming a full participant."

Michelle graduated from Princeton in 1985 and attended Harvard Law School, graduating in 1988. She took a job at Sidley Austin, a corporate law firm. Her position came with a forty-seventh-floor office that overlooked Lake Michigan—and an assistant. Michelle wore Armani suits and bought herself a Saab. She was enjoying the new rhythm of her seventy-hour workweeks when she was assigned to mentor a summer associate, a guy from Harvard named Barack Obama. She was skeptical of the rumors she had heard about him before they met, including that he was among the most gifted law students ever to grace Harvard. Over an introductory lunch, Michelle, who had grown up feeling torn between different communities— Black and white, poor and rich—was impressed by the ease with which Barack, the son of a white woman from Kansas and a Black man from Kenya, had navigated a childhood spent in Hawaii and Indonesia. He was at once cerebral and charismatic, a bookworm and a brilliant legal mind who loved basketball and had an off-putting smoking habit.

"To me, he was sort of like a unicorn," she wrote. "Unusual to the point of being almost unreal." They fell in love over a summer of mixing with other associates at firm functions and spending evenings at his cramped walk-up apartment on Fifty-third Street. She followed him to a meeting at a Black church in the Roseland neighborhood, where he spoke emphatically to South Side residents about their collective ability to register voters and persuade local leaders to deliver more resources to the community. "Do we settle for this world as it is," he asked in a booming voice, "or do we work for the world as it should be?" It was a moment she would later mythologize in her 2008 convention speech.

They married on October 3, 1992, at the Trinity United Church of Christ in Chicago. Michelle wore an off-the-shoulder white dress, with her hair swept up and adorned with a veil. Her groom wore a black suit, a white satin bowtie, and, in several photos, a smear of cake frosting on his nose. The next handful of years were a whirlwind, with Barack picking away at a book manuscript and taking a job for the advocacy organization Project Vote, where his goal was to register thousands of Black voters throughout the state of Illinois. Michelle had switched from Sidley to city hall, where she worked for the city of Chicago's Department of Planning. That job brought her into contact with Valerie Jarrett, who became a top adviser and confidante in the Obama administration.

In 1995, Barack published *Dreams from My Father: A Story of Race and Inheritance* while teaching at the University of Chicago and soon thereafter went into politics, winning a seat in the Illinois Senate in 1996. After a struggle to conceive and a round of fertility-stimulating drugs—which Michelle administered on her own while her husband toiled away in the state legislature—the Obamas got pregnant. They welcomed their first daughter, Malia, in 1998, and another, Natasha— they would call her Sasha—in 2001. Michelle, who at that point was the associate dean of student services at the University of Chicago, became a bleary-eyed working mother. Barack set his sights on higher office, running unsuccessfully to unseat Representative Bobby Rush, a popular Democratic incumbent, in the 2000 primary, before winning a Senate seat in 2004. It was around this time that Michelle began feeling a growing resentment about sharing her husband with the demanding world of electoral politics.

"As Sasha and Malia grew, I found that the pace only quickened and the to-do lists only got longer, leaving me operating in what felt like a never-ending state of overdrive," she wrote. Michelle, at the time, was an executive at the University of Chicago Medical Center— a high-powered professional trying to parent two young girls. She was in love with her husband, but they were two different people who were raised on different sides of the world. Barack was gone often, pursuing his future and working long hours. The pace of his life had become a source of deep-rooted tension. A round of couple's counseling, she said, helped her see "that there were ways I could be happier and that they didn't necessarily need to come from Barack's quitting politics."

So she began powering down her own career to support her ultra-ambitious husband, and to be there for their girls. By the time Barack convinced her to stand by his side for a presidential campaign, Michelle had tempered her own professional ambitions, and in the process had developed a blunt, almost cynical sense of humor about her life.

She initially told reporters that it had been no trouble to step away from her job to be a wife and mother in the White House, though she later said the decision pained her. On election night in Chicago, as the Obamas prepared to greet supporters in Grant Park, the soon-to-be First Lady glanced at her husband and shot him a one-liner: "You actually pulled this off?"

AFTER THE OBAMAS MOVED into the White House, Michelle spent much of the next eight years refining her public identity, constantly negotiating how much to share of herself. In the beginning, everyone seemed to want everything from the self-described mom in chief.

"The political committees wanted her to raise money for them, campaign for every candidate in every state. Members of Congress wanted her to come to their district," said Bill Burton, who served as a deputy press secretary in the Obama White House. "Lots of people out there in the world wanted her to be the spokesperson for American women or to be out in front when some sort of race-based incident occurred. She just had a different path."

Even though she had decided years ago to try to make peace with the demands of her husband's political career, at times she lost her patience when presidential duties interfered with family time. During a vacation to Hawaii in December 2009, Burton recalled being assigned the unfortunate task of pulling the president away from a waiting motorcade to give a statement about the arrest of a man who had tried to detonate explosives hidden in his underwear aboard a flight from Amsterdam to Detroit on Christmas Day. When Burton went back outside, he saw an annoyed First Lady standing next to a waiting SUV, looking right at him.

"She had these big sunglasses on and turned and walked to the car," Burton said. "She was clearly annoyed that her kids had been made to wait in a car as they were going to go someplace, with the final result that he wasn't even going to go with them."

At first, Michelle had pledged to only work—unpaid—as First Lady twice a week, a decision designed to ensure that her daughters were thriving and happy in a new city and at Sidwell Friends, one of the most elite schools in Washington.

"She was fiercely protective of the girls," said Jen Psaki, who served as deputy press secretary and deputy communications director in the Obama White House. Michelle was also far more removed from her husband's political orbit than other First Ladies, including Jill Biden, have been. "She kind of ran her own orbit more. She used her world to drive things and make changes in a way that her husband would never have the interest or capacity to do."

That included, Psaki said, making the First Couple "cool." While Barack was the brainy policy wonk, Michelle was interested in the arts and pop culture. With a personal style that was both straightforward and warm—a contrast with a husband who was politically gifted but often reserved and cerebral—Michelle became a star. She was relatable; people wanted to know what she was wearing because there was a chance they could afford it, too. And she was funny: A visit to CVS with the comedian Ellen DeGeneres, in which the two poured out boxed wine for shoppers and tried to operate a self-checkout machine, racked up sixty-three million views on YouTube. State dinners soon evolved from stuffy diplomatic affairs to star-studded South Lawn blowouts that drew A-list performers like Beyoncé. Guest lists ran the gamut from Frank Ocean to Jerry Seinfeld. (Even some Biden aides feel that Michelle had a rare star quality that her Democratic successor does not: "Michelle is iconic," one of them told me. "Jill is not.")

After her daughters settled into life in Washington, Michelle, who had been careful not to oversubscribe herself during her first year, focused on developing a significant policy initiative. Let's Move was centered around lowering childhood obesity rates and encouraging children to make healthy choices. On the program's launch day in February 2010, the East Wing announced that several medical groups, including the American Academy of Pediatrics, had agreed to issue revamped recommendations for measuring obesity in children. Professional athletes participated in public service announcements promoting "60 Minutes of Play a Day." And major suppliers of school lunches, including Aramark and Sodexo, agreed to begin curbing the amount of salt, fat, and sugar in prepared meals over the next five years. More than that, the president signed an executive order mandating "optimal" coordination between government agencies to ensure the initiative was taken seriously. She had not only her husband's support but the power of his pen. Over the next several years, she partnered with the Department of Agriculture to unveil MyPlate, a child-focused version of the food pyramid, and announced plans to ban the sale of junk food and sugary sodas in schools. Her efforts were celebrated by health experts and assailed by conservatives.

But as she delivered a speech unveiling her initial plan, she spoke with characteristic pragmatism. She wanted to leave politics out of the effort.

"We know that solving our obesity challenge won't be easy and it won't be quick, but make no mistake about it, this problem can be solved," she said. "This isn't like putting a man on the moon or inventing the Internet. It doesn't take a stroke of genius or a feat of technology. We have everything we need right now to help our kids lead healthy lives."

The following year, she worked with Jill to unveil the Joining Forces initiative, which provided education, health, and employment resources for military families. According to several people who have worked for both women, the two were not close at first. Jill and Joe were in a different stage of life, with grown children and a cluster of grandchildren who were in and out of the vice president's residence so often that the Bidens installed bunk beds. Michelle and Barack, on the other hand, were in the thick of child-rearing. But the two women were also just very different people—"as Dr. Biden herself would say a lot," said one former Biden official. Another former Biden official said that Jill had to adjust to the fact that she was not always going to be able to work together with Michelle on projects. "She's the first Black woman to live in the White House," the person said of Michelle. "She didn't need Delaware Barbie as a sidekick."

Michelle could be reserved, and she had come to the White House with a tight-knit group of friends she'd collected from every period of her life. Jill, on the other hand, was focused on her family and juggling a full-time career while Michelle lived under the klieg lights. The two families gelled over time, particularly in the wake of Beau's death, but even now, Jill and Michelle remain at a distance. Instead, they share what a person who knows them said is a "mutual respect and appreciation for each other's differences." Michelle did develop a closer bond with Laura Bush, whose daughters reached out to Sasha and Malia to offer advice.

Year after year, it seemed, Michelle was becoming more comfortable with the position—or, really, with herself in a role that she had hoped to hold at arm's length. In 2012, she delivered a convention speech that was watched more times than those of all the speakers at the Republican National Convention combined, according to the Princeton professor Lauren Wright. Michelle's popularity, combined with her up-front speaking style, had turned her from a reluctant First Lady to an in-demand asset for her husband's reelection campaign. "Don't tell me that's not a serious person," Wright said. "Those are just skills that most people in politics don't have."

A striking scene that showed just how much Michelle had evolved came on May 9, 2015, when she delivered a commencement address at Tuskegee University, a historically Black college in Alabama. In a cap and gown onstage, she was a battle-tested version of the woman who stumped for her husband in 2008.

"It made me wonder, 'just how are people seeing me?'" she said at one point, recounting a time when she had appeared as a cartoon wearing an Afro and holding a machine gun. She had been called a "baby mama" and "uppity" and one of her husband's "cronies of color." Those experiences, she said, made her realize that she'd always just had one choice.

"And at the end of the day, by staying true to the me I've always known, I found that this journey has been incredibly freeing," she said. "Because no matter what happened, I had the peace of mind of knowing that all of the chatter, the name calling, the doubting—all of it was just noise. It did not define me. It didn't change who I was. And most importantly, it couldn't hold me back. I have learned that as long as I hold fast to my beliefs and values—and follow my own moral compass—then the only expectations I need to live up to are my own."

With each of their choices, First Ladies are often unfairly expected to represent the kaleidoscope of the experiences that encom-
pass American womanhood, but Michelle's mere existence had placed
her in the middle of a national discussion about race. Within a handful of years, she had gone from a reserved mom in chief to a powerful
messenger, passionate about celebrating the potential and scope of
Black life in America.

The following fall, when she delivered her last convention speech
as the First Lady, she urged voters to support Hillary Clinton as the
Democratic nominee, and uttered the now famous line, "When they
go low, we go high." She never used Trump's name in that speech. Her
remarks encouraged Americans to take the high road instead of engaging in the below-the-belt antics favored by the firebrand Republican nominee. It took Trump's corrosive politics—along with a number
of women who accused him of sexual assault and misconduct—to
prompt her to go on the offensive just weeks before the 2016 election.

"I can't believe that I'm saying that a candidate for president of the
United States has bragged about sexually assaulting women. And I
have to tell you that I can't stop thinking about this. It has shaken me
to my core in a way that I couldn't have predicted. So while I'd love
nothing more than to pretend like this isn't happening, and to come
out here and do my normal campaign speech, it would be dishonest
and disingenuous to just move on to the next thing like this was all
just a bad dream," she told supporters at a New Hampshire event for
Hillary in October 2016.

In the years since leaving the White House, Michelle has spoken
more forcefully about the destructive influence Trump has had on
American politics, a system she never had much faith in to begin
with. At the 2020 Democratic National Convention, she delivered a
fiery prerecorded speech in which she called Trump the "wrong president for America" and acknowledged how divided the nation had
become.

"You know I hate politics. But you also know that I care about this
nation. You know how much I care about all of our children. So if you
take one thing from my words tonight, it is this: If you think things

cannot possibly get worse, trust me, they can; and they will, if we don't make a change in this election. If we have any hope of ending this chaos, we have got to vote for Joe Biden like our lives depend on it."

It had felt good. And she had felt free.

"Maybe more than I ever had," she wrote in *The Light We Carry* about the speech, "I'd experienced the kind of volcanic clarity that comes when you speak from the absolute center of your being."

CHAPTER FIVE

RELUCTANCE

AHEAD OF JOE'S DECISION TO LAUNCH A BID FOR THE presidency in 2020, there was no single moment that pushed Jill from "no" to "yes." She told me that she instead reached her decision after hearing from people, repeatedly, that Joe should run. Among them was their eldest granddaughter, Naomi, who called a family meeting to assure Joe that the family would be fine. Naomi and the other grandchildren told him that they could weather any attacks coming their way, and that they could share their grandfather with the public one more time.

Jill had been looking forward to returning to civilian life. The simple things, like throwing the dogs in the car and going on a drive, were luxuries. So was having dinner with her husband without having the evening turn into an impromptu photo line.

"We were in the in-between and we had really no intention of running for president," she said. "I mean, we were done. Yeah, we were done." She paused. "I mean, do you realize how much you'd miss driving if you could never drive again? How would you feel about it?"

But she knew that a violent white-supremacist rally in Charlottesville in 2017 had pushed Joe toward considering a run. And she couldn't avoid what she said was a rising chorus of voices—from people at work, from people in town, from people she didn't even know—who approached her and told her that Joe was the best chance.

"In some ways she was a less excited political spouse," said Jen Psaki, who served as Joe's first White House press secretary. "I think when he says he wasn't going to run and felt like he had to, I almost think he's speaking for her."

Jill knew that she couldn't shield her family from the attacks from Trump and his supporters if Joe decided to run, but she slowly came around to the idea that her husband might be the only one who could beat him.

"Things were happening in the government that I was like, 'Oh, my God. This cannot be happening in our country, in the America I love,'" Jill said. "And then I started realizing, 'Everybody's right.'"

Her dislike for Trump was a driving reason behind her support for Joe's campaign for the presidency, and it remains so for his reelection effort, even if that means he will not leave office until age eighty-six at the end of a second term. The amount of work Joe takes home with him from the Oval Office each night is daunting—he brings stacks of briefing books to the residence each evening—and she knows how much the job is draining him. Still, she was willing to again be a force on the campaign trail and in her husband's political operation if Joe's opponent embraced antidemocratic beliefs.

"I would rail against injustice if I feel like somebody who would be Joe's opponent would not be a good thing for this country," she said when asked about Donald Trump being the possible Republican nominee. "I think I would work even harder."

In recent decades, the idea of a reluctant First Lady has become the rule and not the exception. Several women, including Michelle Obama, have been less than thrilled to leave their jobs and tend to their families under the harsh glare that comes with a life in national politics. Others, including Jill Biden, have had to overcome an initial distaste for public life.

But only one First Lady has been so uninterested in the role's traditional expectations that she refused to join her husband in the capital after his election.

———

MELANIA TRUMP HAD LONG believed that her husband could win the presidency. Back when she was his girlfriend, she'd even entertained the idea of what it might be like to be the First Lady: "I would be very traditional. Like Betty Ford or Jackie Kennedy. I would support him," Melania told *The New York Times* in December 1999. ("She's light, she's fun, she's exceptionally wonderful to look at," Joyce Wadler, the reporter who interviewed her, wrote of the experience. "Two hours later you walk away and the conversation disappears into the air. Pop! If anything substantial was said, it is difficult to recall. She might, in other words, be the perfect political spouse.")

At that point, though, being First Lady was about as distant a possibility as being the third Mrs. Trump. Indeed, shortly after she gave that interview, Donald broke up with her. They were back together by spring, though, and were married in Palm Beach on January 22, 2005.

Born under communist rule in the western region of the former Yugoslavia, Melania had been raised since birth to aspire to a comfortable life, complete with fine clothes, a powerful husband, and a grand home. She wanted to lead the kind of life that would force others to take notice. She had grown up with a clear idea of what it would take to find and—to the degree that she could—manage a man like the one she married. But, contrary to her passing comments about wanting to emulate Jacqueline Kennedy, she had not spent much time anticipating what might happen to her life if her husband's interest in politics transformed from a publicity stunt to a formal presidential campaign.

Born Melanija Knavs on April 26, 1970, she grew up in Sevnica (pronounced SEH-oo-nee-tsa), a small town about fifty miles outside the Slovenian capital of Ljubljana. The daughter of Amalija, a factory worker, and Viktor, a car salesman, Melania was known as a beautiful, quiet child. She and her older sister, Ines, went to school dressed in perfectly tailored frocks, the handiwork of their mother, whose job as a patternmaker allowed her to dress herself and her family in a way that gave them the appearance of wealth.

Throughout her youth, Melania was approached by photographers and asked if she'd ever considered modeling. Understanding that her looks could fast-track her to a life in more stylish parts of Europe and perhaps even the United States, Melania abandoned her pursuit of an architectural degree. (In a typically Trumpian flourish, she would later say in her official White House biography that she received her degree in architecture, a claim that was quickly walked back after observers caught the fib.) Melania, who Westernized the spelling of her name to Melania Knauss after winning a modeling contest as a teen, said remarkably little about herself to the people who knew her at different phases in her career as a model. Still, one constant was her desire to make her mark.

"I want to do something great," Melania, in her early twenties, told a onetime roommate, the model Victoria Silvstedt, when they lived together in a sixth-floor Manhattan walk-up, the journalist Mary Jordan reported in her book *The Art of Her Deal: The Untold Story of Melania Trump*. Back then, Melania had designs to be as big as one of her idols, Sophia Loren.

Melania met Donald Trump in 1998. According to their telling, they met at a party at the Kit Kat Club in Manhattan when Trump noticed her sitting next to a better-known model. By that point in her career, Melania had worked hard to become semi successful. Her biggest jobs were cigarette campaigns, notably a billboard for Camel cigarettes in Times Square. But she was older than the young women and teens who were trekking across Manhattan to book jobs for editorial shoots and runways. She was a homebody, former roommates recalled, interested in at-home beauty treatments and walking around the house with weights on her ankles. She quickly sized up Donald, who was out on the prowl even as he had a date by his side, and declined to give him her phone number when he asked.

"He wanted my number, but he was with a date, so of course I didn't give it to him," she told *Harper's Bazaar*. "I said, 'I am not giving you my number. You give me yours, and I will call you.'"

When she met Donald, the twice-divorced father of four was a ticket to the notability she craved. Neither of them has ever pretended that their relationship wasn't mutually beneficial: Donald helped Melania secure glossy magazine profiles written by people he was connected to either personally or professionally. In return, he had a more bankable and better-known (thanks to him) model on his arm. In 1999, he started his own modeling agency, Trump Model Management. One of his first clients was twenty-nine-year-old Melania Knauss, who had left Elite to join his agency. "If I couldn't do that," he said at the time, "then I don't know what I could do for her."

By 2000, Melania was fully embracing the perks of being associated with the flamboyant real estate developer. That year, she appeared nude on the cover of British *GQ* for the magazine's "Naked Supermodel" special issue, with the caption "Melania Knauss: cleared for takeoff!" She posed for a photo shoot aboard Trump's Boeing 727 in various states of undress. In one photo, she held a pistol and wore a red bikini, looking like a Bond villain. In another, she wore a gold lamé bodysuit with an open front, next to a briefcase overflowing with jewelry. In yet another, she wore a chain mail tunic and sat in the cockpit with one of her nipples nearly exposed.

Dylan Jones, the editor of the magazine, later recalled that he had been "bombarded" with requests to shoot Melania. The story they came up with featured Trump, then a prospective candidate for the Reform Party nomination, gamely playing along with the Mile High Club theme. "I'm going to do everything I can do," Donald said, to "see that regular Americans can fly as high as their wings will take them," he told the magazine. Melania, for her part, said that she would be along for the ride.

"I will put all my effort into it," she said, "and I will support my man."

Jones said that Trump had requested photos from the shoot immediately, so *GQ* quickly sent along a framed cover and a set of photos to Trump Tower.

Throughout their relationship, both made it clear to the public what each prized about the other. Donald Trump, a person motivated by power and money, shared that he felt that the third thing on his

list—women—should take less effort than the other priorities on his
agenda.

"I don't want to have to go home and have to work at a relationship. I mean that's it. A relationship where you have to work at it, in
my opinion, doesn't work," Trump told Larry King in May 2005, the
year the Trumps married.

Melania, whom her associates have said is largely motivated by the
security and comfort of her lifestyle, has often spoken, with a certain
degree of pride, of her ability to handle a man like Trump. The fact
that she could stay with him, she has signaled, is a testament to her
strength.

"We are very equal in the relationship, and that's very important,"
Melania told Larry King in the same interview. "You know, to marry
a man like Donald, you know, you need to know who you are. And
you need to be very strong and smart. He needs to know he can rely
on me sometimes, you know? And we share a lot of stuff together."

As his political power grew, Melania became one of the few people in her husband's orbit who could deliver an unvarnished opinion
to him. "He's 'Donald' to her," said Thomas J. Barrack, Jr., a Trump
ally.

The Trumps functioned as a tag team long before he became president. Donald was the bawdy and unruly one, and Melania occasionally came along and defiantly backed him up. Until he circulated the
lie that the 2020 election was rigged, one of Trump's defining misinformation campaigns had been spreading around the unfounded
claim that President Barack Obama was born in Kenya and not eligible to serve as president. Melania helped with this, too.

In 2011, Donald made the rounds on several talk shows, including
The Joy Behar Show and *Fox & Friends*, delivering his incendiary
claims with a shrug—a tactic he only perfected as his political career
advanced.

"Why doesn't he show his birth certificate?" he wondered aloud on
The Joy Behar Show in March 2011. "There's something on that birth
certificate that he doesn't like."

By that point, Donald had refashioned his image from that of a bankruptcy-prone real estate investor to an American success story, thanks to the help of reality television. With his fame from *The Apprentice*, his deep connections in New York media, and a seemingly endless flirtation with a life in politics, he had commanded the attention of the media class. Trump had refashioned himself in the public's imagination as a tough, rich, straight-talking business mogul. With his newly bolstered relationships, he began spreading the sort of misinformation that had no business surviving outside of the bowels of the internet.

In April 2011, Trump claimed on NBC that he had sent a team of investigators to Hawaii, the state of the president's birth, to dredge up information. At the time, Trump was polling in first or second place among prospective Republican presidential candidates who could mount a challenge to the Obama reelection campaign.

But Donald was not the only Trump who had an interest in the birth certificate controversy. That same month, Melania appeared on *The View*, echoing her husband's concerns about Obama's birthplace. "It's not only Donald who wants to see [it,]" she told one the show's hosts, Joy Behar. "It's American people who voted for him and who didn't vote for him. They want to see that."

On April 27, 2011, the Obama White House—which had publicly battled birther rumors among Barack's critics since his presidential campaign and had previously been harassed into providing a short-form birth certificate—published a long-form version of the document on its website. Trump has long been credited and derided as the high-profile figure who provoked the White House into releasing the document. But it was Melania Trump who lent her gold-plated image—as a 2005 *Vogue* cover model, a QVC entrepreneur, and doting mother—to put a softer lens on an ugly theory.

LESS THAN SIX YEARS LATER, I stood in the crowd at President Donald Trump's inauguration ceremony and noticed how angry the people there seemed—and how angry the new president seemed—

even though he had won. Donald Trump did not have the popular vote, but he had surfed a tide of anger to the White House. He had channeled the fear and racial resentment of millions of Americans. At his side was Melania, the second foreign-born First Lady in history, who had not only recognized the forces capable of elevating her husband but had willingly helped stoke them.

"We must protect our borders from the ravages of other countries making our products, stealing our companies, and destroying our jobs," Trump told the hooting, hollering crowd as rain began to fall that day. "Protection will lead to great prosperity and strength. I will fight for you with every breath in my body, and I will never, ever let you down."

Melania was no longer a striving former lingerie-and-swimwear model, no longer a playboy's girlfriend, and—perhaps most crucially—no longer a candidate's wife who spent a campaign season being humiliated by revelations about her husband's piggish and abusive behavior toward women. Now she was a First Lady draped in cashmere.

When Donald was sworn in, Melania held the Bible as his children, including Ivanka Trump, looked on. Melania, standing at five foot eleven, with glossy brown hair and sapphire-blue eyes, wore a baby-blue outfit designed by Ralph Lauren, the country's foremost purveyor of sartorial Americana. The choice of designer was a nod to the America-first promise her husband had made, and the color of her outfit was an intentional choice of the shade worn by Jacqueline Kennedy on President Kennedy's Inauguration Day.

Though she had her pristine outfit handled, Melania did not yet have a formal plan for how she wanted to operate her East Wing. She had helped her husband weather a brutal campaign, one that had angered her at several different points. Her top agenda item was protecting herself and Barron, their young son. When she wasn't in the spotlight, the pre-presidency Melania was a homebody. In Palm Beach, where the couple spent their winters at Mar-a-Lago, their gilded fortress by the sea, Melania rarely went out with friends or participated in the social scene. She supported some charities, including the American Heart Association, but rarely attended events she was not personally hosting. Lore Smith, a real-estate agent in Palm Beach and a frequent Mar-a-Lago visitor, said that Melania's circle included "her family and her home and whatever charity that she's involved with."

Donald had flirted with the idea of a political run for decades, but he was usually more interested in the success of his various entertainment endeavors and commercial interests. In 2015, he said that he had finally decided to run because various "tremendous developments" in business had been completed, including his run with *The Apprentice*. He also hinted that his family had grown tired of hearing him say he could do it better.

"I didn't want to look back in ten years and say I could have done that or I could have done that," he told *Time* magazine. "My family would look at me and say, 'Ugh, stop.' I had to do it for myself."

When he announced his campaign for the 2016 election, Melania would become instrumental in helping soften her husband's image with voters, particularly with women, even though she had little to no interest in campaigning, and knew day-to-day life on the trail would be hectic. Melania's highest-profile moment in politics came in July 2016, when she delivered a speech on the opening night of the Republican National Convention. The Trump campaign hired Matthew Scully and John McConnell, two veteran speechwriters, to draft her remarks. Their assignment was to write something that would introduce Melania, a woman who had almost zero interest in public speaking. Scully and McConnell were experienced writers who had drafted remarks for some of the most memorable events in recent history, including President George W. Bush's address to Congress after the September 11, 2001, terror attacks.

Melania disassembled the draft and recruited Meredith McIver, an aide at the Trump Organization, to help her create a speech that was all her own. McIver, a former ballerina, had cowritten several books with Donald. Almost as soon as Melania had finished delivering the speech, accusations of plagiarism overshadowed the relative novelty of her appearance. Passages of Melania's speech matched, word-for-word, a speech Michelle Obama had given at the Democratic National Convention in 2008. After the tried-and-true tactic of outright denial failed, the Trump campaign quickly blamed the press for overreacting, then pointed a finger at McIver, who apologized for lifting the excerpts from Michelle's speech.

"This was my mistake," McIver wrote, adding that the Trumps had rejected her offer to resign. "Mr. Trump told me that people make innocent mistakes and that we learn and grow from these experiences."

Things went from tense to worse in October 2016, when Melania defended her husband after a leaked video from an *Access Hollywood* appearance revealed that he had bragged to the show's host, Billy Bush, about grabbing women by their genitals.

"You know, I'm automatically attracted to beautiful—I just start kissing them. It's like a magnet. Just kiss. I don't even wait," Donald said during the conversation with Bush, which took place in September 2005. At that point, he was hosting *The Apprentice*, and the Trumps were newlyweds. In the video, Donald kept going. "And when you're a star they let you do it. You can do anything . . . Grab them by the pussy," he added. "You can do anything."

In the hours after the Trump campaign learned of the video's existence, Melania coolly and angrily told her husband that his mouth might have just cost him the election and refused all talk of appearing with him in a joint interview to downplay what he had done. Instead, she released a statement on her own the day after the tape appeared.

"The words my husband used are unacceptable and offensive to me. This does not represent the man that I know. He has the heart and mind of a leader. I hope people will accept his apology, as I have, and focus on the important issues facing our nation and the world."

Ten days later, in an interview with Anderson Cooper of CNN, Melania, Trump's wife of eleven years, told the world not to feel sorry for her. "People think and talk about me like, 'Oh, Melania, oh poor Melania.' Don't feel sorry for me. Don't feel sorry for me. I can handle everything." She also dismissed the comments on the *Access Hollywood* tape as "boy talk" and said that her husband had been provoked by Bush "to say dirty and bad stuff."

Melania Trump was not finished fishing her husband out of a

media hurricane that treatened to tank his campaign. A week before the election, she made a rare appearance at a campaign event in a Philadelphia suburb, asking a group of women voters to put their faith in her husband.

All the while, she had closely followed accounts given by an ever-growing list of women who claimed that they had been sexually harassed, abused, or assaulted by Trump. She had even called several of those women liars. But by the time she became the First Lady, Melania was starting to embrace the idea of declaring independence from her husband in unprecedented and potentially explosive ways.

From the beginning of her tenure as First Lady, it was clear that Melania was going to do her own thing, starting when she declared that she would not be joining her husband in Washington immediately after the inauguration. Instead, she returned to New York City, where Barron was finishing out the school year. In February 2017, during a meandering and combative news conference, Donald momentarily softened when a reporter asked what his wife was doing for the country while stationed in Manhattan.

"I think she's going to be a fantastic First Lady. She's going to be a tremendous representative of women and of the people," the new president said. "And helping her and working with her will be Ivanka, who is a fabulous person and a fabulous, fabulous woman."

Back at Trump Tower, Melania monitored every mention of her name in the press and often trawled Twitter to see what the press, her critics, and her supporters were saying about her. She was aware that her husband had suggested that his eldest daughter would be helping to share the responsibilities of being First Lady, and this was not a development that pleased her. At the time, Ivanka was staking out office space in the West Wing but was eyeing the potential of a re-vamped East Wing that could be geared to serving the entire First Family, not just the First Lady, according to people familiar with her plans. The suggestion irritated Melania, who put a stop to the talk of a family-led wing. A month later, Ivanka announced that she would become an official government employee, working as an unpaid ad-viser for her father. For her four years in the White House, Melania would wage an internal power struggle with her stepdaughter. Melania called her "the princess" so frequently that a coterie of East Wing aides had adopted the nickname.

Meanwhile, discord grew between several East Wing officials and Stephanie Winston Wolkoff, a Manhattan-based adviser whose social cachet in the city included a long stint at *Vogue,* about Melania's official platform. Winston Wolkoff, who had helped oversee the inauguration festivities, was pushing Melania to develop a platform that promoted social and emotional learning in children. Armed with binders full of planning documents and a phone stuffed with high-powered connections, she had assumed a degree of control that made East Wing officials bristle.

As tense as the dynamics were inside of the building, in the early days, Trump advisers and White House officials had been reasonably successful in convincing the Washington press corps that Melania's absence was proof that she was going to be detail oriented, strong-willed, and nontraditional. With characters from central casting like Anthony Scaramucci and Steve Bannon practically swinging from the rafters in Trump's West Wing, the comparatively dormant East Wing said that the First Lady's slow-walking into the role was proof that she wanted to get this right on her own terms. The explanation was, of course, spin, but, given the chaotic backdrop of the Trump White House, it seemed almost reasonable.

"I think she felt important and empowered," said Stephanie Grisham, the former White House press secretary who served as a senior adviser to Melania. "I think she liked having her office, her own people. She finally had a real voice."

For the first time, Melania had a staff who could support her, defend her, and, crucially, serve as a firewall between her and her husband. Melania would direct her staff to make decisions without checking in with the West Wing—"This is our office, we do our own thing," she would tell them.

Also important to Melania was the matter of her and her son's financial futures. The journalist Mary Jordan reported in her book that Melania renegotiated the particulars of her prenuptial agreement before moving to Washington. A particular focus, according to Jordan, was obtaining written guarantees that Barron would be on equal footing with Donald's other children. At the time Jordan's book was published, Grisham, at the First Lady's request, released a statement that assailed Jordan's reporting: "Yet another book about Mrs. Trump with false information and sources. This book belongs in the fiction genre," Grisham wrote at the time, without addressing any specific claims.

Grisham would go on to have a change of heart about her role in the Trump machine, and in 2021 published a tell-all memoir: *I'll Take Your Questions Now: What I Saw in the Trump White House.* The book reads as repentance by someone who says she willingly lied to protect her standing as a senior aide. She had also prized being a confidante for a woman she believes was blindsided by the level of scrutiny she would endure as First Lady, and who failed to anticipate the amount of work the role requires.

"She's so private that she doesn't let a whole lot of people in. When she does let you in, you feel special. You feel, then, more responsibility to protect her because she's giving you the honor of letting you in," Grisham said in an interview in the summer of 2022. She was speaking from her home in Kansas, where she moved during the pandemic to decompress after several tumultuous years in Washington. Since moving, she says, she has tried to lead a more peaceful life, with the occasional appearance on network television to discuss her former boss and his assortment of legal predicaments. As we spoke, she was preparing to bottle-feed a kitten. She has since opened a nonprofit animal sanctuary.

Grisham is mostly comfortable with her new mission to tell what she says is the truth about how both Trumps and many of their aides operated. The Trumps, of course, have responded by calling her a liar or worse. Max Miller, an ex-boyfriend turned Republican congressman, filed a defamation lawsuit against her for accusing him of abusing her during their relationship; the case was scheduled to go to trial but was dismissed in the summer of 2023. She has endured threats for her public criticism of the Trumps, she says, and has abandoned much of the life she knew.

But Grisham has continued talking about what happened to her, and what she saw, which includes the existence of ongoing prenuptial renegotiations that were first reported by Jordan. Grisham said that, as First Lady, Melania often held meetings with teams of lawyers to examine her assets and attend to matters associated with her pre- and postnuptial agreements with her husband, which suggests that negotiations were ongoing not only before Melania moved from New York but throughout the Trump presidency.

"I know that she had very separate finances that she watched very carefully, and she had her own lawyers that she met with a good amount," Grisham recalled. "It often had to do with prenups and money in the bank that she had personally."

Through a spokesperson, Melania said that Jordan's book was "false" but told me that Melania had met with lawyers while living in the White House. "Mrs. Trump had a successful career before she met her husband and has always had her own businesses and assets," that person said. "As an accomplished professional, she frequently meets with her counsel."

Although Melania didn't appreciate the onslaught of news coverage while she was First Lady—she never quite understood that she could not just "kill" a story, Grisham said—there were parts of the role that she came to cherish. Most of them had to do with the aesthetics or the pageantry of presidential life.

Before moving from New York, Melania had chosen some furniture for the White House residence. But her husband—whose tastes veer more toward Louis XIV than the modern, clean lines she favors—replaced her choices with several pieces he liked better. Without so much as control over the décor, Melania still wanted to signal to the public that she was optimistic about her future in Washington. After she and Barron moved in, Melania peered out a window of the residence, took in her stunning new view of the Washington Monument, and posted a message to Twitter: "Looking forward to the memories we'll make in our new home!" she wrote, with a snapshot of the grounds.

She set up her own suite in the White House residence—separate from her husband's. She settled Amalija and Viktor into a bedroom that had been lived in by Michelle Obama's mother, Marian Robinson. Melania, Barron, and her parents often spoke exclusively in Slovenian to each other throughout their time in the White House. While Melania relied on her husband's credit cards to pay for most things, she personally paid for her parents to travel back and forth to Slovenia. (She always booked them in coach, Grisham said.) She often mailed personal packages from her online shopping sessions to her aides, who carried them into the White House to bypass lengthy security screenings.

Melania's earlier promise to support her husband ended up being conditional. She did not seem to mind standing apart from her husband on some of the most divisive matters of his presidency. In 2017, after a gathering of white nationalists turned deadly in Charlottesville, she quickly discouraged violence on Twitter while her husband would all but excuse the episode: "Our country encourages freedom of speech, but let's communicate w/o hate in our hearts. No good comes from violence," she wrote. When Trump criticized Black athletes who decided to kneel during the national anthem to protest racial injustice, she had Grisham issue a statement praising the basketball star LeBron James, whom her husband had insulted publicly.

Her tweets were small gestures that amounted to little more than digital ephemera. Still, compared with her husband's bridge burners, Melania's missives established her as a rare figure in the Trump administration who seemed more interested in calming a cultural divide than widening it. Americans are not used to seeing daylight between a First Couple, so her unwillingness to always side with her husband caused some critics of the administration to hold out hope that maybe she could be a mediating force in a White House that only seemed to deal in extremes.

As First Lady, Melania launched Be Best, a child-focused platform with three primary areas of focus: curbing bullying, promoting childhood well-being, and fighting opioid abuse. Melania drew the program's logo herself, but the East Wing became engulfed in another plagiarism scandal when eagle-eyed observers discovered that staffers had repurposed an instructional pamphlet that had first been created during the Obama administration.

"At its launch, the program was comprised of little more than a pamphlet and cookies decorated by White House chefs," said Stephanie Winston Wolkoff, who has said her plans for a more expansive platform, focused on social and emotional learning, was nixed by Melania's advisers. She left the Trump White House in February 2018.

Days after the Be Best launch, Melania Trump was hospitalized at Walter Reed National Military Medical Center to treat what the White House called a benign kidney condition and was not seen again in public until early June. The president assailed his critics for asking questions about her multiweek absence from the public eye. "The Fake News Media has been so unfair, and vicious, to my wife and our great First Lady, Melania," Trump tweeted. "During her recovery from surgery they reported everything from near death, to facelift, to left the W.H. (and me) for N.Y. or Virginia, to abuse. All Fake, she is doing really well!" he wrote on June 6, 2018. Trump had told reporters at the White House that his wife had endured a four-hour operation and was unable to travel.

"She wasn't dying or anything like that, but she definitely had a medical issue that had to be taken care of," Grisham, who did not write about the incident in her book, said. "It wasn't cancer or anything. We didn't hide anything, we just protected her privacy."

For a long time, observers had questions about whether Melania was willfully sabotaging her husband with her contrary comments and body language in public. Throughout the presidency, she raised eyebrows by swatting her husband's hand away on international trips, at a state dinner, and on the South Lawn.

She also traveled separately to Trump's 2018 State of the Union speech and wore all white—the color of suffragists. The event was also known as the first time she had been seen in public since reports surfaced in late 2018 that the porn star Stormy Daniels was paid $130,000 just before the 2016 election to keep quiet about a sexual encounter she had had a decade earlier with Trump. The affair, Daniels said, happened soon after the Trumps were married, and soon after Melania had given birth to their son, Barron. In the wake of the news, Melania had canceled a trip to an overseas conference with her husband and absconded to Mar-a-Lago without him for two days. Grisham, who traveled with her on that jaunt, said that the First Lady had wanted to communicate her anger to the president.

"I think she was pissed at Trump and wanted him to be a little humiliated that she took off," Grisham said.

There were so many questions that swirled throughout the Trump presidency about Melania Trump. Was she a secret resistance figure? Did she secretly hate her husband? The answer was always no to both. For every defiant action she took, she took another that confounded legions of rapt observers. Members of her small circle defended her character. Karen LeFrak, the wife of the real estate developer Richard LeFrak, called her "a real example of strength, character, and grace."

In June 2018, Melania received a rare bit of public credit when Donald agreed, largely at her urging, to issue an executive order that stopped his administration's policy of separating migrant families at the southwestern border of the United States. The administration had been under heavy criticism for days as news reports detailed horrific and inhumane conditions in migrant shelters. In large part, the bullheaded Donald had been cowed into action because Melania had been adamant that wrenching children away from their parents was wrong. Amid the din of voices who tried to persuade the president to change his mind—including members of Congress and his oldest daughter, Ivanka—the First Lady's concern seemed to stand out.

"My wife feels very strongly about it," Donald said as he signed the order.

There was no mention of the fact that the First Lady was an immigrant herself. There would have been little reason to bring it up.

From his earliest hours in office, Trump approved plans meant to block the flow of both legal and illegal immigration into the United

States. Some of the changes were so restrictive in scope that they encountered immediate legal challenges—including a travel ban, filed within the first week of Trump's presidency, that barred foreign nationals from seven predominantly Muslim countries from visiting the United States. The ban underwent several rewritings, expansions, and reductions, but it existed until the Biden administration revoked it.

Hundreds of other changes were quietly worked into government memoranda and application forms. His immigration policies, with his primary immigration policy architect, Stephen Miller, at his side, added a chilling heft to Trump's embrace of racist language.

An immigrant herself, Melania represents how selective the American Dream can be, and how much access to resources and power it relies on. As her attorney Michael Wildes told Mary Jordan of *The Washington Post*, Melania Knauss first arrived in the United States in August 1996 on a B-1/B-2 visitor visa. Two months later, she was issued an H-1B visa, which is described by the Department of Labor as a document that "applies to employers seeking to hire nonimmigrant aliens as workers in specialty occupations or as fashion models of distinguished merit and ability." In 2020, Trump issued an executive order that suspended the H-1B visa program.

Melania relied on H-1B visas until March 19, 2001, when she became a permanent resident and received her green card, according to Wildes. She received her card under the EB-1 program, also called the "Einstein visa," which is reserved for people who, according to the State Department, "demonstrate extraordinary ability in the sciences, arts, education, business, or athletics through sustained national or international acclaim." At the time, Melania's most visible modeling gigs had included the Times Square billboard and a photograph hugging an inflatable orca in a swimsuit issue of *Sports Illustrated*.

She became a naturalized United States citizen in 2006, a status that would allow her to sponsor green cards for her parents, Viktor and Amalija Knavs, who became United States citizens in 2018. The Knavs are technically an example of so-called chain migration, in which immigrants rely on their relatives who've become citizens to establish their own citizenship. The process was assailed by Trump.

"Some people come in, and they bring their whole family with them, who can be truly evil. NOT ACCEPTABLE!" he wrote on Twitter several months before his in-laws used that very practice to obtain citizenship.

But as soon as Melania earned a bit of recognition for helping persuade her husband to bring a stop to separating migrant families, she found herself in a media firestorm of her own making. The day after the order was signed, on her way to visit detained children in shelters along the border, Melania wore a jacket emblazoned with the phrase I REALLY DON'T CARE, DO U? It was a chaotic message to send a day after receiving public credit for pushing the president to walk back a deeply unpopular decision. Grisham later recalled that Trump summoned the two of them to his office, yelled at them, and then decided that the official explanation for the jacket would be that Melania was speaking directly to the media.

But it was not the only explanation. A popular one, circulated by Trump administration officials, was that the jacket had not been directed at the media but at the Trumps—specifically, the president's eldest daughter, Ivanka. The two were locked in a quiet competition for press coverage and, to that end, Melania did not think that it was appropriate for Trump's children to be enmeshed in White House operations. If she ever waged a battle over the issue, it is one she clearly lost: For four years, it was hard to see where the operations of the family business stopped and the Trump administration started. Ivanka and her husband, Jared Kushner, were two of the president's closest advisers. Donald Trump, Jr., and Eric Trump were both attached to the Trump Organization and fixtures of the Trump campaign.

Months later, on a solo trip to Africa in October 2018, Melania sat for a television special with Tom Llamas of ABC. She sided with her husband's version of events.

> You know, I often asking myself, if I would not wear that jacket, if I will have so much media coverage. And it's obvious I didn't wear the jacket for the children. I wore the jacket to go on the plane and off the plane. And it was for the people and for the

left-wing media who are criticizing me. And I want to show them that I don't care. You could criticize whatever you wanna say, but it will not stop me to do what I feel is right.

No account has ever really explained why she did something so unbecoming of her office. For a woman who enjoyed soaring popularity ratings—at least compared with her husband—Melania Trump undercut any previous idea that she was the less-impulsive Trump. If anything, the episode showed how sympathetic she could be to her husband's belief that he was unfairly treated by the news media; Melania also used the ABC interview to declare herself the "most bullied person in the world."

"She wasn't a big-picture woman." Grisham said, reflecting on her former boss's tendency to approach her role through impulse rather than strategy. She said that the interview on the Africa trip had been one of her proudest days. Melania had not wanted to give any interviews or explain herself at all.

The Africa trip also highlighted how comfortable Melania was with being a mix of contradictions. In Egypt, East Wing staff positioned her in front of the Great Sphinx of Giza. Speaking to reporters in front of the ancient wonder, she defended her husband's disparaging comments about African nations—he'd called some of them "shithole countries"—and lamented the news media's coverage of her trip. A story I had written of her decision to wear a white pith helmet—a symbol of British colonial rule—in Kenya had visibly frustrated her.

"I wish people would focus on what I do," an exasperated First Lady told a group of us as we gathered in front of her at the Sphinx, "not what I wear."

Then came the fashion show. She spent several minutes sauntering around in front of a wall of cameras. Wearing Ralph Lauren and Chanel, she posed as the desert wind whistled and a group of drummers played background music. There were plenty of surreal events I covered during my years covering the Trump White House, but the First Lady's fashion outburst in the desert was near the top of the list.

———

FOR MOST MODERN FIRST LADIES, there are parts of the role that align with their personal interests and others that don't. Melania did not enjoy receiving requests to make appearances on behalf of her husband's political agenda. Though she was one of the most popular people in her husband's orbit, she did not want to appear at fundraisers; the first one that had ever made it onto her public schedule was canceled during the pandemic.

She avoided being overscheduled, and at times avoided being scheduled at all. Her chief of staff, Lindsay Reynolds, and other East Wing officials grew adept at trying to convince the First Lady to do multiple events on days they knew she would already be camera ready, with a full designer ensemble, dewy makeup, and a pristine blowout. They were only successful about half the time. When she did travel, her aides were tasked with lugging along an item they called The Brick, a large cosmetics case that the First Lady would crack open before events.

But Melania did fully embrace the part of the role that expects the First Family—particularly the First Lady—to be caretakers of the White House. Melania loved the idea that she was helping preserve a part of American history, in part because she was interested in architecture and design. She was not as interested in putting on public-facing events as she was in choosing the place settings and floral arrangements for exclusive state dinners.

Some of Melania's lasting contributions as First Lady included upgrades to facilities and features most members of the American public will never be able to see in person. She wanted to make life more comfortable and beautiful for the people living in the Executive Mansion and the people who visited. Hilary Geary Ross, another transplant who moved from Palm Beach to Washington when her husband became Trump's commerce secretary, was one person who experienced Melania's modifications up close. Geary Ross said in an email that her favorite was the upgraded tennis pavilion, completed in 2020, and glossily described the project as including "an elegant limestone exterior, a copper roof, and palladium windows with wide, round columns that reflect those of the White House." Geary Ross also praised the revamped Rose Garden, which contains a sculpture by Isamu Noguchi. The bronze piece, called *Floor Frame,* is the first piece of art from an Asian American artist to be featured in the White House.

None of those changes came without surrounding controversy. Melania hailed the tennis pavilion's completion and was instantly criticized for celebrating an architectural upgrade in the middle of the coronavirus pandemic. The Rose Garden redesign, while approved by a preservation committee, was derided by the public as an unnecessary facelift.

"I think it is challenging for anyone and everyone who goes from the private sector onto the world's stage," Geary Ross wrote. "What microscopic scrutiny!"

Like her husband, Melania is an avid consumer of news, particularly if it is about her and her husband, and like him, she can aggressively rail against stories she feels are unfair. In the White House, she watched CNN voraciously while her husband watched Fox News. A house divided.

Their differences in media diet at times became a pain for White House aides. In July 2018, I obtained emails that were circulated among several members of the White House military office. Donald was incensed that his wife's television was tuned to CNN aboard Air Force One during an overseas trip. Going forward, televisions on the plane were to be tuned to Fox News, the officials wrote. So were the televisions in both the president's and the First Lady's separate hotel suites. The emails also illuminated another pressing concern voiced by the Trumps: They wanted military cargo plane ramps to be covered in a nonslip material during dignified-arrival ceremonies. "Yesterday, POTUS (and FLOTUS) was concerned about his shoes and almost slipped while either walking up or down the back ramp," a military aide wrote. At those ceremonies, which are solemn moments where soldiers' remains are returned, Donald was particularly preoccupied with how he might appear in photos.

Like him, Melania pays close attention to how her image is used and distributed. She made sure Hogan Gidley, a former deputy press secretary, was admonished after he mistakenly tweeted an unsanctioned photo of her, Grisham said.

Earlier in her husband's presidency, Melania was the first in the Trump family to issue a statement urging peace when a tragedy had sent the nation into shock and introspection, as she had done after the Charlottesville tragedy. Scores of Americans spent much of the Trump presidency trying to read the tea leaves of her public appearances and tweets, searching for signs that she was secretly more in tune with those who were horrified by her husband's actions than aligned with people who fervently supported him. There just was never much evidence that she was.

"The fact that the Trumps gathered and apparently still maintain a devoted following makes me think that a segment of the public was ripe and ready for a sea change of the sort that the Trump White House era was," said the historian Katherine Jellison. "He certainly said he was going to tear things down and rebuild in a different direction, and one could look at Melania Trump's approach to the role of First Lady in the same way."

AS TIME WENT BY, Melania's sporadic efforts at traditionalism lost steam, undermined by her husband's public spectacles as well as her own self-inflicted public relations disasters and the hostility she felt from the news media. In her private moments, she was frustrated and angry that anything she tried to do as First Lady would not be enough to quell the torrent of criticism directed at the White House because of Trump's policies, particularly his stance toward immigration.

"They say I'm complicit. I'm the same like him, I support him. I don't say enough, I don't do enough where I am," she complained to Winston Wolkoff, who'd secretly recorded their phone conversations and later used them as fodder for a tell-all memoir.

In Melania's view, nothing she did—not even the most simple and rote of First Lady duties—would be enough to escape scrutiny. Everything the Trumps touched, they politicized. Not even the Christmas decorations were safe.

"I'm working my ass off on the Christmas stuff," she complained to Winston Wolkoff in the summer of 2018. "Who gives a fuck about the Christmas stuff and decorations? But I need to do it, right?"

By 2020, when the pandemic was setting in, Melania had taken to wearing elegant robes at all hours. In the evenings, she would occasionally visit her husband in his bedroom, perching on his bed and listening as he placed calls to and received calls from advisers. She busied herself with assembling photo albums of her aesthetic contributions to the White House.

As First Lady, she visited the East Wing only a handful of times, according to several former members of her staff. There were only two visits that those former aides could remember: Once, she made the journey from the Executive Residence when Winston Wolkoff had visited and called for a meeting. Another visit, aides recalled, occurred when she was nearby and felt like surprising her staff.

Her major contribution to the East Wing itself was the creation of what her aides referred to as a "swag room": unused office space converted into a gifting suite. The swag was kept under lock and key, and entry required a signature on the sign-out sheet. Ikea-like shelving had been installed and stuffed with First Lady–themed coins and keychains, bowls etched with the image of the White House, an array of dishes made of pewter, plush robes for guests at the Executive Residence, leather desk sets, salt-and-pepper shakers, crystal bookends, baby rattles, golf balls, and golf towels. Melania enjoyed selecting and sending items to friends and Trump allies. From the residence, she kept watch over a binder of inventory, which was constantly updated with new photos of the items and sent to her in the residence so she could select gifts.

Since Melania's vacant East Wing office had been transformed into a large gift-wrapping suite—her desk *was* the only empty surface large enough for gift assemblage, several of her aides reasoned—the White House military office annexed a suite of Trump East Wing offices, turning the unused space into a sensitive compartmentedinformation facility, a secure place where secret and classified information can be viewed or exchanged. The facility still exists today, to the annoyance of several Biden East Wing aides who say they could use the real estate.

HAD SHE VISITED THE East Wing more often during her four years in Washington, Melania might have grown to appreciate the appeal of a place that exists, in large part, to shield First Ladies from the prying eyes of the public and the media. She might have turned her East Wing into something more than a gifting suite.

Instead, she preferred to spend much of her time in the residence, where she would occasionally summon members of her staff to update her on the day's gossip and would shake her head at the infighting taking place on the floors below. (With her cerulean gaze and her knowing smile, she was a master at procuring juicy information without engaging in the backbiting combat taking place under her feet.)

Several aides said that her interest in expanding her role dwindled over time. In the early days, she would meet with her aides in the Map Room, which is near the elevator to the family residence and required little effort in the way of a daily commute. Often, Grisham and the rest of the staff would try to catch the First Lady on days when she had her hair and makeup done—usually for events where she appeared with her husband—and convince her to shoot a video or attend a planning event for Be Best. It always felt like a win when she said yes. The Map Room planning meetings, which were held about once a month, had all but disappeared by the fourth year.

Seeking to shield herself, Melania had assembled a small and loyal staff whose members acted as a firewall between herself and the public and, at times, a buffer between herself and her husband. This force field, as fragile as it turned out to be, offered her a sense of freedom and equality that she had not experienced in her relationship before.

"I think she felt very independent and strong," Grisham said, "and that seemed to completely evaporate at the end."

By January 2021, when her husband was fighting to stay in the White House, Melania was ready to go home.

In the waning, wintry days of the Trump administration—when millions of Americans were terrified by an unchecked coronavirus pandemic—Melania had even less interest than usual in attending more than a dozen raucous holiday parties that were unofficially dedicated to shoring up her husband's (disproven) belief that the election had been stolen by Joe Biden. Throughout Donald's presidency, Melania had wanted to be viewed as an independent woman. Bombastic husband aside, though, it was unclear if she ever really understood how much her own behavior—which included sporadic attacks on real or imagined foes and long periods of absence—had contributed to poisoning her experience in Washington.

Instead, she longed to return to Palm Beach, where she enjoyed visiting the in-house spa at Mar-a-Lago and taking long walks, while Barron and his friends would zip around the patio, sometimes sitting at the bar to order food. In the evenings, if her husband was in town, they'd sometimes dine together. When they entered the patio, it was customary for club members to stand up and applaud.

Mar-a-Lago was both her home and a haven from Washington, so she spent her last holiday season making plans to return. Instead of taking the elevator down and mingling with the crowd at the White House, she summoned friends upstairs to see her during at least one holiday party. When she appeared at the soirée held for East Wing employees and White House residence staff—traditionally the most lavish party of them all—she stayed for only two minutes, according to an aide who took time-stamped photographs of her arrival and departure. She was "pretty checked out and exhausted, is my impression," that aide recalled.

Melania, who still lingered nearby as her husband raged on the phone to friends and advisers, began to absorb what she was overhearing him say. And eventually, Melania began to repeat her husband's false belief that the election had been rigged and stolen from him.

"Something *bad* happened," she told them, according to Grisham.

Unlike her husband, Melania ultimately accepted the election outcome, in large part, aides said, because it meant she could return to her old life. Within days, she began making plans to pack up—or directing others to pack up—the residence, searching for schools for Barron, and putting other plans in motion to move from Washington to Palm Beach. She had enjoyed the perks of her role but abhorred the scrutiny that came with living in the White House. When her husband lost the election, her main concern was whether she would still have access to security and to people who could drive her around, Grisham said.

But even a dormant East Wing is still difficult to pack up and move. During the last weeks of the Trump presidency, several young aides were doing the literal dirty work, which included cleaning, packing, and answering a never-ending stream of calls from Melania's team in Florida, who needed help setting up her office in Palm Beach. Their preparations were interrupted on January 6, 2021, when legions of cursing, spitting-mad Trump supporters broke through the metal barricades protecting the United States Capitol. The mob was there to interrupt the certification of the 2020 election, because they had been told by Donald and his supporters that votes had been tampered with and that the election had been stolen. This accusation, of course, was a lie, but that did not stop groups of instigators from breaking windows and surging through the broken glass.

"What I saw was a war scene," Caroline Edwards, one of the more than 150 police officers who were injured that day, testified to the House Select Committee to Investigate the January 6 Attack on the United States Capitol. "I saw officers on the ground. They were bleeding. They were throwing up." She added, "I was slipping on people's blood. It was carnage. It was chaos."

That day, the First Lady could not be relied upon to do the bare minimum: separating herself from the chaos associated with her husband's leadership with a tweet or a statement. She was busy having photos of a rug taken as the mob attacked the Capitol. ("All she cared about was the fucking photo albums," said Grisham.)

Grisham finally realized that her boss was much more likely to mirror her husband's beliefs—and his grievances—than she was to challenge them. As the mob descended on the Capitol, Grisham made a last-ditch effort, texting Melania to ask if she wanted to denounce the violence and rioting that was fomenting a mile away.

"Do you want to tweet that peaceful protests are the right of every American, but there is no place for lawlessness and violence?" Grisham asked her. The reply was definitive. "No."

Grisham was no fair-weather Trump supporter. She had endured a series of indignities from the Trumps, including, she wrote, when Donald asked Max Miller, her former boyfriend, about her sexual prowess. But for Grisham, the First Lady's listless response to a riot at the Capitol was the last straw. She still thinks about the flat no she received when she asked Melania if she'd like to make a statement denouncing the violence.

"I kick myself now," Grisham said. "I almost texted her back that day and asked, 'Why?' I wish I would've."

MORE THAN ONE HUNDRED miles away from Washington that day, Joe Biden watched the coverage from his home in Wilmington and later journeyed to his makeshift transition command center, a music venue called the Queen.

"The work of the moment and the work of the next four years must be the restoration of democracy, of decency, honor, respect, the rule of law," he said that day. "Just plain, simple decency." He quoted a line from one of Lincoln's annual addresses to Congress, delivered during the Civil War: "We shall nobly save, or meanly lose, the last best hope of earth." The next day, Biden used the sort of harsh words he has since employed sparingly as president. He called the rioters "extremists" as part of a "mob" whose "insurrection" had threatened the stability of American democracy.

As the violence unfolded, Jill watched the coverage from home. Just hours before the attack, Jon Ossoff had won a Senate runoff against David Perdue in Georgia, clinching Senate control for the

Democratic Party. Ossoff's victory, coupled with another win in the state by Raphael Warnock, had delivered an unexpected boon for Joe. He had already done the improbable by defeating an incumbent president, and now he was headed to Washington with a Democrat-controlled Senate.

Michael LaRosa, Jill's press secretary and a well-connected former television producer, quickly saw that the victories could mean that her interest in free community college might become a reality.

"GA, Dr B!" LaRosa said he texted Jill, using an abbreviation for the state. "We might actually be able to get free community college done! It could actually happen now!"

"Yes!" she replied, adding a heart emoji, one of her texting signatures.

Any elation she and her staff felt in those moments, though, was quickly dashed as rioters descended on the Capitol. She texted with her friends and several aides, including LaRosa and Anthony Bernal, who were both in Washington touring apartments. She was in disbelief, and her fears for her family were only deepening. Jill had given her blessing for Joe to run for the presidency a third time and had done all she could to support his efforts, but the chaos of the day only heightened her anxiety about what had been a dark and uncomfortable transition period.

"I hardly ever see Jill unsettled," Mary Doody said. Doody was one friend exchanging texts with Jill that day. "It was so unpredictable. They weren't getting any help from the previous administration about what they needed to do to get into the White House."

For a politician who thought that he had seen it all, Joe never imagined that, at age seventy-eight, his presidency would be centered around selling the benefits of a functioning democracy and lucid leadership to Americans.

The January attack on the Capitol had come months after a summer of protests meant to draw attention to the police killings of Black men and women. In response to those protests, the Trump White House had been turned into a fortress. Joe was about to take control at a moment of upheaval not seen in generations. The unchecked violence unfolding on January 6 only deepened Jill's sense of worry about what might lie ahead.

"I can remember just thinking about what we were walking into, and the hatred and the violence of it all, and the haters, and it was a little frightening," she told me. "I mean, you know, to think about going into that, that's where I was going to live."

As the Bidens prepared to move from Delaware to the White House in the days after the attacks, several Trump aides either had resigned or were in the process, including Grisham and Rickie Niceta Lloyd, the White House social secretary. The two of them had left in a hurry, leaving behind East Wing offices stocked with personal effects—framed pictures, gifted trinkets, stacks of old newspapers. Their abrupt departures meant that email accounts and phones were turned off and access to the White House complex was immediately restricted, leaving the offices of the departed unreachable and frozen in time.

On the day of Joe's inauguration, just two weeks after the attack on the Capitol, it seemed like everyone in Washington was prepared to—at least momentarily—take a break from the Trump chaos. That included the departing First Lady.

When the Trumps left the White House on the morning of January 20, 2021, Melania Trump was dressed in a black suit and carrying a Birkin bag. By the time the couple touched down in Palm Beach, Melania, a fan of designer clothes tailored to fit her figure, had changed into a body-swallowing patterned dress. Her sunglasses were on. She was even wearing flats. For a woman who had spent four years communicating to Americans through the clothes she wore, this time the message was unmistakable. It was the fashion equivalent of an out-of-office reply.

GENE SPERLING, THE MIDNIGHT-OIL-BURNING perma-aide to Democratic presidents, has a saying about what Inauguration Day feels like when a new government takes over. He likens it to "some kind of mix between the first day of summer camp and the French

Revolution." At 11:59 A.M., the White House is occupied by the head of one government. Once the clock flips to noon, the order effectively dissolves and another crew rushes in, bright-eyed and ready to deliver on promises made, or at least arrive somewhere in the general vicinity of promises kept.

Sperling's comparison, first made in the nineties when he was a young gun burning oil for President Bill Clinton, was perhaps a little on the nose to describe the mood that characterized the Biden Inauguration Day, given that a horde of rioters had accosted the seat of American government weeks earlier.

But, for all of Donald Trump's bluster about winning the election, and amid fears that he may not vacate the White House, he did leave Washington. Access to the White House was indeed turned over to the Bidens—just not seamlessly. As the new First Couple hugged in front of their new home, posing at the North Portico, there was a delay in opening the front door. The Bidens lingered as the usually highly choreographed event went awry. It was the sort of pause that only a well-trained observer would've noticed. Several of them did.

"There was a protocol breach when the front doors were not held open for the first family as they arrived at the North Portico," said Lea Berman, who served as a White House social secretary for President George W. Bush. Although it is unclear exactly what caused the delay with the doors—which are normally opened by marine guards—the chief usher of the White House, who manages the residence, had been fired that morning.

The job has traditionally been nonpolitical, but Melania's 2017 decision to hire Timothy Harleth, a Trump Organization employee who had been poached from the Trump International Hotel, added partisanship to the role, even though Harleth had believed his work there was one stop in a long career in the hospitality industry. The White House job is well compensated—former chief ushers say salaries run in the $200,000 range—but the days are long, particularly if the president is an early riser or a night owl. Donald Trump, who rarely slept more than five hours a night, was both.

Since Election Day, Harleth had found himself in an untenable position: trying to begin preparations for a new resident in the White House, even as its occupant refused to concede that he would be leaving the premises. But Harleth had hoped to keep his job.

This, of course, was a fundamental miscalculation of the degree to which the Bidens guard their privacy: They do not trust residence staff and security officials they have not directly hired or chosen, multiple people familiar with their thinking have said, which is partly why they spend so much time at their homes in Delaware. On Inauguration Day, Harleth was dismissed about an hour before the Bidens arrived at the White House, and it would take the Bidens nearly a year to decide on a suitable permanent replacement: Robert B. Downing, a caterer who had once worked in the Reagan administration.

On Inauguration Day, desks and offices across the West Wing were freshly claimed, and binders were snapped open. The East Wing staff also got to work. Jill was taking over an office that had undergone some renovations under her predecessor, including the swag-room shelving installation, but had remained largely untouched as a workspace. That was about to change.

As soon as the Biden family had settled into the White House residence, Jill traveled to the fourth floor of the Eisenhower Executive Office Building to videotape a message addressed to the American people. Because of the strict restrictions around the coronavirus, only a few staff members were authorized to be with her at that time, including Bernal and Jordan Montoya, a senior aide who helped manage her schedule and plan trips.

Aside from Carlos Elizondo, the White House social secretary, everyone else on the East Wing staff was awaiting a coronavirus vaccine and working remotely on the day of the inauguration. Because the Biden administration had committed to strict coronavirus protocols, it was the first of many events in the early days of the Biden presidency that felt isolated and muted rather than communal and celebratory.

The new First Lady, still dressed in her inaugural ceremony outfit—a turquoise tweed coat, complete with a matching dress and face mask, by the New York designer Markarian—recorded a message that thanked Americans and the authorities for ensuring that the transfer of power had been peaceful. As surreal as it was for the First Lady to imagine, she had not known that morning whether a safe outcome would be guaranteed. She made it a point to thank members of the military and first responders.

"It was the culmination of thousands of people working together to create something incredible, especially in this uniquely difficult year," she said, speaking into the camera.

Unlike her predecessor, Jill wanted to immediately convey the idea that the First Lady was engaged and thinking about the American people. Her message was one of hope but also one that illustrated, in the first hours of her husband's presidency, how political her role would be, and how in sync they were.

BY THE TIME THE Trumps arrived back in Palm Beach on that day, Jill had discovered that, at some point during her listless final days in office, Melania had performed one last act of decorum. The outgoing First Lady had dictated a series of notes to a young woman on her staff, who then transcribed the messages and typed them out on official White House letterhead. Copies then would be sent upstairs for her approval.

One such note—a stripped-down version of a more fulsome letter three aides had workshopped days before—sat awaiting Jill on her first day, along with a bouquet of flowers. Outgoing presidents often write letters for the next commander in chief. Biden thought the handwritten (in Sharpie, of course) letter Trump left was more gracious than he'd expected. But the practice is less common among First Ladies.

Instead, departing First Ladies have traditionally hosted their successors for private conversations to impart advice over tea at the White House. Michelle Obama invited Melania over for a tour, despite what the Trumps had put the Obamas through over the years, starting with their work seeding the conspiracy theory that Obama had not been born in America. (Michelle has said she will never forgive Trump for spreading viral misinformation that had the potential to endanger her family.)

Melania did not extend the same invitation to Jill. Communication lines between the Biden and Trump camps were so broken that it had even become an open question among Biden aides whether the Trumps would offer the Bidens Blair House, the dwelling across the street from the White House where incoming presidents traditionally stay. In the end, the Bidens, who had flown from Wilmington to Joint Base Andrews a day before the inauguration, were given the house.

Melania's note contained no reflections or advice. It only wished her successor good luck. Jill was not swayed by the note, or the bouquet of flowers left for her. And Jill especially didn't like that the letter—which she would only describe in an interview as a "typical good-luck letter"—was typed and not handwritten.

"I do a lot of correspondence," Jill told me of her penchant for writing notes in her own hand. "I know how important it is."

Her husband had remarked to his aides that Donald's letter had been nice. Jill, the family grudge holder, has said the same thing about hers, just in a very different tone. "It was *nice*," she has said privately, with a tinge of sarcasm in her voice. Anyone with even the faintest familiarity with her fierceness in protecting her family knew what this meant. It meant the letter was nice for a woman whose husband maintained that Biden's win was illegitimate, who had suggested her husband's mental health was in decline, and who had attacked her children.

Jill's dislike of the Trump family runs deep, but she has reached out to Melania since taking office, according to several people familiar with their correspondence. In April 2022, Jill sent a birthday card to Melania. In June, when Jill turned seventy, a card arrived from Melania.

This small gesture is both curious and counterintuitive, given how deeply the ideological battle lines between the parties—and between these two families in particular—have been drawn, and it perfectly illustrates how the First Lady is one of the only remaining figures in American politics still expected to be governed by the dictums of decorum. These two women with very little in common have remained in communication—despite the violence, the vitriol, and the deep public animus between Joe Biden and Donald Trump—only because of the strange, singular, and increasingly anachronistic nature of the role they have shared.

CHAPTER SIX

"THE PROFESSOR
MUST TEACH"

T

HE CHARACTERISTICS THAT PERSONIFY MODERN FIRST
Ladies since Hillary Clinton—on themes involving ambition, tradition, expectations, and reluctance—culminate in Jill Biden, the first of
them to work outside of the White House. In interviews, she has insisted that the path to teaching came easily, but the truth is that she
had to fight to convince her husband and his advisers that she could
really handle both roles. Here is the full backstory.

On a brisk afternoon a little over a week before the 2020 presidential election, Jill and Joe walked onto an outdoor stage adorned with
pumpkins and hay bales in Dallas, Pennsylvania. They were both
wearing masks—Jill's said VOTE—and the couple waved to supporters
who had been welcomed with an acoustic set by Jon Bon Jovi. The
applause they received from the crowd was curiously muted, but since
this event was held during a pandemic, this was not a typical campaign gathering: it was a drive-in rally, where supporters pulled up
and cheered from within the safety of their own cars.

With states across the country reporting record numbers of hospitalizations from COVID-19, and with vaccines still in development,
the Biden campaign had been cautious about organizing in-person
gatherings and sending Joe, then a seventy-seven-year-old Democratic presidential candidate, on barnstorming trips.

Donald Trump, his Republican opponent, had contracted the coronavirus during the first week of October, and he had been relentless in downplaying the illness, telling Americans that the virus was nothing to be afraid of and calling his own diagnosis "a blessing from God." He had been sicker than the public knew, but he had barely slowed the pace of his raucous in-person rallies.

For the Biden campaign, a summer without in-person events had turned into a mad dash to visit several battleground states, including Pennsylvania, by the fall. Jill was hitting the campaign trail and traveling so much in the weeks before the election that her team was using two private jets: One of them carried one-half of her staff and a contingent of Secret Service agents to campaign destinations, and a second jet carried everyone else. In rare moments of downtime, she'd binge-watch *Mrs. America,* a miniseries about the Equal Rights Amendment. Her schedule far outpaced that of her husband, who was widely criticized by the president and others for not holding enough in-person campaign appearances. ("He's in his damn basement again" was one of Donald's favorite rally refrains.)

As Joe and Jill rode in a motorcade from their home in Wilmington, Delaware, toward their first event in Bristol, they held a call with dozens of senior campaign officials. Those who dialed in included Ron Klain, a skilled Democratic operative whose ties to Joe dated back to 1989, when he first worked in the Biden Senate office; Anita Dunn, another longtime strategist who had first entered the Biden orbit in 2015, when Joe was considering another run for the presidency, and who ultimately stepped in as a course corrector when his 2020 campaign was broke and rudderless; and Jen O'Malley Dillon, an experienced Democratic hand who replaced the original campaign manager, Greg Schultz, shortly before Joe clinched the nomination.

On the call, O'Malley Dillon—who had taken over as the operation had gone remote during the pandemic and instituted testing protocols to protect the septuagenarian nominee—assured Joe that Jill had been traveling extensively, and that Kamala Harris, his running mate for vice president, had been crisscrossing the country as well. But the candidate was unsatisfied and did not understand why his appearances were not keeping pace.

"I didn't ask you what she was doing," Joe replied gruffly, in a reference to Harris. "I'm asking you why I'm not doing more."

That day in Pennsylvania, instead of standing near the stage and yelling, supporters showed their excitement by honking their horns, only occasionally pausing to open their doors and shout. Even though more than two hundred cars were pulled up to the rally, it was a sedate affair compared with Trump's anything-goes campaign productions.

Two days before the Pennsylvania event, both candidates had appeared for their final in-person presidential debate, an episode that showcased a mutual disdain for each other and the gulf between their views on handing the virus.

"We're rounding the turn, we're rounding the corner, it's going away," Trump said in the opening two minutes of that debate.

Joe shot back: "220,000 Americans dead," speaking directly into the camera. "Anyone who's responsible for that many deaths should not remain as president of the United States of America."

Within the sprawling lore of Joe's life, there were plenty of examples that illustrated just how different he was, both in style and background, from Trump, a real estate developer turned reality-television star turned president.

THE FIRST THREADS OF Joe's story start with his birth on November 20, 1942, and his upbringing in Scranton, Pennsylvania, where his mother, Jean, dispensed an endless supply of uplifting and politically expedient Bidenisms. ("Joey, no one is better than you. Everyone is your equal, and everyone is equal to you" was one of her favorites.) With the support of his mother, he tamed a childhood stutter, but not before being bullied by fellow students and even a teacher at his elementary school. "I learned so much from having to deal with stuttering," Joe said in a 2016 speech at an American Institute for Stuttering gala. "It gave me insight into other people's pain."

He had overcome the death of Neilia, his first wife, and daughter Naomi, and then he had found Jill, who had healed him and his boys before the couple had a daughter together. By the time the two of them had been married for a decade, Joe had survived a plagiarism scandal that sank his first run for the presidency. He overcame the political blow by returning to the Senate and working furiously to dispatch Robert Bork, a Republican-appointed Supreme Court nominee. Months later, he survived a more serious threat when he underwent two surgeries to address aneurysms doctors had discovered in his brain. Joe's second presidential run, in 2008, was rerouted to the vice presidency, where he reintroduced himself to Americans as the assured, affable statesman who would assist the younger, cooler President Barack Obama. Talks of a third campaign were dashed after Beau died—and after Barack had privately concluded that Hillary Clinton stood the best chance to win a presidential election.

Donald Trump had coaxed Joe out of a short-lived retirement, but in March 2020, his third presidential campaign was broke and limping after poor performances in Iowa and New Hampshire. It became a told-you-so comeback story after Super Tuesday. No one could say that Joe wasn't the master of his own remarkable story, one defined by starry-eyed pride and resilience through unthinkable tragedies.

But he could be undisciplined. He tended to pepper his recollections with inconsistencies or outright falsehoods. On the campaign trail, however, no one was a more adept and disciplined keeper of the best—and most accurate—version of the Biden story than Jill. And at this point in her political-spouse career, she knew how to assemble a team. At the Biden campaign headquarters in Philadelphia, there was a mini East Wing in the making, existing alongside other established teams, including communications, finance, scheduling, and advance.

"People don't think about it in this way, but in a primary of twenty-five people, we got in and we had basically two candidates from day one," one former campaign staffer said in an interview, noting that no other spouse in the field was nearly as polished as Jill. "We could cover twice the ground."

As she stood amongst the hay bales in Pennsylvania and spoke to the citizens of Luzerne County—a pivotal blue-collar area of the state that had swung for Trump after years of voting Democratic—

Jill reminded the people who'd gathered that Joe had returned to work as vice president just four days after Beau's funeral.

"Through it all, he learned how to heal a broken family," she told the crowd in a speech she has since repurposed. "It's the same way you heal a country: with love and understanding and small acts of kindness. With bravery, with unwavering hope. Joe has spent his entire career listening and bringing people together. He will be a president for all Americans. And he has a plan to calm the chaos of Donald Trump's America." The crowd exploded into a chorus of honks and beeps. Minutes later, Joe took the stage, just a local "Scranton guy," he said, beaming over his "Philly girl."

"You know, people wanted to hear optimism and hope and something to look forward to—a future to look forward to," she said in Rehoboth in 2022. "I think that's what I was offering—what Joe was offering. And they had had enough of that negativity every single day on TV."

The pair had done this so many times, across so many years and campaigns, that there was little need for a playbook. Jill could do this kind of speech alone, as she often did, or alongside Joe. She could do this live on television or standing in front of hay bales in rural Pennsylvania. Whatever the moment demanded.

But it had never been enough for Jill to be known simply as Joe's wife, and she liked being a part of the world that exists outside of Beltway politics. At Northern Virginia Community College, where she had taught English since 2009, many of her students were immigrants or first-generation Americans who struggled with mastering English. Others were single mothers trying to balance education with work and family demands. Concerned with retaining women students, Jill and a handful of colleagues even created a mentorship program designed to provide advice and support.

Jill had come to NOVA because her life had changed. She had just finished getting a root canal when Joe told her that Barack Obama had called. It was 2008, and the senator from Illinois and a Democratic presidential candidate had asked Joe if he would like to come onto the ticket as the vice-presidential nominee. Joe had dropped out of the Iowa caucuses that January, leaving a campaign that was, in part, driven by Jill's anger that President George W. Bush was re-elected in 2004. Jill had encouraged him to run. He had failed. Now Barack was offering him a path to the White House, even if it wasn't Joe's preferred route.

"He said, 'Barack called and asked me to be the vice president,'" Jill told *CBS News Sunday Morning* in 2009. "And I just burst into tears. And I said, 'Joe, you deserve it. I'm so happy for you.'"

At first, Joe wasn't sure he wanted to be the "second banana" to anyone, a moony sentiment he had shared with his aides. He wasn't used to having a boss. He gathered his children and Jill in his study at the Wilmington home, and they debated the options. In his memoir, *Beautiful Things,* Hunter Biden wrote about sharing his father's reticence: Staying in the Senate, his younger son reminded him, would allow him to continue as one of the most powerful Democrats in the chamber, with a chairmanship of the Senate Foreign Relations Committee. He could keep his voice. Beau took a wider view of the situation.

"Turning down the nominee of your party in a historic election just isn't done, out of protocol," Beau told him. "The vice president's job will become what you make of it."

And Jill, who had heard Joe's complaints about not being in charge any longer, wasn't sympathetic. She told him to "grow up," according to a longtime aide who was familiar with the discussions. Joe took the job.

As Second Lady, Jill would not be able to keep her day job at Delaware Technical Community College, but she quickly found that schools in the Washington area were publicly vying for her to come teach: "We would love it," a spokeswoman for Montgomery College told *The New York Times* as the Bidens prepared to move to Washington. "I think it would be a really pleasant surprise."

Jill was assessing her options when an email arrived from Jimmie McClellan, a dean at a nondescript campus of Northern Virginia Community College, about nine miles outside of Washington. Within reach of a TGI Fridays, a Target, and a strip of Ethiopian restaurants and markets, the campus feels far away from the cramped confines of official Washington. Jill hadn't even heard about the school until McClellan came calling.

"He would write about what a great college NOVA was—and great teachers—he said it was perfect for me," Jill recalled in an email to colleagues, sent in November 2019. "He said this with all his wit and humor. I wasn't quite sure if this was real or not."

McClellan is beloved at NOVA. Born in East Texas to parents who ran a small grocery store, a young Jimmie grew up catching fish in the Brazos River and watching his parents extend credit to folks who were down on their luck or give away their catch so others could eat. A folksy and funny character, he charmed the incoming Second Lady, who was unsure about continuing her teaching, and enticed her to visit.

"But he did make me laugh, and soon, I looked forward to meeting him after our election," she wrote in that email. "The moment I walked through the doors of NOVA, I felt like I was home. Jimmie was right." With the perfect school in mind, Jill decided to continue to teach.

"I told Joe when we were elected—when he was elected as VP, I said I'm going to continue to teach," she told Symone Sanders, the former press secretary to Kamala Harris, in an interview on Sanders's MSNBC show. "And my staff said, you can't do that. You can't do that. And I said, 'Yes, I can, and I will,' and I did."

During her eight years as Second Lady in the Obama administration, Jill became the first person in that role to keep her career, and she often changed in the bathroom at the school, slipping out of her teacher's uniform of blazers and skirts and into cocktail dresses for receptions at the vice president's residence.

Jill and her advisers have never agreed to let reporters into the classroom to see her teach, but the broad facts are these: For most of her years at NOVA, Jill has taught English 111, an introductory college composition course, in which she covers the basics of research, critical thinking, and using facts to support a thesis. One of Jill's regular lesson plans, a colleague at NOVA said, involves having students write a "This I Believe" essay, and she also asks that her students keep a regular journal; both projects give her a better sense of the obstacles her students face at home.

Nazila Jamshidi, a former NOVA student who moved to the United States from Afghanistan in 2016, remembered that Jill stood out for the time she spent working with students who were struggling to learn English or who were new to the country.

"She would sit there with them until the end of the class," Jamshidi recalled in an interview. "She was listening to people when English is not their language. She was so easy about that and patient about that, instead of asking, 'What, what? I can't understand that.'"

Another time, Jamshidi said, Jill was kind and attentive to a fellow student who suddenly went into labor and couldn't make it to class: "I remember she was saying, 'This is the community, this is the people with whom we interact. We need to make ourselves familiar with every student's circumstances.'"

(The woman who went into labor, who gave her first name as Nooria, said in an interview that Jill had responded promptly to her email notifying her that she was in labor and could not make it to class.)

Another student, Mikaela Stack, said that when she took Jill's English class in 2014, the Second Lady took extra time to help her find a doctor when she came down with bronchitis.

"I didn't have insurance," Stack told *The Washington Post*. "I didn't even know where to go to the doctor. She didn't have to do that. No one else did it."

To most of her students, Jill was just "Dr. B." Few ever asked what the "B" in her last name stood for, and until she became First Lady, her name was listed as "Staff" or "Tracy, J"—a reference to her middle name—on class schedules. Stack was one of the few who noticed that her English teacher had mysteriously appeared on television next to Michelle Obama during President Obama's State of the Union address: "'Why . . . is my English professor sitting next to Michelle Obama?'" she recalled thinking to *The Washington Post*.

As Second Lady, Jill rarely talked to students about her life beyond campus. She relished the relative anonymity teaching provided. Indeed, on the website Rate My Professors, former students have more to say about her teaching style ("tough grader" is common) than her connection to two presidential administrations.

"She's their teacher," said Kathy Wax, a friend and fellow teacher. "She doesn't belong to the wider world."

As First Lady, maintaining anonymity has been more difficult. Students must now slip their backpacks through metal detectors, and Secret Service agents roam the hallways. Still, she says that her students remain generally hard to impress.

"It's kind of funny," she said of her return to the classroom in 2021. "My students are really nonplussed."

THOUGH SHE WANTED TO keep teaching after Joe declared that he was running for president in April 2019, Jill was soon asked to take time off to help him.

From the first months of his campaign, it was clear Joe's storytelling needed some work. He was criticized for speaking warmly of his work with Southern segregationists early in his career. Hunter's business dealings overseas, along with his personal problems— including a paternity suit filed against him by a woman in Arkansas and ongoing public disclosures of his battle with addiction—were also putting the Biden family under an uncomfortable amount of scrutiny. It was around that time that Joe and his brain trust of aides started to ask Jill if she'd consider joining him more frequently— which really meant full-time—on the trail.

"I am getting pressure to take off a semester to campaign," she wrote by email to a colleague in July 2019, around the time a lengthy profile of Hunter titled "Will Hunter Biden Jeopardize His Father's Campaign?" was published by *The New Yorker*. "You know where my heart is."

She was unable to decide, just then, about the course load for a fall semester schedule: "I'd like to talk to Joe first. If I ever see him!!!!" she wrote in an email, as reported by Katie Glueck and Steve Eder of *The New York Times*. Jill decided to join the campaign and tried to keep teaching, but by the end of the year, she had taken a leave from her day job to help her husband win the presidency.

By the day of the car rally in October 2020, Joe and Jill were near the end of a roller coaster that had taken them from a fourth-place finish in the Iowa Democratic primary, only to be anointed the party's front-runners after the South Carolina primary. He was now the candidate, and things were looking positive. Jill decided it was as good a time as any to remind her husband and their advisers that she intended to go back to work if she became First Lady.

That afternoon, she sat in a cramped conference room at Dallas High School in Dallas, Pennsylvania, with her husband and several top advisers, including Bruce Reed, a longtime Biden hand who had served as chief of staff to Joe during his vice presidency; T. J. Ducklo, a campaign press secretary who was dispatched because of aggressive behavior shortly after the Bidens were inaugurated and later reinstalled for the reelection effort; Michael LaRosa, Jill's press secretary; and Anthony Bernal.

Still wearing their face masks, the Bidens sat on a sofa, with Jill perched on the arm of the couch, as several aides worked to prepare them for two local television interviews. Jill had announced earlier in the year, during an interview with Rita Braver of *CBS News Sunday Morning*, that she intended to return to the classroom should her husband win the presidency.

"Do you think you'll keep teaching if you become First Lady?" Braver had asked during that interview.

"I hope so. I would love to. If we get to the White House, I'm gonna continue to teach. It's important, and I want people to value teachers and know their contributions and lift up the profession."

"So, you're really planning to do it as First Lady?" Braver asked again.

"Yeah, yeah," Jill responded.

But as they prepared for a new round of interviews in Pennsylvania, Joe mentioned to Jill that continuing her career might not be possible if they made it to the White House. "Baby," Joe said to his wife at one point, using a frequent pet name she dislikes, according to a person in the room, before he asked a series of questions: Did she really want to be that definitive to the press? If she decided to keep a paying job, how would that even work? He tried to stress to her that there were still open questions about whether she'd take a salary and, if she did, how she could be paid without running afoul of ethics laws.

During the campaign, the worry among the Biden brain trust was that Jill's $81,000 salary at NOVA, paid out through a state school, could violate a provision of the Constitution's Domestic Emoluments Clause, which prohibits the president from reaping income from the United States or any single state. Some Biden campaign officials thought it would be risky for an operation that was running as the antidote to what Democratic voters saw as four years of corruption and ethical violations punctuated by an impeachment (with more to come). And conservative attacks on Hunter's attempts to drum up business overseas were not going anywhere. The last thing Joe wanted was to have his wife's career scrutinized as a potential ethical violation.

Jill is known among her allies as a fierce guardian of her family. Joe is similarly protective over her, but his old-school sense of chivalry toward his "Jilly" can sometimes veer into *over*protectiveness. As they discussed whether she would teach, Joe was concerned with subjecting his wife to even a fraction of that level of criticism. Inside the Biden circle, sending her back into the classroom "was not the most popular idea," a Biden aide recalled. "We had to ease ourselves into it."

During the meeting in Pennsylvania with her husband and his aides, Jill fell quiet as Joe and the poobahs outlined their concerns. LaRosa recalled that, after months of Jill publicly saying that she intended to teach, the matter had suddenly become a "third rail" discussion topic. But Jill was determined. Behind the scenes, she deployed Bernal to reach out to campus advisers.

"The professor MUST teach," Bernal wrote in an email to Jimmie McClellan, the dean of the school, on October 30, 2020, just days before the election, and just days after Joe had gently suggested teaching might not be possible. "Will discuss with her later today and be in touch over the next few days."

After the Biden-Harris campaign won the election, the incoming First Lady was adamant that the details be hashed out, and quickly: On November 9, an official at NOVA messaged her with a class schedule that included a full day of teaching her usual English III class once per week. During the presidential transition, attorneys spent weeks figuring out how to make it possible for Jill to keep teaching and receiving her yearly salary. NOVA officials, working with White House lawyers, eventually arranged for her to be paid out of a nonprofit fundraising account affiliated with the school, a solution that would keep her income from running into the ethical provisions surrounding the presidency. The matter was not fully settled until weeks before the semester started. Privately, however, she had already advised a NOVA administrator that she would be returning to the classroom.

There was still the matter of formalizing her plans with the rest of the Biden inner circle. When the Bidens joined a prep call with a senior group of aides to the president-elect, including Klain, Dunn, and Mike Donilon, Joe's chief campaign strategist and a longtime Biden whisperer, ahead of a joint December 18, 2020, appearance on *The Late Show with Stephen Colbert,* a back-and-forth ensued as the incoming First Lady answered questions about her decision to teach.

Some of what she said was a surprise to her husband, according to others briefed on their exchange.

When an aide during the prep session asked Jill if she planned to teach full-time, her answer was a matter-of-fact "Yep."

At this point, the president-elect chimed in: "You are?"

Joe wanted to know how many credits—only a handful, right?

"I'm teaching fifteen credits. It's a full course load."

With that, the matter was settled. Being First Lady was the honor of a lifetime, but it was not her day job. Jill spent the next days and weeks trying to learn how to teach online—"I took the training, but it is hard stuff," she emailed to a colleague on January 3, 2021. She began a new year relieved that she was going to be able to hold on to her identity while working as First Lady.

In a later interview, Jill said she told Joe, "If we win, I'm gonna keep teaching." She said her husband was concerned that "it might be too much" but ultimately said, "'If you want to, you should do it.'"

She added: "And of course, you know, people around me said, 'No, no, you can never do it.' And I said, 'I'm going to do it. So figure it out.'"

CHAPTER SEVEN

"THE KIND OF WOMAN
I'D LIKE TO MEET"

J ILL BIDEN MIGHT OWE HER UNEXPECTED JOURNEY TO THE
White House to a Delaware-based photographer named Tom Stiltz.
One day in the early 1970s, one of Stiltz's closest friends—a guy
named Bill Stevenson—had called to ask if he would photograph his
wife, who was thinking about a modeling career. Days later, Stiltz
stood outside of his studio in Newark, Delaware, waiting for his newest client to show up.

Stiltz watched as a 1972 Cutlass convertible pulled up to the
curb—"a look-at-me car," he recalled decades later. A group of women
across the street had been sitting outside shelling beans, but when
that car rolled up, they all had stopped what they were doing to gaze
at the petite blond woman who emerged from it, her hair still curled
up in rollers. Jill wrote in her memoir, *Where the Light Enters,* that she
was friends with Stiltz, and she met with him as a favor to help him
build his photography business. But he said he did not know her before that session. He said small talk did not come easily between
them.

"She was just staggeringly beautiful," Stiltz said, recounting his
encounter with a young Jill, whose married name, back then, was Jill
Stevenson. "I kind of almost couldn't talk to her."

He did eventually muster the courage to speak with her, and the
two headed over to Brandywine Park, which straddles the Brandy-

wine Creek in Wilmington. The two of them walked to a section of the park that houses a large limestone fountain, which was donated by a grieving widower in the 1930s. With dozens of Japanese cherry trees, the space serves as a haunting mourner's grove.

Stiltz didn't get the impression that his young client seemed particularly interested in the idea of pursuing a modeling career, but she gamely posed in a few outfits, including, he recalled, one with a leather vest and no bra. (It was the seventies.) But it was a shot of her in a faded tank top that captivated him. With her elbows resting against stone, a twenty-something Jill looked directly into the camera. Her long blond hair had shaken out of the roller-tight curls and fallen behind her shoulders. Her arms were strong and tanned. On her left ring finger sat a diamond ring. She was stunning, and her expression betrayed nothing.

That photo eventually became part of a display for the New Castle County Parks Department, which was hanging in the airport in Wilmington in 1975. In the long scope of Biden mythology, it is said to be here that Biden first encountered Jill—or a two-dimensional version of her. Joe, whose floppy brown hair had gone from boyish to thinning at the top, and whose shiny forehead had started to crease even when he was expressionless, peered at the ad and saw someone carefree gazing back at him. He found himself wondering who might be sitting alongside her, gazing at the trees and the ponds in the parks.

"That's the kind of woman I'd like to meet," Joe, in his memoir, recalled thinking as he shuffled home to his children and siblings, who were always in and out of the home, pitching in to take care of his boys, Hunter and Beau.

The widowed senator had spent the years after his wife's death dating around in Washington, his grief never leaving his side. Still, Joe was ready to find love and settle down with someone who could care for his two young sons in the same way that he did. His anguish seemed to arouse the curiosity of local journalists, who frequently pitched the Biden press team stories about his eligible bachelorhood.

The most bruising of these was a tell-all interview with the writer Kitty Kelley, cruelly headlined "Death and the All-American Boy," published in June 1974. Over the course of three hours, Joe showed Kelley a bikinied photo of his "beautiful millionaire" first wife, the daughter of a wealthy family from the Finger Lakes region. "She looks better than a Playboy bunny, doesn't she?" He talked at length about the sexual and emotional connection he and Neilia shared, and about the kind of woman he was looking for in the future.

"I do indeed want to get married again. I hate the image of the gay, young bachelor about town. That's just not my style. I am not a womanizer. I would like very much to fall in love and be married again because basically I am a family man. I want to find a woman to adore me again," he told Kelley. Yet even as he waxed wistful about all that he had lost, and even in the midst of his grief, Joe turned back to his ambition, speaking of his desire to win the presidency.

"I know I could have easily made the White House with Neilia," he told Kelley. "And my family still expects me to be there one of these days. With them behind me anything can happen."

In his memoir, Joe, who is in every other case a vague and circuitous storyteller, recalls the exact day—Friday, March 7, 1975—when he first laid eyes on the woman in the poster. That evening, he joined his family for dinner at the house he had named North Star. His brother Frank mentioned that he had the phone number of a woman he might like. Joe had wanted to swear off dating, but he found himself dialing the woman's number the next afternoon.

"Um, this is Joe Biden?" he said to the woman on the other end of the line. "Do you think you could go out tonight?"

The woman replied that she already had a date. He asked her to break it.

"When I called back an hour later, she was free," he wrote. "And when I got to her door, there was the woman I'd seen in the airport photographs . . . in person." The two of them went out to dinner and a movie.

Jill's own retelling fleshes out their origin story, but her version is slightly different.

In her own memoir, she adds a wrinkle to the tale by saying Frank had picked Joe up at the airport that evening, and that Joe had showed his brother the parks poster. "Look, Frankie," Joe said, pointing to the photo of the woman he'd like to date.

"I know her," Frank volunteered, according to Jill's retelling. In her memoir, Jill says that she'd befriended Frank Biden before she ever knew who Joe was, but as the reporter Ben Schreckinger notes in his book *The Bidens: Inside the First Family's Fifty-Year Rise to Power,* Bill Stevenson, her husband, was already supporting Joe's Senate campaign in 1972. That year, Frank still would have been in high school.

Still, in Jill's retelling, Frank looked at his brother looking at the poster and added a point in her favor: "She doesn't like politics."

According to Jill, that is when the senator called her up and convinced her to break her date. He picked her up from her rented townhouse in Chadds Ford, Pennsylvania. ("My God, what have I gotten myself into?" she thought to herself when she saw the straitlaced senator, dressed in a suit and leather loafers, on her doorstep.) He drove them to Philadelphia to evade curious members of the Delaware news media. In her memoir, she recalls—though is not certain—that they saw a French movie, *A Man and a Woman,* which is about a widow and widower whose romance is haunted by their dead spouses.

OF COURSE, JILL'S LIFE did not begin when Joe first spotted her on the airport wall.

Jill Tracy Jacobs was born on June 3, 1951, in Hammonton, New Jersey, the eldest daughter of Donald Jacobs, an Italian American navy signalman turned bank executive, and Bonny Jean Jacobs, a homemaker who raised five girls. Hammonton calls itself "the blueberry capital of the world," and it sponsors the longest-running Italian festival in the United States.

The family moved around while Donald climbed the local savings-and-loan ranks, and Jill spent her teen years with her parents and four sisters in a split-level home in Willow Grove, Pennsylvania, a middle-class suburb of Philadelphia, where she proudly claims her "Philly girl" roots. (As First Lady, she has made it known that she is a diehard fan of the Philadelphia Eagles, the Flyers, and the Phillies.) She is the oldest of five daughters, including younger sisters Bonny and Jan, and twins Kim and Kelly, who were born when Jill was a teenager.

A sandy-haired beauty with blue eyes, she wasn't a standout student at Upper Moreland High School, but she gravitated to subjects that interested her, including English and history. She didn't grow up dreaming of Hollywood or of Washington or even of life as a single girl in a big city, but she did want to go to college.

(If you visit the Upper Moreland Free Public Library now, there is no trace of the First Lady who grew up down the street. The yearbook from 1969, her senior year of high school, is missing. None of the librarians at the reference desk had any idea that a First Lady spent years in Willow Grove until I showed up in the summer of 2022 and asked to see the evidence.)

But a former classmate and neighbor, Liz Leonard, told me that Jill was popular, "not shy," and a lot of fun to be around. In ninth grade, Jill was a cheerleader, and later, she was involved in her senior-year prom-planning committee. Jill usually had a boyfriend, Leonard recalls, and she was part of a tight-knit group of friends who ran around Willow Grove and enjoyed attending Friday-night football games. At least once, Jill hosted a postgame party at her parents' house, the kind of affair where boys always tried to sneak in booze.

"A couple of times it got a little rowdy," Leonard recalled. Then Leonard seemed to remember that she was talking to a journalist about the First Lady of the United States. "We didn't imbibe! But that was going on in 1969," she quickly added.

Leonard texted me a few high school yearbook photos. In her senior-year photograph, Jill smiles into the camera. Around her neck is a string of pearls, and her hair falls past her shoulders in blond waves. Leonard wears a similar outfit: a black dress and pearls. One of their biggest capers came in the spring of 1969, when Jill was part of a group of students who cut school and went on a picnic. They were all punished with a six-month assignment to weed and garden on the school grounds.

Still, Leonard remembered her childhood friend as focused and ambitious, even back then.

"She was always determined and wanted everything to be perfect," Leonard said. "I knew she was going places."

And Leonard confirmed Jill's description of her childhood in Willow Grove as idyllic, the sort of *Happy Days* backdrop that kept a mostly middle-class, mostly white group of teenagers sheltered from a roiling civil rights movement and a war overseas.

"It wasn't Shangri-la all the time," Leonard said. "But we were pretty close."

Jill grew up with that tension of rebellion and responsibility that often exists within eldest children. She believes she inherited a stoic nature from her mother. She has often said she saw her mother cry just once in her life: at Donald Jacobs's funeral in 1999. Her mother's sense of emotional reserve became a model for her to control her own emotions. When Bonny Jean died in 2008 after a long battle with cancer, Jill remembers feeling like she was not allowed to be upset.

"As the oldest of five girls, I was the parent," Jill said in Rehoboth. "So I had to hold it together. I couldn't go home and be with my sisters and cry, because maybe they were crying, and I had to be strong. And then one of my sisters said to me recently, she said, 'Jill, it really surprised me that you cried at Mom's grave.' And I thought, *Wow, even* you *expected me to be strong at all times, no matter what.* And so, I think I learned it from my mother. She had such an inner strength, and I saw how important that was to me."

AS PLACID AS HER upbringing was, Jill inherited a defiant streak from her parents, who eloped before officially marrying and then kept the elopement a lifelong secret. As a child, once Jill was old enough to understand that her maternal grandmother was unaccepting of her father, she refused to stay the night at the woman's house.

"They weren't quite the Montagues and Capulets," Jill wrote in her memoir.

This is true. The setting wasn't fair Verona. It was Hammonton,

New Jersey. But her parents were what their daughter called "star-crossed lovers from literal different sides of the tracks." The pair met in the late 1940s in Godfrey's Rexall Drugstore on Bellevue Avenue, the pharmacy owned by Bonny Jean's parents. Donald was a World War II veteran—boyishly handsome, with blue eyes, big ears, and an inscrutable smile that he passed on to his daughter. Strong, with a stocky build, he had just returned from the navy, where he had served as a signalman after enlisting at the age of seventeen.

When young Donald met his future bride, he'd been working nearby as a bank teller. Bonny Jean, who was three years younger, was working the soda fountain. Jill said that her mother was nineteen when she met Donald.

The Godfreys made their displeasure known and tried to keep the youngsters apart. They were against their daughter marrying a man who didn't come from a wealthy family. Harold was a pharmacist, and Mabel, whom her grandchildren called "Ma," had attended college before becoming a teacher, a relatively rare achievement for the time.

The pair secretly eloped to Elkton, Maryland. Neither ever told their parents of that first ceremony, and they lived separately until they were married (again) in July 1950. They were married for fifty years before Donald died in 1999. Their five daughters were raised at home by Bonny Jean, and Donald used the GI Bill to get a business degree. Their eldest daughter would go on to become the First Lady of the United States, a woman who wastes few public opportunities to conjure up a childhood heady with the touches of Americana. In one particularly saccharine graduation speech delivered in September 2022, Jill recalled her upbringing as "ribbons of pasta drying on the linoleum counter in my grandfather's Italian kitchen, tomato sauce bubbling on the stove. I'm from five sisters, glued together—messy rooms and borrowed jeans and standing up to bullies who lived on our block. I'm from running through the yellow streetlights on hot July nights, feeling like summer would never end."

Still, the Godfreys had never warmed to the union, and Mabel was particularly confrontational with her oldest granddaughter, whose blond hair and blue eyes and strong temperament were just like her father's. "Ma wasn't a warm woman with any of us girls, but her lack of affection seemed most pronounced with me," Jill wrote in her memoir. "We all just ended up sidestepping her anger."

Rather than banishing her daughter, son-in-law, and grandchildren, Mabel Godfrey required their presence each weekend at stiff family dinners served on fancy plates. A similar request was issued by Donald's family. With each matriarch trying to outdo the other with their respective Sunday spreads, the Jacobses spent most weekends traveling between the dueling households of Hammonton. When the rest of the family stayed overnight with Bonny's parents, Jill would stay with her father at the Jacobs house, where both felt comfortable and accepted.

"My mother's mother realized that there was no way she was ever going to get my parents to separate," Jill told Darlene Superville and Julie Pace for their biography of her. "I had sealed the deal, my birth."

Despite the anger that Jill felt was directed at her from her maternal grandmother, she did inherit Ma's love of reading and education. Mabel had attended the Glassboro Normal School, which later became known as the New Jersey State Teachers College at Glassboro and is now Rowan University. Glassboro Normal School opened its doors in 1923 to young women who were interested in a two-year teacher training program. In her senior yearbook photo from the 1925 class, Mabel, whose nickname was Mae, listed "rowdy-dow" as her favorite expression, an exclamation that doesn't quite match up with the serious, almost impatient-looking young woman who posed for the photo with short dark curls, a cocked head, and a Mona Lisa smile. An inspirational quote listed near her photo was adapted from *Hamlet:* "She smiled and smiled and was a villain still."

Jill's grandmother bought her subscriptions to book clubs, and she grew up immersed in the world of Nancy Drew, among other favorites. And it was Ma, a longtime teacher, who would bring the future First Lady into the one-room schoolhouse where she taught, giving Jill a look at the inside of a classroom from the teacher's perspective for the first time. Ma Godfrey would find a way to get clothes and gloves to give to her students, many of whom were low income, when it was cold outside.

That instinct exists within her granddaughter, who holds teaching as central and sacred to her identity. She makes it a point to keep extra granola bars in her bags for students, many of whom she knows do not always have time to eat between class, work, and childcare.

"I had to give a couple of students books because they couldn't afford them," Jill said during an interview in the fall of 2021. "Every teacher has done that."

As a teenager, the young Jill clashed with both of her parents, but most often with her father. She has described herself as the curfew-crashing, often-grounded eldest daughter who became adept at devising workarounds for parental boundaries. Growing up on Greyhorse Road, Jill sometimes slipped out of the house in the evenings with a friend to sneak into the local swim club. And when her father fished an ashtray out from under her bed, her punishment was to smoke—and inhale—three cigars on the back porch. But the stubborn Jill smoked all three of them and continued smoking cigarettes until college.

Jill has said that she can be a lot like her father: bullheaded, judgmental of others, and self-critical. Donald was from an Italian family whose surname, Giacoppa, had been taken as a "warped Ellis Island interpretation" when they alighted on American shores, his daughter has noted. His grandparents, Gaetano and Concetta Giacoppa, brought the family to the United States from the tiny village of Gesso, Sicily, and took Jacobs as the new family name.

By the time Jill was a teenager, the Jacobs house was crowded, and eventually, Jill's parents allowed her to move ninety miles away to Ocean City, New Jersey, after her junior year of high school. During the summer of 1968, Jill shared a rented house with four friends and worked at a restaurant, relishing a life that had few responsibilities outside of feeding herself—with lobster tails and other treats snuck from the restaurant's kitchen—and catching a deep tan.

She worked as a waitress at Chris' Seafood Restaurant, which served fish caught by fishermen who docked several boats outside. The restaurant's owner, an Italian fisherman named Chris Montagna, ran a fleet of boats from the dock and would often take patrons out to the open sea on a World War II–era torpedo boat he called the *Flying Saucer*.

"In the sixties and seventies, OC was like a college town," said Bill Kelly, a writer who maintains a blog about his youth spending summers in Ocean City.

"We dated the lifeguards. We'd date the guys who worked at the restaurants who were the cooks and flipped the burgers and made the sandwiches, and it was fun," Jill told Superville and Pace. In a later interview with me, she said it wasn't tension with her parents or even a crowded house that made her leave home. She said it was because she wanted to make her own money. Her parents had agreed to help pay for college, but they had little extra money to help cover expenses.

"I had to make money for college," she said in that interview. "Five kids." She also wanted to keep up with her friends. "I wanted the nice pocketbooks that all the other girls had. If I wanted them, I had to pay for them."

Near the end of her second summer in Ocean City, the eighteen-year-old Jill met Bill Stevenson, a tall twenty-one-year-old who played football for the University of Delaware and drove a yellow Z/28 Camaro. It was the car that brought them together, Stevenson recalled in an interview, when Jill and a couple of friends approached him at a car wash. More than fifty years after they first met, Stevenson still gets wide-eyed when he recalls what it was like to meet her.

"I looked at her and said, 'You gotta be kidding me,'" Stevenson recalled when I met with him in Wilmington. "She was beautiful."

As he remembered it, they were a natural fit as a couple: They both liked muscle cars, the beach, and having fun.

In 1969, Jill began studying fashion merchandising at Brandywine College, a two-year college that later became part of Widener University. The school was located about a half hour from Jill's parents in

Willow Grove. She spent nights hanging out with girlfriends, including Liz Leonard, her childhood friend, studying in the halls or, more
likely, waiting to use the only available pay phone.

Jill's interest in fashion merchandising began to cool as her relationship with Stevenson grew serious. According to Stevenson, it was
Jill who first proposed the idea of marriage. Stevenson, who lived in
Newark, said Jill told him one evening that she could more easily be
accepted into the University of Delaware as an in-state resident, and
at a lower tuition rate, if the two of them married and lived full-time
together.

He proposed on Christmas Day in 1969, and what followed was a
no-frills engagement. Jill's parents trusted their daughter's judgment,
even though she was eighteen years old. The two married in February
1970. Liz Leonard attended the event, which she called a "lovely, normal church" wedding.

Stevenson described Jill's parents as traditional and kind. "Don,"
he said, shortening Jill's father's name, managed a savings and loan,
and Bill remembered him as gray-haired, Italian, and strong. Bonny
Jean, he said, was a *Leave It to Beaver* type of mother. Both had a good
sense of humor, and Stevenson said the stories Jill has told of her
youthful rebellion—including sneaking out late at night and smoking
in her parents' house—were just blips in what he sees as an idyllic
upbringing.

"Her parents really paid attention to her," Stevenson said. "She
was very close to her parents and really respected them."

Over the years, Stevenson's and Jill's accounts of their marriage
have diverged on several key details, but both agree that her parents
were loving toward her and welcoming of him.

"I truly believed we were destined for each other," she wrote in her
memoir of that relationship. "Looking back, it may seem like that
relationship was a mistake of youth."

While Bill and Jill were falling in love, America was undergoing
societal and political upheaval. In 1969, the number of Americans
serving in the Vietnam War had reached its peak, bolstered in part by
the first draft lottery since the 1940s. That December, two months

before marrying Stevenson, Jill and a group of friends packed into the apartment she and Stevenson shared in Newark to watch the draft. The group included several young men, including Stevenson, he said, who had gathered around the television to see if their lottery numbers, which corresponded to their birthdays, would come up. The men in the group that night were spared.

"It was surreal to think of the lives wrapped up in those flimsy plastic capsules," Jill wrote in her memoir. "They seemed too small to hold the future of so many men."

By 1970, students at college campuses across the country, incensed by President Nixon's decision to reverse a commitment to withdraw 150,000 American troops from Vietnam and instead send several thousand into Cambodia, waged large-scale protests on campuses across the United States. Donald Scott Mackenzie, a childhood friend of Jill's, was shot and injured walking home from class when the National Guard began firing on a group of peaceful protesters at Kent State University.

But Jill's life was punctuated by the rhythms of school and married life, not the war. Her upbringing was tranquil and had sheltered her from the rest of the world. She was not interested in branching out. She cared little for politics, and when she became old enough to vote, she registered Republican, mostly because that was how her parents had registered. The moment that changed her marriage came in 1972, when Bill opened the Stone Balloon, a bar on 115 East Main Street in Newark, Delaware. He was twenty-two. She was nineteen. He has said he didn't tell her he bought a bar until after the sale was complete.

The bar attracted locals, many of them college students who were lured in with cheap beer specials. Mondays were movie nights, and Thursday was Mug Night, when guests bringing in the bar's glass mugs could get cheap beer refills. Stevenson also offered big meal portions at lunchtime for young people short on cash—he always insisted that the meat and cheese on the sandwiches served there be at least four or five inches deep, Sherry Hynson Kitchen, who worked at the bar in the early days, recalled.

"The Balloon," as it was called, was an unassuming, even dingy-looking building with green awnings and a stone facade. Stevenson was a charismatic owner, and he lived and breathed rock 'n' roll. He was always leveraging connections, attending shows, and begging musicians to come and play at his bar. There weren't big acts in the beginning, but he was also a tireless networker. By the time the bar was two years old, Stevenson had convinced Bruce Springsteen to play the Balloon.

After a day full of classes, Jill would circle back to her husband and friends at the bar in the evenings, but she was not much of a scenester. People who worked for Bill at the time say they viewed her as the owner's wife.

"I didn't know Jill," Kitchen recalled. "Except I knew she was married to Bill."

The Balloon, Stevenson has said, was what led him to Joe Biden. Stevenson said that in January 1972 he asked Biden, then a county councilman, to help him obtain an occupancy permit for the bar. Stevenson has also said he helped fundraise for Joe's first Senate campaign, and recalled in interviews that the first meeting between Joe and Jill came in the summer of 1972—years earlier than when the Bidens have said they first met.

"We got married in '70. I introduced Joe to Jill in '72. Right before the election in '72, Jill, Joe, Neilia and I were in his kitchen. How do you forget that?" Stevenson, who voted for Trump, told the tabloid site *Inside Edition* in an interview published about six weeks before the 2020 presidential election. He went on to claim that a romantic relationship began between Joe and Jill in 1974, when she was still married to Stevenson.

Over a long lunch in Wilmington in the summer of 2022, Stevenson, who is affable and came toting photos and documents, declined to provide evidence to support his claim that Jill and Joe were romantically linked while she was still married.

"The relationship of Joe and Jill Biden is well documented," Michael LaRosa said in a statement around the time Stevenson participated in the *Inside Edition* interview. "Jill Biden separated from her first husband irreconcilably in the fall of 1974 and moved out of their marital home. Joe and Jill Biden had their first date in March of 1975, and they married in June of 1977."

Jill is the fourth woman in American history to have been divorced before marrying a future president, following Florence Harding, Betty Ford, and Rachel Jackson. The failure of her first marriage, people who know her say, profoundly destabilized Jill, who had, until then, lived a relatively sheltered life. Stevenson's decision to go public with claims that she had an affair deeply angered both Bidens, but especially Jill. "She hates him," a person close to her said. Another person close to her said she was basically indifferent.

As he looked back on their relationship, Stevenson seemed to want to telegraph that he was not bitter about the marriage ending, and that he had moved on—a difficult task when your ex is the First Lady of the United States. He said he shared the blame for the dissolution of their marriage because he had turned his attention to the Stone Balloon. "I think she thinks she was left behind," he said.

Stevenson is planning a book that will delve into the details of their divorce, including a contentious trial that he claims saw Jill unsuccessfully trying to take half-ownership of the bar, in addition to other property. He said at lunch that he has no ill will toward her and that he still worries about her.

"She's a target," he said. "The bad people in the world would love to hurt anyone in this family."

As Joe pursued Jill, she was reluctant to meet his family or get her heart broken again, but she was also wary of the Biden family's complexities. Fitting into the Biden family would require her to put parts of herself and her ambitions on hold. On top of everything else, she would be taking the place of Neilia Biden, the woman who had married Joe and helped make him a senator.

WHEN JOE FIRST MET Neilia Hunter in the spring of 1964, he was a cocky junior at the University of Delaware. He had arrived on campus after overcoming a persistent childhood stutter and enduring years of bullying, and he was ready to reinvent himself. He was interested in becoming an attorney, but he spent his first several years trying to make the football team and chasing girls.

Joe was beginning to realize that he might need to get his act together and bring his grades up in time to apply for law school when he and a friend traveled to Nassau, the Bahamas, for spring break. Carrying just eighty-nine dollars from his tax refund, Joe had no idea where he was going to stay that evening. Luckily, the pair ran into some classmates who let them crash at their rental. Looking for action on Paradise Island, the pair snuck into the exclusive British Colonial Hotel. They found a couple of discarded resort towels, wrapped them around their waists, and acted like they belonged.

A pretty blonde was lounging by the pool. Neilia.

"When she turned toward me, I could see she had a beautiful smile and gorgeous green eyes," Joe wrote in his memoir. "She was lit by the unforgiving glory of a full afternoon sun, and I couldn't see a single flaw. Basically, I fell ass over tin cup in love—at first sight."

He liked that she was easy to talk to. She liked it when he talked. Neilia was raised in Skaneateles, New York, and was a senior at Syracuse University. She had plans to teach at a nearby high school that fall. Her father owned the Hunter Dinerant in Auburn, and she spent her childhood summering along Skaneateles Lake in the Finger Lakes region. She had attended Penn Hall Junior College and Preparatory School, a boarding school in Pennsylvania. Athletic and graceful, Neilia came from a different background from the scrappy, working-class Joe.

According to Joe's retelling, on the first day they met, she shrugged off a posh young suitor to go to dinner with Joe. It was a heavenly development, except for one snag: He only had seventeen dollars left to his name. Neilia, seeing him look panicked when the check arrived, slipped him cash to pay for dinner.

Neilia and Joe were inseparable for the four days they were together in Nassau. He loved talking to her, and she made him feel special. The young, swaggering Joe had decided before he left the island that he was not going to live without her.

"You know, we're going to get married," he told her, at the end of their trip.

"I think so," she whispered back. "I think so."

After their time in Nassau, the couple returned to their respective schools, and Joe began a commuting habit that stuck with him over the decades. He turned down a chance to take a spot on the University of Delaware football team and instead traveled hundreds of miles each weekend to visit Neilia in Syracuse. And if he couldn't borrow a car to drive the 320-mile, five-hour trip to see her, he would hitchhike.

"I guess the only time I ever had trouble with my parents," Neilia told *The News Journal* in an interview in December 1972, "was when I wanted to marry Joe. He was Irish Catholic and we were Scotch Presbyterian, but they liked him too much to say no."

The two of them spent hours plotting out the course of their life together: a beautiful home, a gaggle of sandy-haired Biden children (she had wanted five), a booming law career for him, and a life in public office.

"Once I had Neilia with me, it became more of a plan than a daydream. Nobody outside my family believed in me the way Neilia did; seeing myself through her eyes made anything seem possible," he wrote. "'We can do this' was how she'd say it. 'I promise you.'"

Valerie Biden Owens, Joe's younger sister, recalls in her memoir, *Growing Up Biden,* that her brother's new girlfriend was beautiful and kind, but she also cleverly navigated the dynamics of the close-knit Biden family—winning each of them over, one by one. When Neilia and Joe eventually married, she asked Valerie to be her maid of honor. It was Neilia who persuaded Valerie to go on a blind date with Jack Owens, the man she would eventually marry.

"I took mental notes," Valerie wrote. "This was how I wanted to treat my future sisters-in-law, whoever they may be—with grace, with strength, with love, and with understanding. She became my role model."

A year after Joe graduated from the University of Delaware, he entered law school at the Syracuse University College of Law, while Neilia taught English at the Bellevue Heights School. The pair married on August 27, 1966, at St. Mary's of the Lake Church, a Roman Catholic church in Skaneateles near the northern tip of the lake where Neilia had spent her summers. She had converted to Catholicism to marry Joe, a decision that had been difficult for her father to stomach. (And to make matters worse for her father, she switched her political affiliation from Republican to Democrat.) In 1968, after Biden received his law degree, the family moved to Wilmington, where he set up his own firm.

While Joe worked and made plans to run for local office, eventually winning a seat on the New Castle County Council in 1970, the Bidens got to work fulfilling their ambitions to have a family. On February 3, 1969, Neilia gave birth to Joseph Robinette Biden III, whom they called Beau. One year and one day later—February 4, 1970—Robert Hunter Biden, whom they called Hunter, or just Hunt, was born. And on November 8, 1971, came their baby girl, Naomi Christina. They called her Amy. In less than three years, Joe and Neilia had accumulated three of the five children they had envisioned.

Neilia had entered her relationship with Joe with a full understanding that his campaigns for public office would be the product of their shared political vision and attentive work. Along with Valerie, who ran Joe's first Senate campaign, Neilia hosted parties in their home so voters could come and meet with Joe in a personal setting. Then the two of them wrote thank-you notes by hand to each attendee.

Much of what is remembered about Neilia by those who knew her is her beauty. She had an easy, wide smile. Her hair was thick and blond. She is less remembered for her interest in politics, her zeal for campaigning, and the astuteness she used to size up her husband's political opponents.

"'Oh, boy, you're going to have Neilia Hunter? She's beautiful, Sue,'" a former student named Susan Spooner remembered being told by a friend the day she received her classroom assignment at Bellevue Heights. When Spooner got a look at her new teacher on the first day of school, she understood what her friend had meant. "When she started speaking, she was exactly what my girlfriend had told me: very soft spoken and beautiful personality," Spooner told *The Daily Orange,* Syracuse's student newspaper.

In the last year of Neilia's life, the Biden family posed for a photograph that they would use to give out as a campaign souvenir to supporters. In the photo, Neilia is cradling an infant Naomi, feeding her a bottle. Despite her having three children under five years old, Neilia's hair is swept perfectly into an updo, with tendrils framing her face. Hunter sits in his own little chair, while Joe holds Beau, a towhead in saddle shoes, on his lap. On the back was a recipe for a fast-and-easy chicken dish that the dynamo mother of three said she could whip up in a flash.

"Hi! I'm Neilia Biden and this is one of our family's favorite recipes for chicken that can be baked in a jiffy. Hope you enjoy this. Neilia Biden."

Two weeks before he turned thirty years old, Joe won his first Senate race in November 1972, wresting a seat away from J. Caleb Boggs, a two-term Republican incumbent and former two-term Delaware governor. When Joe had announced his intentions to run against Boggs, the local paper published a list of the many candidates who had tried and failed to unseat the affable senator, who had a nice-guy reputation on Capitol Hill.

"Biden is 29 and has been a county councilman for 16 months," the columnist Al Cartwright wrote in *The News Journal* in March 1972. "Boggs is 62—he has shoes older than Joe—and has been a Delaware congressman, governor, and senator for 26 uninterrupted years. He is 7-for-7 in the election majors."

The Biden campaign, a scrappy operation run by Biden's relatives, made the decision to let Joe's age work for him. Using a strategy that his own critics would deploy against him over four decades later, Joe painted Boggs as too old and out of touch to understand the concerns of modern Delaware.

"Cale Boggs' generation dreamed of conquering polio," read one ad. "Joe Biden's generation dreams of conquering heroin."

"To Cale Boggs, an unfair tax was the 1948 poll tax," read another ad, posted under a story about Joe's campaign strategy two weeks before the 1972 election. "To Joe Biden, an unfair tax is the 1972 income tax."

"Joe Biden. He understands what's happening today" was each ad's coda. Joe squeaked past Boggs and won by 3,162 votes.

"There were only two people who made important decisions in the campaign," Joe said in a 1972 interview with *The News Journal*. "Myself and Neilia. She was the brains. And she also prevented me from blowing my top when I got angry late in the going."

In an interview given to *The News Journal* shortly before she died, Neilia hinted that she shared her husband's ambition to not just take on the political establishment but have her family take its rightful place in its firmament. And she didn't much like comparisons to the most well-known family in American politics at the time: "I don't know the Kennedys," she said, "but I don't think they could be half as great as the Bidens."

Neilia also shared a family ethos that has held true of the Bidens to this day: "We have very few close friends outside of the family."

She and her husband had just bought a house near Washington, one they planned to fill with new rugs and reupholstered furniture fit for entertaining. They were primed and ready to join the political and social mix as a young and attractive power couple.

"She was just a dynamo. She was bubbly, enthusiastic. She could get you to do anything on the campaign. You could never say no to Neilia," Karen Peterson, a former Democratic Delaware state senator from 2003 to 2017, who knew Neilia and volunteered on Biden's first Senate campaign, recalled.

There was something too lucky about the whole thing for Biden to completely accept. The day after he won the Senate election, according to Richard Ben Cramer's 1992 presidential doorstop of a book, *What It Takes*, Joe turned to Neilia and told her he was worried that something was going to happen.

"I don't know," he told his wife as they sat in a car. "But it's too perfect. Can't be like this. Something's gonna happen."

In the long span of Joe Biden's political career, this brief snapshot in time, when his family of five felt complete and ready to chart the post-victory course that he and Neilia had plotted, must have felt no longer than taking a breath.

ON DECEMBER 18, 1972, Joe and Valerie were interviewing staff in Washington when Neilia piled her three children into the family station wagon to go Christmas shopping and pick up a Christmas tree. She had pulled away from a stop sign when a tractor-trailer carrying corncobs hit the driver's side of the Chevrolet she was driving. After the collision, the Chevy spun for 150 feet, striking a row of evergreen trees and a highway sign before it hit and stopped against another tree. Neilia and Naomi were killed in the crash, while Hunter suffered head injuries and a broken arm, and Beau a series of broken bones, including a hip, an arm, and a leg. Afterward, campaign literature that Neilia had been carrying was found littered along the road.

Their brother Jimmy called Valerie: "Come home." Emergency responders called Joe, who flew with his sister to Wilmington in a rented plane that Jimmy had arranged for them. Joe was so devastated that he was given sedatives. At the hospital, he was given a bed to sleep in next to Beau and Hunter. His brother Jimmy slept nearby in a cot.

"I would never have made it here without her," Joe would tell Kitty Kelley about Neilia years later. "It's hard to imagine ever going through another campaign without her. She was the most intelligent human being I have ever known. She was absolutely brilliant. I'm smart but Neilia was ten times smarter. And she had the best political sense of anybody in the world. She always knew the right thing to do."

Jill says her first and only encounter with Neilia came about a month before the accident, in the opulent Gold Ballroom of the Hotel Du Pont in downtown Wilmington on the night of the election. It was a glittery, vibrant affair and the only big celebration that Neilia, who had worked so hard to get Joe elected, would live to see.

Husband and wife took turns with the microphone addressing the crowd that evening, but in her memoir, Jill writes that her only interaction was with Neilia.

"She had an easy, natural beauty that made her look almost out of place in the frantic crowd," Jill wrote. "On the spur of the moment, I decided to say hello. I walked up to her, held out my hand, and said, 'Congratulations on your win.' She took my hand, smiled graciously, and said, 'Thank you so much.'"

Jill, who had attended the party with Stevenson, wrote that she left with the same impression that so many Biden supporters had gotten after encountering the picturesque family for the first time: "Here they were, with the world at their feet, taking on the political establishment and *winning*." Stevenson said that he and Jill stayed at the hotel that evening, in a suite he had arranged for a victory celebration.

BY 1977, JILL, WHO had spent much of her young life vacillating between yearning for freedom and building a life of domesticity, was facing another marriage proposal, this time from the senator whose life she had admired from afar in that victory gathering at the Hotel Du Pont.

It wasn't the simplest of proposals. She was being asked to sign up to be not just Joe's wife but his second wife, replacing the beautiful first one who had been the core of his political operation and, according to everyone near the burgeoning Biden machine, loved the energy of campaigning as much as Joe did. The entire Biden family had made it clear to her that Joe wanted to run for the presidency. Joe's brothers, Jimmy and Frank, had even taken Jill out to dinner to suss her out and make sure she was on board.

"They were letting me in on this, and kind of warning me that if I was going to marry him, that this was part of the plan," Jill told PBS in September 2020. "But I sort of brushed it off, because I figured, well, maybe, you know, maybe not."

She was also being asked to take over the caregiving responsibili ties for two young boys who were still adjusting to a life without their mother and baby sister. In the years since the accident, Joe, Valerie, and Jimmy Biden, along with their mother, had pooled their time and energy to raise the boys. Valerie's first marriage ended and her second one, to Jack Owens, began while the newlyweds lived under Joe's roof, taking care of his sons. But Joe wanted a permanent fixture in their lives who could be a force of calm and stability.

He saw the potential in Jill, who had taken her time getting to know the Biden family, including Valerie—a towering figure in the boys' lives who had adored Neilia and who, by her own account, had taken some time to adjust to the new woman stepping in to care for the boys.

"I had to be 100 percent sure that if Joe and I got married, it would be forever—for Beau and Hunter's sake," Jill wrote in her memoir.

That spring, Joe appeared on the doorstep of her apartment. He was, he told her, too much in love with her to just be friends. But there was also his political future to think about. He was thirty-five years old—which, as anyone around him at the time would have noted, made him eligible for the White House.

"I've been as patient as I know how to be, but this has got my Irish up," Joe, folksy even then, told her, she recalled. "Either you decide to marry me, or that's it—I'm out. I'm not asking again." On that try—his fifth—she said yes.

AFTER TWO YEARS OF DATING, Jill Jacobs, wearing a white eyelet dress, married Joe Biden on June 17, 1977, at the chapel at the United Nations in New York City. The service was punctuated by Biden's two young sons approaching the couple during the ceremony and standing beside their father. Still new to the public relations game, the young bride let her new husband handle the media rollout around his second marriage. The next month, the Sunday *News Journal* published a story—"Son Told Joe to Marry Jill"—featuring an interview between Biden and the columnist Al Cartwright. In it, the senator first told what would become a well-trodden story. His son Beau had run out of patience with his father's courting of Jill: "We've been dating for over two years. Are we getting married or aren't we?" In Joe's mind, his eldest son's question had confirmed Jill's new role within the family: "It was understood right along that we would be a family unit—that Jill would be the mother of the boys," Joe told Cartwright.

The story featured a two-columns-wide photo of his new wife, who was, Joe said, "entitled to a little privacy." He said that she had started volunteering at the Child Abuse Center in Wilmington, tending to plants, and learning the piano. But Joe did not mention that Jill had been married and divorced before. That development threatened to create complications for the senator, a practicing Catholic whose church teaches that marriages are unbreakable and remarrying after a divorce is a sin. A week later, Cartwright issued an update from the senator: "I thought the fact that Jill was married before had no relevance," he told the paper. "She married very young, when she was 18, and there was a separation for a year or so before the divorce. There were no children. I thought all that was common knowledge in Wilmington."

As far as both Jill and Joe were concerned, her past had little to do with her new life, where she had found renewed purpose as a wife and teammate in raising Beau and Hunter. Beau was outgoing like his father and shared Jill's playful sense of humor. They were both blond and blue-eyed, and they both enjoyed it when strangers would say Beau took after Jill. Hunter was the soulful one who did not always express every emotion he was feeling, a personality trait that Jill recognized. Jill, who wasn't used to touchy-feely displays of affection, had grown to love both boys, who "were like puppies who always wanted to snuggle up and climb in my lap," she wrote.

As she adjusted to the life of a political wife, Jill would make occasional trips into Washington to meet with other Senate spouses over lunches and volunteer meetings. In September 1981, Jill brought an infant Ashley to a Senate Wives Club luncheon on Capitol Hill, where a group of the wives assembled baby dolls and kits to donate to the Red Cross. Barbara Bush, then the Second Lady and president of the spouses' club, was present, as was Catherine Stevens, the wife of

Senator Ted Stevens of Alaska. Stevens, who at the time had an infant daughter of her own, bonded with Jill as a fellow young mother. Stevens recalled that one of Jill's main concerns was integrating Ashley into the boys' lives. Joe was taking the train back and forth to Washington each day, but Beau and Hunter's world was largely managed and organized by Jill, who now was caring for a newborn.

It was enough pressure to make any woman crack, Stevens recalled, but she said she felt like there was very little about her new friend that seemed demanding or self-involved. Most of what Jill did, and most of what she talked about, appeared to be in the service of bringing her new family closer together.

"She is such an unusual human," Stevens said. "She has been through so much and she is smart and thoughtful, and she is the same person she's always been." Stevens paused before continuing: "He is so lucky to have her."

CHAPTER EIGHT

"A FORCE TO BE RECKONED WITH"

JILL SPENT THE FIRST DECADE OF HER MARRIAGE JUGGLING motherhood and making her way back to her teaching career. Her life as a political spouse was low on her list of priorities.

After graduating from the University of Delaware with an English degree in 1975, Jill had taken jobs as a substitute teacher in the Wilmington schools and, later, became a teacher at Saint Mark's High School, a private Catholic school in the city. She was also slowly working toward a master's degree in education, with a focus on reading, from West Chester University.

"I wanted a degree in remedial reading because I saw so many kids who couldn't read," she said in Rehoboth. "Then I decided, 'Oh, I should get a master's in English.'"

She left Saint Mark's in 1977, right after she married Joe, and began working one day a week at his Senate office. Eventually, she chose to become a full-time mother to Beau and Hunter, taking over for the assorted Bidens who had stepped in to help raise the boys after Neilia's death. In 1979, she was hired as a reading specialist at Concord High School in Wilmington but, in January 1980, was transferred to Claymont High School in Claymont, Delaware, the first school in the state to racially integrate. She received her first master's degree in teaching, with a focus in reading, in 1981, eking out one course a semester while working as a reading specialist at Claymont.

(Claymont was closed by the Brandywine School District in 1990 because of low enrollment and racial imbalance.)

Jill returned to work two years after Ashley was born, as an English and history teacher at the Rockford Center psychiatric hospital in Newark. She left in 1987 but was still taking classes to earn a second master's degree, which she eventually received from Villanova University in 1991.

As Jill was juggling, Joe's star was rising in the Senate, with seats on the Senate Judiciary Committee and the Foreign Relations Committee. Jill, a natural introvert, had mostly avoided requests from her husband or his family to campaign or give speeches on his behalf. After a shaky early attempt at delivering remarks at a fundraiser in Kent County, she had told her husband her political career was done, but, of course, it wasn't. In 1978, Joe had a Senate reelection campaign to win, which required her to travel to state fairs and donor events. Jill was not a creature of Washington, but she was willing to publicly support Joe if she felt her presence could benefit him.

"I don't think Jill ever sat around in her younger life and thought, 'I want to have a life in politics,'" Cathy Russell, Jill's former chief of staff and a close friend, said in an interview. "That's just not who she was. I think she loved him and she was going to support him in this effort. That's really how I would think about the beginning."

During the reelection campaign, she defended Joe against a Republican challenger, James H. Baxter, Jr., who accused Joe of absenteeism. At an event hosted by the Hadassah Women's Zionist Organization, she stood up in front of her sons—and Baxter—and told the group that her husband was dedicated to the people of Delaware. "I just cannot let this go by," she said, according to an account by Superville and Pace. "I just can't let you go out that door thinking that Joe just sloughs off down in Washington! Joe is a smart man and he knows which votes are important . . . If he misses a vote because it's an amendment to an amendment, he's made a good decision on that!"

Joe's campaign-manager sister, Valerie, and several of his earliest loyalists, including an attorney named Mark Gitenstein, all thought of Jill as smart and charming, though not particularly interested in politics. She hadn't even switched her party affiliation to Democrat before the Senate primary, Superville and Pace write. (Luckily, Joe handily won reelection and did not need her vote.)

She was fonder of small gatherings than large political fundraisers or debates. As a Senate spouse, she had developed friendships with other political wives, including Catherine Stevens and Marcelle Leahy, who was married to Senator Patrick Leahy, a Democrat from Vermont. She'd also introduced Senator John McCain, the late Republican from Arizona, to his future wife, Cindy, at a cocktail party in 1979. His new bride never forgot that the Bidens "were the first couple to invite us to their home." John's work as a Navy liaison to the Senate, in which he served as one of the main military points of contact for elected lawmakers, brought him closer to the Bidens. As McCain accompanied them on one trip to Greece, Jill and McCain danced on tables, and he had a "red bandana clenched in his teeth," wrote Robert Timberg in his biography of McCain.

All the while, Joe flirted with the idea of running for the presidency—casually in 1984 and then more seriously as the 1988 campaign drew near. A moderate Democrat who staunchly occupied the center of a party that was shifting to the left, Joe believed he could sell voters on a candidacy that could bridge the intraparty divide. (He'd dust off the same playbook in 2020.) Later in his life, Joe realized that it had been ego, not policy, that had guided his decision to run for the first time.

"I started looking at the race through the wrong prism," he wrote in *Promises to Keep*, recalling that first presidential race. "I looked around, judged myself against the other potential candidates for the nomination, and by the beginning of 1987 I decided I could beat them."

Joe entered a primary field that included Senator Al Gore of Tennessee, Representative Richard A. Gephardt of Missouri, and Rev. Jesse Jackson. With a fiercely loyal campaign team and a natural ability to connect with people—a "gut politician"—Joe stood out from the beginning. So did his tendency to play loose with facts, embellish stories, and lift material from other speeches.

In February 1987, Joe told a crowd in New Hampshire that he had marched during the civil rights movement. (He hadn't.) That month, he took material from a speech by Robert Kennedy without crediting him. In April 1987, Joe got into an argument with a voter over his IQ score before embellishing his academic credentials, an interaction that initially went unnoticed. When Joe got the feeling that he might not be ready, it was Jill who convinced him to officially declare his candidacy in June of that year.

Three months later, as reporters began to dig up his past comments and scrutinize his speeches, and amid accusations that he had plagiarized some of his public remarks from Neil Kinnock, then the British Labour Party leader, Joe dropped out of the 1988 race.

He told reporters that it was important to return to his role as chairman of the Senate Judiciary Committee and lead a fiery opposition to the nomination of Robert Bork, President Reagan's choice for the Supreme Court. Biden went right from his meeting with reporters into a nomination hearing. Afterward, he was walking with an aide toward the Senate when they ran into a fired-up Jill in the hallway.

"Jill turns to him and says, 'You better win this Bork fight,'" the aide recalled. "I remember looking at Joe. It was like, 'Oh shit.' It was the first time I realized she was a force to be reckoned with."

It surprised several advisers that Jill had so deeply shared her husband's anguish about dropping out. The setback had ignited a stoic, fiery streak in her that paired well with her husband's ceaseless sense of ambition. A month after Joe pulled out of the race, the Senate voted 58–42 to reject Bork's nomination.

The Bidens had survived Joe's plagiarism scandal, but it would only be a few months until a more serious obstacle appeared. In February 1988, Jill was teaching a class at Claymont when she was told something had happened to Joe.

"We got a call, Jill," another teacher told her. "You need to go home."

Joe, who was then in his midforties, had been suffering from daily headaches, popping Tylenol by the handful. Days earlier, he had been lifting weights in the Senate gym when he felt a pain in his neck and a numbness in his body. He continued his schedule until that day in February, when Jill was summoned home and found him lying on the bed, his skin gray, "as if he were slowly becoming an old family portrait," she wrote. Jill, who over time had become deferential to the other decision makers in Joe's family, felt herself taking control.

"We have to get him to the hospital now," she told Joe's brother Frank and an aide named Tom Lewis. Joe was transported to Saint Francis Hospital in Wilmington, where a team of doctors rushed outside to greet him. A CT scan and spinal tap showed that there was blood in Joe's spinal column, the telltale sign of an aneurysm. Doctors eventually confirmed there were two aneurysms located near the base of Joe's brain.

The decision was quickly made to send Joe by ambulance to Walter Reed National Military Medical Center in Washington, where a doctor told the Bidens there was roughly a fifty-fifty chance that he would not survive the surgery. If he did survive, there was a chance that the part of his brain that governed his speech would be damaged.

For Jill, the diagnosis was the latest setback after a stressful year. She had spent months campaigning on his behalf, despite her discomfort with public speaking. She was raising their three children, Beau, Hunter, and Ashley, who were all in different stages of adjusting to school and life in Delaware. She was exhausted. In the hospital, as she watched Joe's mother, sister, and brothers debate the best path forward for Joe's treatment, something in her broke.

"Wait a minute!" she yelled at the group. "He's my husband. I should be making the decision here."

The Bidens were stunned, until Joe's mother eventually agreed: "She's right," Jean Biden told the group, settling the matter. That was the moment, as Jill has recounted, that she felt she had become a full-fledged Biden. Joe survived the first surgery and had another four-and-a-half-hour procedure to correct the second aneurysm in May of that year. Before he was wheeled in for the second surgery, Joe reached up and grabbed the arm of Dr. Neal Kassell, the neurosurgeon who performed the procedure.

"He looked me in the eye and said, 'Doc, do a good job, because someday I'm going to be president,'" Dr. Kassell recalled to *The Daily Beast*. Even at the lowest points of his life, Joe's ambition always prevailed.

THE STRESS OF 1988 pushed Jill into a more powerful role within her family, and her influence would only grow. When it came time to weigh future bids for the presidency, Jill's opinion could halt or green-light a campaign, in large part because she understood the effect each campaign would have on the rest of the family. She had become the center of a family that is notoriously tight-knit, politically and personally.

In 2004, John Kerry announced a presidential run, and Joe's advisers were urging him to try as well. During a meeting at his home in Wilmington, several aides—including Ron Klain, who had dialed in by speakerphone—were imploring him to get into the race. But then Jill entered the room in a halter top with the word "NO" scrawled on her stomach. "At that point, it was all over," a person in the room recalled in an interview. (Klain, who had not seen her parade through the room, came away from the conversation deeply confused about why the mood had suddenly changed, that person said.)

As her husband weighed decisions, Jill made sure that the people near her him were also people she trusted. "She has a very good sense of people and whether they're good for Joe or bad for Joe," said Mark Gitenstein, a Biden ally whom Joe nominated in 2021 as ambassador to the European Union. "Unerring."

Maybe it was domestic bliss. Maybe it was the Sharpie. But in 2006, Joe still seemed more interested in staying home with Jill than in running for the presidency, and he said as much to a group of supporters that year: "I'd rather be at home making love to my wife while my children are asleep," he said of his interest in the job. The remark might've surprised some in the audience, but it drew little more than a shrug from a spokesman, who explained that the senator was "frankly totally in love with his wife." (Joe may have tamped down on his public bedroom declarations winning the presidency, but he has joked to aides that "good sex" is the key to a lasting and happy marriage, much to his wife's chagrin.)

In 2008, the Bidens decided the time was right for another run, only to drop out after finishing fifth in the Iowa caucus. Joe eventually accepted Barack Obama's offer to run as the vice-presidential nominee, but the campaign season was not without its moments of tension. On occasion, the Biden team—including Joe himself—groused about his second-class treatment. One former campaign official recalled asking Biden to give a statement on immigration policy. "You mean the one I've had for twenty-five years?" the senator snapped. "Or this guy's?" Jill could be impatient, too. At campaign events, she would chide aides who crafted speeches that were too long-winded. "You see these boots?" she told one former speechwriter, Jeff Nussbaum, pointing toward her heels. "Shorter speeches!" She was playful when she said it, Nussbaum recalled, but he said he knew better than to cast off her criticism as a joke.

According to several accounts, the Bidens and Obamas were friendly but never grew particularly close. Several people in the Biden orbit have privately pointed to the fact that Joe and Jill never attended dinner in the White House residence during the eight years the Obamas were in office as evidence of the distance. A person close to the Bidens said that invitations were issued, but the then vice president and his family were usually too busy with their own engagements. Michelle Obama did venture to the vice-presidential residence for cocktails "a couple of times," that person said, and she had joint meetings with Jill, often about their shared initiative centered around military families, about every six weeks.

It would take time for the president and vice president to grow comfortable with each other, but during eight years as vice president, Joe provided the legislative experience and key political instincts that the younger president lacked. He helped sell the Affordable Care Act, helped oversee the drawdown of troops in Iraq, and helped shepherd the country out of one of the largest financial crises in its history. His public image had been burnished by playing the easygoing, assured

In the early 1970s, a young Jill Biden—who was then Jill Stevenson—posed for this photo with the Delaware-based photographer Thomas Stiltz.

The image was later used as part of an advertisement for a nearby park. According to the memoirs of Joe and Jill Biden, this image of her is what first caught Joe's eye.

After marrying Senator Joe Biden in 1977, Jill Biden became a Senate spouse. Throughout the year, the Ladies of the Senate Red Cross Unit would meet periodically to volunteer their time for good causes. Jill was not always present, and focused much of her time raising her children in Delaware. The meeting on September 22, 1981, included Catherine Stevens with two-month-old baby Lily (far left), Peatsy Hollings (second from left), Second Lady Barbara Bush (fifth from left), Nancy Murkowski (visible behind Jill Biden), and Jill Biden, with baby Ashley (far right).

Senator Joe Biden announced his first campaign for the presidency in Wilmington, Delaware, on June 9, 1987. Here, riding on the Biden Express, "Amtrak Joe" is flanked by Jill Biden and the Biden children (from left to right) Hunter, Ashley, and Beau.

Jill Biden grasps her husband's arm on September 23, 1987, the day Joe Biden, beset by accusations of plagiarism, announced that he would no longer seek the Democratic presidential nomination. Dropping out of the race devastated both Bidens and ignited a competitive streak in Jill, who urged her husband to return to his role as chairman of the Senate Judiciary Committee and lead a fiery opposition to the nomination of Robert Bork, President Ronald Reagan's choice for the Supreme Court.

As President Donald J. Trump is sworn into office on January 20, 2017, Michelle Obama, the outgoing First Lady, and Jill Biden, finishing eight years as Second Lady, huddle under an umbrella together. The two women were not exceptionally close during their time in office, but they have both spoken fondly of each other.

Joe Biden had revived his third presidential campaign and was fresh off a Super Tuesday campaign victory on March 4, 2020, when two protesters rushed the stage at his rally in Los Angeles. Jill Biden attempted to push a protester away, while Symone Sanders, a senior campaign adviser, grabbed the woman and pulled her from the stage. One of the glowing headlines of the episode was from *The Philadelphia Inquirer:* "Jousting Jill Biden Showed Us a Fightin' Philly Girl Straight Outta Willow Grove."

On October 22, 2020, two very different political couples faced off ahead of the final presidential debate before the 2020 election. The debate between Donald Trump and Joe Biden showcased their mutual dislike for each other and exposed the gulf between their views on protecting Americans from the coronavirus pandemic. Since taking office, Jill Biden has exchanged birthday cards with her predecessor, Melania Trump.

The Bidens celebrate their Inauguration Day fireworks display from the White House Blue Room Balcony, alongside their children and most of their grandchildren.

First Lady Jill Biden meets with the actress Jennifer Garner as they travel to a West Virginia high school for a coronavirus vaccination event on May 13, 2021. That day, Jill was the first high-ranking Biden administration official to publicly appear without a mask after the Centers for Disease Control began a brief period of advising Americans to dispense with face coverings.

Anthony Bernal, a longtime Biden aide and confidant, is known as Jill Biden's enforcer. He is also the person who pulls off marquee East Wing events, including a secretive trip to Ukraine.

During a secret trip to Ukraine in May 2022, First Lady Jill Biden meets with Olena Zelenska, the Ukrainian first lady. Their meeting was kept completely secret until after it happened. "I thought it was important to show the Ukrainian people that this war has to stop, and this war has been brutal, and that the people of the United States stand with the people of Ukraine," Jill told reporters that day. Her visit to Ukraine occurred months before her husband was able to make his own trip there.

After spending much of their first year eschewing traditional celebrations because of the ongoing coronavirus pandemic, Joe and Jill Biden began to open up the White House to events, including trick-or-treating, in 2022. Between her Halloween costume and the pranks she has pulled above her government aircraft, Jill appears to have an extensive wig collection.

First Lady Jill Biden addresses lawmakers during the White House Congressional Picnic on July 12, 2022, as President Joe Biden and Vice President Kamala Harris look on. Relations between the First Lady and vice president were tense during the presidential campaign when Harris attacked Biden for his past stance on student bussing. "She's an Italian," one person close to her said. "She's all about loyalty."

Following a modern tradition set by her predecessors, First Lady Melania Trump traveled to Africa in the fall of 2018. On that trip, she lamented that the press seemed to cover only her attire, and then she posed for several minutes, with drums thumping behind her, in front of pyramids in Egypt.

As First Lady, Melania Trump hosted her first state visit, for President Emmanuel Macron and Brigitte Macron of France, in 2018. Her wide-brimmed white hat, commissioned by her longtime collaborator Hervé Pierre, made headlines and later became the inspiration for her future ventures with NFTs.

First Lady Hillary Rodham Clinton chaired the Clinton administration's sprawling effort to reform health care in the United States. In September 1993, she takes questions from members of the House Energy and Commerce Committee on Capitol Hill. "If I had known that being First Lady and doing this would cause so much cognitive dissonance," Hillary said in an interview decades after the effort had failed, "I would have shown up in meetings, I would have traveled the country, but I wouldn't have taken on a formal role."

First Lady Hillary Clinton and her daughter, Chelsea, visit an air base in Bosnia in 1996, shortly after a peace agreement ended a civil war in the country. Later, Hillary would use this trip as evidence of her foreign policy work as First Lady, though she eventually walked back claims that she'd landed under sniper fire there.

First Lady Laura Bush co-founded the National Book Festival in 2001. On September 8, 2001, thousands of authors, Olympians, celebrities, and book lovers gathered in Washington to celebrate. Just three days later, the September 11 attacks instantly transformed both her husband's presidency and her East Wing role.

First Lady Michelle Obama, seen here on Inauguration Day in 2009, was the first Black woman to hold her role. She left her career to support her husband's political ambitions and focus on settling her children in Washington. But by the end of her tenure, she had grown more comfortable with her closely watched life. "By staying true to the me I've always known, I found that this journey has been incredibly freeing," she said in 2015.

On June 1, 1990, First Lady Barbara Bush delivered a commencement speech to the graduates of Wellesley College alongside Raisa Gorbacheva, the wife of the leader of the Soviet Union. The students of Wellesley had protested the choice of Barbara as commencement speaker, but the First Lady won the graduates over with a speech that acknowledged a new generation of women who were more interested than ever in balancing careers with their home lives. "That, for me, is really a signal for the modern age of the First Lady," said the historian Anita McBride.

counterpart to Barack's cerebral and cool commander in chief, and his relative popularity prompted whispers of a third presidential run.

It was not to be. In May 2015, Beau, a bright star in the close family's orbit, died of brain cancer. Broken again by tragedy, Joe backed away from the 2016 race. Another element of the story, commonly circulated among Biden aides, is that Obama's support of Hillary Clinton as the first female Democratic presidential candidate in history played more of a role in Joe's decision to duck out than anyone involved in those deliberations has publicly admitted. In any case, the loss of Beau profoundly reorganized the tight-knit family. Once again, it was Jill who stepped forward to try to heal a broken link in the chain, taking more of a role in her husband's political decision-making than she had before.

Joe's retirement from public life was brief. In August 2017, when a group of white nationalists stormed Charlottesville, Virginia, the demonstration soon turned violent, and a man driving a Dodge Charger ran over a young woman in a crowd of protesters, killing her. Both Bidens were astonished when President Trump said that there were "very fine people on both sides" of the protest line in Charlottesville, but only Joe was immediately convinced he should run. Though Joe has credited Charlottesville for reigniting his interest in trying to unite the country, Jill took more convincing. She was enjoying the brief respite from politics.

Advisers had also warned that there would be intense scrutiny from the news media and right-wing critics, not just of Joe but of their children and their grandchildren. The Bidens were privately told that struggles within their family, including Hunter's ongoing battle with substance abuse, which was not widely known at the time, might bleed over into Joe's campaign should he seek the 2020 Democratic nomination.

Hunter had become "unmoored" by Beau's death, as one former Biden adviser described the situation. Hunter was, that person said, "an untethered emotional kind of slow-moving cyclone." His marriage had fallen apart, he was engaged in a tumultuous relationship with his brother's widow, Hallie Biden. He had long struggled with alcoholism, but now he was sliding into a devastating addiction to crack cocaine.

Through it all, Joe, that adviser said, remained deeply protective of his family, and particularly his son, the adviser said. But his devotion had left him unwilling to take "an accounting of the vulnerabilities in his life," that person said. Donald Trump had shown little restraint in attacking the Clintons in 2016. If Joe chose to run, the Bidens—especially Hunter—could not expect to be spared.

Beau's death changed the family. Joe was without one of his closest advisers, whom he often described as "me, without all the downsides." Without their older brother, Hunter was in shambles and Ashley, who has also struggled with addiction, was bereft. Once again, it fell to Jill to hold her family together. After Beau died, Jill's place in the family yet again shifted toward the center. Instead of calling Beau several times a day to check in or run decisions by him, Joe began relying on Jill more than ever.

"She's in a different place than she ever was before," said a close friend of the couple. "She's one of the few people that can really tell him what's up."

Joe made his final decision on December 5, 2018, when he and Jill traveled to Washington for the state funeral of President George H. W. Bush. All five living presidents attended the service held at the Washington National Cathedral. The Bidens sat in the second row, in the space reserved for vice presidents, including Dick Cheney, Dan Quayle, Mike Pence, and their wives. The appearance of the Trumps was the awkward elephant in the room, but there were glimpses of bipartisan comity, like when President George W. Bush slipped Michelle Obama a cough drop. The service was replete with a show of military honors to mark the life of the naval aviator who had enlisted on his eighteenth birthday and went on to fly fifty-eight combat missions.

The heartfelt eulogies were all laced with a hearty sense of humor. Jon Meacham, Bush's biographer, recalled that the president had once accidentally shaken a mannequin's hand on the campaign trail. The younger Bush told the crowd his father was a terrible dancer who had been "born with just two settings: full throttle, then sleep." Then he deftly drew comparisons between his father and the sitting president.

"To us, his was the brightest of a thousand points of light," George said, using a phrase Donald Trump had ridiculed. "He showed me what it means to be a president who serves with integrity, leads with courage, and acts with love in his heart for the citizens of our country."

When the service was finished, Jill suggested to Joe that they skip a formal reception and go to dinner, just the two of them, at BlackSalt, an upscale seafood restaurant that had become one of their favorite haunts when they lived in the capital.

"I said, 'Joe, you have to decide. It's time,'" Jill recalled in an interview. "And that's when he said, 'I think I want to run.'" In that moment, they both knew that they were locked in.

The campaign was about to become as bruising as every Biden had expected, but they had all given their blessing for Joe to run.

"HE DOESN'T GIVE UP, as you know," Jill said, giving me her assessment of Donald Trump. "He just pounds, pounds, pounds. And I knew that's what it was going to be. I knew it was going to be hard and I knew we'd have to fight like hell." Joe's advisers were relieved she'd signed on.

"She very much believed he was the right person for the time," Mike Donilon, one of the couple's closest advisers, said. He noted that when it came time to make "fundamental decisions about the campaign message and strategy, she was there, and she really brought it to a close."

The first indication of Jill's influence in her husband's political orbit was the fact that Anthony Bernal, her closest adviser, had served as a deputy campaign manager. "That meant she had a seat at the table, she had a voice, someone who knew her inside and out and could advance her needs, wants, and thoughts, to the senior leadership, and she had someone looking out for her and her husband's best interest, politically and personally," Michael LaRosa said. Jill had been involved in every major decision, from the "No Malarkey" bus tour—a decidedly uncool slogan for the seventy-seven-year-old candidate—to the vice-presidential selection process.

On the campaign trail, Jill became a tireless representative for her husband, often zipping across one area of a state while Joe campaigned in another and reuniting with him in the evenings. And she was adept at neutralizing political grenades lobbed at her husband. In April 2019, when Joe was accused by several women of invading their personal space or touching them in ways that made them uncomfortable, it was Jill who bolstered her husband's apology tour with a personal story of her own. She said her space had once been invaded during a job interview.

"Yes, it's happened to me," she told Robin Roberts of ABC as she sat beside her husband. "I've come home, and I've told Joe about it."

She then reframed the issue in personal terms.

"I think what you don't realize is how many people approach Joe—men and women—looking for comfort or empathy," Jill added during that interview. "But going forward, I think he's going to have to judge, be a better judge of when people approach him, how he's going to react—that he maybe shouldn't approach them."

Joe also faced criticism that he had mishandled the testimony of Anita Hill, a Black law professor who in 1991 accused Clarence Thomas, President George H. W. Bush's nominee to the Supreme Court, of sexual harassment.

Hill publicly said during the campaign that she felt she had not been taken seriously by Joe when he served as chairman of the Senate Judiciary Committee, and that it had been his responsibility to call other witnesses who had information about Thomas's behavior. "I cannot be satisfied by simply saying, 'I'm sorry for what happened to you,'" she told Sheryl Gay Stolberg and Carl Hulse of *The New York Times* after Joe had called her, decades later, to apologize. "I will be satisfied when I know that there is real change and real accountability and real purpose."

Jill was matter-of-fact when she sat for an interview with NPR days later. "He apologized for the way the hearings were run," she said. "And so now it's kind of—it's time to move on."

Back at the Biden headquarters in Philadelphia, several members of the communications team were surprised by what, for Jill Biden, was an uncharacteristically blunt response. But her remarks caught the attention of LaRosa, a television producer turned Senate aide who had long been orbiting Democratic circles and was looking for a way into the Biden campaign.

As a college swimmer at Seton Hall, LaRosa interned for Hillary Clinton's Senate campaign, which brought him into contact with powerful Hillaryland figures, including Patti Solis Doyle, Kelly Craighead, and Capricia Marshall. The trio introduced him to Bernal, who would often solicit LaRosa's advice after Jill's television appearances and interviews. On the day of the Anita Hill interview, LaRosa sent a lengthy strategy memo to Bernal, encouraging him to keep putting Jill up for interviews: "The more people see of her, the more they like her." He felt that Jill should continue defending her husband.

"You can't change the candidate, but you can always change or affect the perceived impression of that candidate," LaRosa wrote. "Those impressions determine what voters FEEL, and politics is much more emotional than it is rational, which is why SHE can shape the perception of Joe Biden as his surrogate-in-chief."

In August, Jill sent her husband's communication staff into a panic when she told a group of teachers gathered at a campaign event in Nashua, New Hampshire, that they should settle for her husband over other Democratic candidates because he could beat Donald Trump. (This was apparently an acceptable message until it was said out loud by a member of the Biden campaign.)

"Your candidate might be better on, I don't know, healthcare, than Joe is, but you've got to look at who's going to win this election," she told the group. "And maybe you have to swallow a little bit and say, 'Okay, I personally like so and so better,' but your bottom line has to be that we have to beat Trump."

Despite the handwringing in Philadelphia—and the pressure on the candidate's wife and her team to walk her comments back—LaRosa, still watching from the outside, was thrilled. In the middle of a bruising campaign, the challenger's wife was being authentic and frankly summing up her husband's entire appeal as a candidate: He could win.

"More of this!!" he wrote to Bernal, who texted back instantly: "Thank you," with a heart emoji. It was virtually unheard of for an outsider to quickly ascend to the outer ring of the Biden inner circle, but Bernal, who had spent the better part of a year vetting LaRosa, eventually called him in November 2019 and offered him a job as Jill's communications director.

The newly assembled team began traveling the country, packing into minivans to tour every county in Iowa and cross New Hampshire, South Carolina, and Nevada. On the road, LaRosa said in an interview, Jill "would grade papers in between events, and I would sit in the back in a panic over whether local press would show up for her next event." Once, Jill insisted on driving to a local newspaper to talk to journalists in person when no one showed up to her campaign event. The small-town paper was closed, so she scribbled a note and taped it to the office door: "Sorry we missed you. Catch you next time. Jill Biden."

"Whenever I was angry or frustrated about something," LaRosa told me, "she would look at me and say, 'Never let them see you sweat.'"

During the heat of campaigning, she was forced to put a women's mentoring project she had organized at NOVA on hold. It was difficult for her to pause the program, which was inspired, in large part, by her life as a working mother. But in an email to a group of colleagues on January 17, 2020, she wrote, "I've just been so busy on the campaign trail.

"Thanks for all your efforts," she continued. "I miss everyone—but hope my efforts make this all worthwhile. Jill."

In living rooms in Audubon, Iowa, and campaign events in Nashua, New Hampshire, Jill fielded question after question and personally approached quiet voters who mingled on the outskirts of each tiny rally. She even offered her email address to answer any lingering concerns they might have. Years of stumping had refined her instincts for knowing what a person looked like when they were unsure of or unenthusiastic about her husband. She was proud of her ability to approach people, even if they might not be friendly to her—or about her husband.

"How can I convince you?" she asked a table of three women she spotted at an event in Iowa, according to a report in *The Washington Post*. She had not wanted to let them get away. "What will it take?"

Jill may have been sad to leave her job, but it was during this period of time that her identity in the press began to rapidly evolve from an understated former Second Lady who had flown, mostly happily, under the radar for eight years while a megawatt Michelle Obama drew headlines, to a Philly girl who was willing to not just stand by her man but put her safety on the line for him.

After Joe had finished fourth in the Iowa caucuses, Jill was with her husband at a campaign rally ahead of the primary election in New Hampshire when she saw a protester approaching. A journalist caught video of her walking toward the man from the side of the stage. She put her hands on the man's chest and gently pushed him back into the crowd.

"You can take the girl out of Philly . . ." was her reply on Twitter to the journalist who shared the video. That evening, she told attendees she had selected the night's music, which featured the song "The Champion," by the country singer Carrie Underwood and the rapper Ludacris. Days earlier, Jill had decided on the song after hearing it in a spin class, and as she played it for Montoya, Bernal, and LaRosa aboard her plane, they nodded along to the lyrics. The song is about being the last person standing after a battle.

The next evening, Joe finished fifth in New Hampshire. The bruised old fighter and his campaign limped on to South Carolina, a state whose Black voters he had long believed would deliver him to the front of the race. He ended up being right.

"The people of South Carolina gave us wings," Jill told CBS News that night of the victory. "So many people had written Joe off. And I kept saying, 'He's resilient, he's resilient. He's gonna come back. He's gonna go forward.'"

In heels, Jill teetered down from the riser and found her husband, who was taking photos with supporters. Her staff was exhausted but euphoric.

"It was a rough few weeks," said LaRosa. "And it turned out, everything he kept telling her was right: 'Just hang on until South Carolina.'"

On March 4, 2020, Joe, fresh off a Super Tuesday victory, was participating in a rally in Los Angeles when a woman rushed the stage yelling, of course, "Let dairy die!" Jill, who was flanking Joe on one side, glimpsed the woman from her periphery. Without batting an eye, she instinctively grabbed her husband's hand and put herself between Joe and the protester. As a second woman rushed the stage, Jill attempted to push that protester away. Meanwhile, Symone Sanders, a senior campaign adviser, came sprinting in from the sidelines, swiftly grabbing the protester and pulling her from the stage.

"We're okay," Jill said quietly—almost to herself, at first. She then repeated herself more assertively to her husband. "We're okay." When she said it a third time, it was in the direction of the microphone, for the entire crowd to hear. "We're okay." Then she led the crowd in a "Let's Go, Joe" chant.

The sight of the two women—one of them a sixty-something white political spouse and the other a twenty-something Black campaign strategist—protecting a seventy-seven-year-old white presidential candidate drew scores of headlines. ("Let's be clear," Sanders told Joe backstage later, according to an account of the episode by the journalists Jonathan Allen and Amie Parnes in their book *Lucky: How Joe Biden Barely Won the Presidency*. "The only people who jumped onstage are the women who work for you.") One of the glowing headlines was from *The Philadelphia Inquirer*: "Jousting Jill Biden Showed Us a Fightin' Philly Girl Straight Outta Willow Grove." LaRosa, who had already left the venue to catch a red-eye flight back to Washington, received a call from Jill and Bernal to give him a heads-up about the exchange.

"Goddamn it," was LaRosa's reply, "why did you have to go viral when I'm not there?"

IF THIS WAS JOE'S last chance to run, Jill and her advisers saw the campaign as one last chance to shape her public identity.

"Does this grab you?" she'd quiz her aides as they went over speeches. "Where's the heart?" she would ask them. Emotion came more easily to Joe than it did for Jill. He had lost so much in his life that his ability to emotionally connect with people was something of a superpower.

Jill was more guarded than her husband, who found himself drawn to others who had experienced loss. But after Beau's death, she had, unwillingly, acquired some of her husband's ability to look into a crowd and see the people who were hurting, who needed some extra time and some eye contact; one administration official likened this ability to a shared "radar" for suffering.

The difference for Jill, though, was that she did not glean energy from those interactions the way Joe did. Speeches about pain came at an emotional cost for her. But she was as invested in her husband's potential to be president, and after decades of marriage, she could be a more effective keeper of the Biden family mythology—an illustrator of its highs and many lows—than her husband.

In August 2020, she got the chance to prove it with one of the most high-stakes appearances in American politics: a video address delivered at the Democratic National Convention. On the first night of the convention, Michelle Obama delivered a fiery speech that all but directly took on Trumpism and offered a forceful update to one of her most famous sayings as First Lady: "When they go low, we go high."

"Going high means standing fierce against hatred," Michelle said in her prerecorded address. "And going high means unlocking the shackles of lies and mistrust with the only thing that can truly set us free: the cold hard truth." It was a more direct and confrontational version of Michelle than the nation had ever seen—so direct that it earned her a defensive tweet from Trump; exactly the sort of fodder that could feed the Twittersphere for the day.

Faced with an onslaught of insults from the Trump orbit, the Biden team could've gone this route when it was Jill's turn to deliver a recorded speech on the second evening. Instead, there was a decision early on not to include any overt punching-out at Trump, one aide recalled, because Jill and her team had decided that they could draw a contrast between the candidates just by describing Joe.

The campaign hired Julie Cohen and Betsy West, Oscar-nominated filmmakers, who positioned Jill inside Brandywine High School in Wilmington, where she'd once taught English. They instructed her to walk through an empty hallway and into an empty classroom to deliver a nine-minute speech, shot live in prime time. But Jill, dressed in a hunter-green dress with her hair in loose waves, was prepared for the moment. She had rehearsed twice.

"When I taught English here at Brandywine High School, I would spend my summer preparing for the school year about to start, filled with anticipation. But this quiet is heavy. You can hear the anxiety that echoes down empty hallways. There's no scent of new notebooks or freshly waxed floors. The rooms are dark, as the bright young faces that should fill them are now confined to boxes on a computer screen."

Jill's speech was a powerful marriage of the concerns of the political moment with the tragic and evocative Biden backstory, and it won her bipartisan praise at a time during the campaign when such a concept was all but extinct.

"You know, motherhood came to me in a way I never expected. I fell in love with a man and two little boys standing in the wreckage of unthinkable loss, mourning a wife and mother, a daughter and sister.

"I never imagined, at the age of twenty-six, I would be asking myself, how do you make a broken family whole? Still, Joe always told the boys, 'Mommy sent Jill to us'—and how could I argue with her?"

It had been over forty years since Biden had first been elected to the Senate, and generations of Americans were familiar with him but not necessarily familiar with his family, what he had endured, or how Jill fit into the picture. Jill had keenly dusted the story off, all in service of showcasing her husband's character to the American public.

As she finished and the camera zoomed out, Joe, who had been watching from the sidelines, rushed toward her and wrapped her in a hug.

"Hey, everyone. I'm Jill Biden's husband," he said into the camera. "As you heard tonight, you can see why she's the love of my life and the rock of our family. She never gives herself much credit, but the truth is, she's the strongest person I know."

It was a political countermove that paid off. The speech did the near-impossible in a charged arena: It earned public praise from Trump allies like Senator Lindsey Graham, a Republican from South Carolina.

"Tonight, Jill Biden did a very good job representing herself and Joe in the causes they believe in," Graham wrote on Twitter. "She's an outstanding person who has led a consequential life."

Graham had been a Biden family friend until he began publicly calling for investigations into the business dealings of Hunter Biden, who had received money from a Ukrainian energy company and pursued business opportunities in China. Once Graham crossed that line, there was no going back into the good graces of the Biden family, as far as Jill was concerned.

Still, she had overcome expectations and garnered some semblance of bipartisan approval. No one from the campaign was surprised that she had pulled it off.

"Her nickname on the campaign trail was 'the Closer,'" Anita Dunn, one of the president's most senior advisers, said—a reference to major-league pitchers who are brought in at the end of a game to protect a winning team's lead.

Dunn, a skilled Democratic operative, also helped Jill conceive of the image she wanted to project to the nation as First Lady: America's mother. If the president was going to be the tell-it-to-you-straight leader during a time of so much fear and division, the First Lady could be the person at his side who could help broaden—and soften—his message.

CHAPTER NINE

"A QUIET ASSET"

THE BIDEN WHITE HOUSE AND ITS WIDE ORBIT—WHICH includes ambassadors and cabinet secretaries—is full of people who stood by Joe and Jill when he ducked out of the 1988 race. It is stocked with people, including Ron Klain, who staffed his Senate office. Several of Joe's closest advisers, including Klain, Bruce Reed, and Steven J. Ricchetti, ran his vice-presidential office. The skill they most share is the ability to manage Joe Biden.

Jill's East Wing is also filled with people who have that same talent, including Anthony Bernal and Elizabeth Alexander, whose relationship with the Bidens dates back to Joe's time in the Senate. Carlos Elizondo, the White House social secretary, worked for the Bidens during the vice presidency. Mala Adiga, Jill's policy adviser, has been in and out of the Biden orbit since the 2008 campaign. Rory Brosius, a former Biden campaign adviser, signed on as a director for the Joining Forces initiative, a program supporting military families that Jill and Michelle Obama had started together during the Obama administration. (Brosius was on staff during the first iteration of the program.) Jill's speechwriter, Amber Macdonald, had helped craft Jill's memoir.

With so many slots filled by loyalists and people who have worked for years to earn the trust of the Bidens, the initial East Wing staff of twenty-one people contained only a few newcomers, including Michael LaRosa, the press secretary, and Julissa Reynoso Pantaleón, Jill's first and only East Wing chief of staff.

Reynoso, a Harvard-educated lawyer and former ambassador to Uruguay, made an impression on Jill and Bernal in December 2019 when she flew to Texas and traveled with Jill across the border into a refugee camp in Matamoros, Mexico. Jill and Reynoso later wrote an op-ed for *The Washington Post* criticizing the so-called Remain in Mexico policy under the Trump administration, a program that the Biden administration fought to rescind.

After she was hired, Reynoso, a longtime ally of Hillary Clinton, spent hours on the phone with the former First Lady and Democratic presidential candidate, fielding her advice for how to set up an effective Biden East Wing.

Reynoso might have been chief of staff and Bernal a senior adviser, but there was no question who had more influence with the First Lady. He has been entrusted with organizing the lives of the extended Biden clan, and once the Bidens were installed in the White House, everything that went on in the East Wing—and a lot of what went on in the West Wing—was routed through Bernal.

Jill and Bernal are, as Jill puts it, in a "work marriage," but his reach extends beyond the East Wing. He weighs in on everything from the Biden family's schedules to the president's motorcade routes. No order is beneath him: He wrangles the dog, carts the White House cat around in her cage, and makes sure that the various Biden children and grandchildren are transported to the appropriate weekend retreats. Camp David or Wilmington this weekend? Call Anthony. When the Bidens take vacations to Rehoboth, Bernal goes with them to make sure the two-minute walk to the beach is properly choreographed.

In the East Wing, Bernal and Jill quickly became fond of hourslong meetings, where they discussed the ins and outs of every decision she could make. Alexander, Reynoso, Adiga, and LaRosa—until he resigned in July 2022—were also central to early marathon meetings. That small inner circle was and is virtually leakproof.

One of the more controlled rollouts overseen by this group was the debut of the White House cat, Willow, who had been secretly living with LaRosa while the drama surrounding Major's biting incidents was sorted out. The story of Willow's ascension was so tightly controlled that the East Wing did not allow photographers to take photos of the animal, out of fear she appeared too paunchy from the wrong angle. ("The Bidens don't do fat," quipped one official about the episode.) The White House distributed handout photos instead. Another example is the East Wing's decision to tightly control information about the wedding of Naomi Biden, Jill and Joe's eldest granddaughter and Hunter Biden's eldest child. It was a private family event, held on the South Lawn of the White House. And covered by *Vogue*.

If Elizabeth Alexander helps keep the office on an even keel, Bernal can be the genesis of the drama, pitting staffers against each other and quizzing them about their loyalty to the Bidens, according to people who have observed his interactions. Bernal is also known to profess his love of and respect for his colleagues in the same breath as telling them they are disliked or disrespected in other parts of the building.

"It's like, 'Oh my god, I love you, but did you know this person hates you?'" a former senior West Wing official said with a laugh, describing a typical interaction with Bernal. Another former senior West Wing official described him as a "trash talker, a little bit, about people—he's not the only one in politics, but he is the only one with the ear of the First Lady."

Several current and former White House officials and Biden-world aides also say that Bernal has a signature move: upending projects at the last minute and, as one person put it, "'fixing' the disaster that ensues." The end result, several people have said, is that Bernal telegraphs to the most powerful people in the White House that he is the only person really looking out for the Bidens.

In August 2021, a report on the news website *Politico* suggested that Bernal seemed to be operating outside of the boundaries of the Biden edict of treating people with respect and kindness.

"If you're ever working with me and I hear you treat another colleague with disrespect, talk down to someone, I promise I will fire you on the spot," Biden had said when he swore in a group of senior officials on Inauguration Day. "On the spot, no ifs, ands, or buts," he said. "Everybody, everybody is entitled to be treated with decency and dignity."

It was Reynoso who was called upon to defend Bernal publicly.

"Anthony's loyalty to our team and the First Family is unrivaled, and he holds himself, and all of us, to the highest standards," Reynoso told *Politico.* "There is no one at the White House with a bigger heart than Anthony, which is one of several reasons why so many in the First Lady's office have worked with him for years. He cares deeply about the personal and professional growth of his colleagues."

Bernal's defenders say that he is working on behalf of the First Lady, and that everything he does is to bolster her reputation.

"It is my job to make sure that we don't make mistakes wherever possible," Bernal said in an interview in the spring of 2023, after which East Wing officials pointed out that staff turnover remains low.

Defending against staff drama was not the kind of role Reynoso had much experience with. She had been hired to help Jill deliver on a modest list of policy goals. Jill wanted to help military families by continuing the Joining Forces initiative that she worked on during the Obama administration. She wanted to push for more cancer research, an interest that was close to her heart after she lost several friends to breast cancer, and especially after losing Beau. She wanted to work on making community college free for Americans who wanted to attend, which, given the Senate Democrats' interest in using budget reconciliation as a tactic to bypass procedural obstacles, seemed like it could be a distant possibility. But other than community college, Jill's portfolio contained few specifics or deliverables.

In the early weeks of the administration, Reynoso was poised to push the First Lady into further involvement with immigration reform, an all-but-intractable issue that had bedeviled four American presidents. East Wing officials had even discussed sending the First

Lady to the border to see conditions for herself, a plan that was soon nixed by the West Wing.

Then, in March 2021, it was reported that Jill would be officially involved with reuniting migrant children with their families. The East Wing balked at the news, and LaRosa tried to walk reporters back. The problem was that it had been true, at one point, that talks to reunite families had included the First Lady, but no one wanted to set her up to be the face of the administration's immigration policies. In the end, it was decided that Reynoso would be involved in the administration's work to reunite families and would brief the First Lady. At that point, a person familiar with Reynoso's reaction said, "She realized there would be no big policy directives" coming out of the East Wing.

"Her life's ambition was not to work for the First Lady," one of Jill's confidants said, citing Reynoso's interest in international issues. "I think it worked out okay, but I think from the beginning it was clear on both sides that this wasn't Julissa's whole ambition in life."

There were murmurs inside the White House that Reynoso was a mismatch for the office—if not the job, then the culture of Biden world. Her presence had given the East Wing gravitas, but it only went so far. The most valuable currency in the Bidens' world is a combination of loyalty and longevity. As the East Wing staff began to travel more frequently, it was Bernal, with his background in advance work and event planning, who emerged as a de facto leader. At visits to schools and vaccination clinics, Reynoso would often appear at a distance, arms crossed and wearing a backpack, while other aides fretted over lighting, or press access, or tried to game out what a journalist in the crowd might ask. On other trips, she didn't attend at all. Few were surprised in July 2021, six months into the Biden administration, when it was announced that Reynoso would be leaving the East Wing to serve as ambassador to Spain.

"This opportunity came about sooner than we both expected, and I will miss her," the First Lady said in a statement. The East Wing chief of staff role has been empty since.

While White House advisers saw few upsides to the First Lady getting involved in a contentious issue like immigration, it made sense for a longtime teacher to be the public face of the administration's efforts on all matters related to education.

Jill, who had participated in the interview process for Miguel Cardona, the education secretary, was also a member of the National Education Association. Her union background came into play nearly as soon as the Bidens moved into the White House: Her first official event as First Lady was a virtual teacher-appreciation event attended by influential teachers' union leaders. The appearance was an early signal to educators around the country that the Biden administration had a plan to safely reopen schools during a pandemic. Educators were divided over how best to reopen classrooms and when, but Jill was on the road within weeks, visiting schools around the country to push the administration's plans to distribute doses of coronavirus vaccines to teachers and to tout the benefits of in-person learning.

Jill was an asset on the campaign trail, where she could deftly weave her husband's story into his larger ambitions for the country. She was less successful in delivering on her early pledge to help make community college free for Americans.

In 2015, President Obama originally unveiled the ambitious plan to provide two years of higher education free for millions of students, and appointed Jill as an adviser. Obama White House officials did not say how it would be financed or whether such a plan had a shot at passing through a Republican-controlled Congress. The plan went nowhere.

Six years later, the Biden administration tried again, tucking a plan for free community college into a sprawling budgetary wish list— a behemoth, $6 trillion plan that would pump government funds into infrastructure projects and bolster the social safety net on a scale not seen since World War II. In April 2021, Joe delivered an address to a joint session of Congress in a socially distant chamber, touting two plans, both costing trillions. One, the American Jobs Plan, would bolster the nation's infrastructure projects, and the other, the American

Families Plan, would deliver tax cuts for families, establish paid leave, revamp a broken childcare system, and infuse colleges with cash.

And then the president told the public that his wife would be "deeply involved" with advancing the education component of the $1.8 trillion American Families Plan, which would increase the amount of grants awarded to low-income students, called Pell Grants, and provide two years of free community college, among other provisions.

"Jill was a community college professor who teaches today as First Lady," the president said. "She's long said—if I heard it once, I've heard it a thousand times: 'Joe, any country that out-educates us is going to outcompete us.' She'll be deeply involved in leading this effort. Thank you, Jill."

As a candidate, Joe pitched the idea of free community college as the key to rebuilding the middle class and restoring what he called the "backbone" of America. Within the broad scope of what Democrats wanted to accomplish, the estimated $88 billion price tag for free community college was relatively modest—smaller than the $449 billion proposed for an expanded child tax credit, or the $225 billion earmarked to support childcare costs.

Given the Democratic control of the House and a fifty-fifty Senate, the Biden White House was feeling bullish. But it would take a show of total unity from Senate Democrats to pass a plan that was, as one senior Biden administration official called it, "a laundry list of pent-up demands on social spending," not to mention a redefinition of the role of the federal government. In the absence of any Republican support, hopes hinged on two Senate holdouts: Senator Joe Manchin of West Virginia and Senator Kyrsten Sinema of Arizona. Both were intent on whittling down the cost of the plan.

There was little appetite for sending Jill up to Capitol Hill to push for the community college component or the particulars of the American Families Plan—it was too politically volatile. But the First Lady did personally appeal to Manchin. In an interview, Jill said the senator "told me the same old story"—that his own son had had to finance his own college education.

"I said, 'Joe, tough,'" as she recalled the discussion in an interview. "My students need free community college. They have no money. I mean, I have kids in my classroom who don't eat, who can't afford books. Just last week I gave somebody a grammar book. They can't afford their books.

"I just thought he couldn't see the bigger picture, and he was hurting so many college students," she continued. "And I wish he could've at least come to my classroom and see how hard they work—two and three jobs to be in their seat in my class."

None of that firsthand experience had swayed Manchin. Jill did not try to reach out to Sinema, the other holdout. What was the point? Neither had interest in the more expensive components of the plan, and there were no lawmakers on the Hill who were championing free community college. In the cacophony of priorities, community college was low on the list. The fact that it stuck around until the fall of 2021, one administration official, who worked directly with lawmakers on Capitol Hill said, was evidence of the First Lady's influence. No one wanted to tell Joe Biden that his wife's initiative was not viable.

Manchin and Sinema ended up doing the hard part and killed the initiative for them: Nine months into his presidency, Joe told the public at a CNN town hall that the plan for two years of free community college was on hold, largely because two Democratic senators would not support the initiative.

It was one of many initiatives to be traded away as the Biden White House tried to pass sweeping social spending and infrastructure legislation. The initial expansive social spending bill—part of the White House's sweeping Build Back Better effort—was rehashed, and key provisions, including universal pre-kindergarten, family and medical leave, and an expanded child tax credit, were whittled away.

Finally, in August 2022, Democrats passed what was viewed as the final version of the effort, called the Inflation Reduction Act, as costs for food and everyday needs like gasoline shot to record levels. The legislation poured billions into combatting global warming and expanding healthcare subsidies. But major parts of the original plan were eliminated, including the entire education agenda.

By the fall of 2022, there were no plans to try again to revive free two-year community college. Instead, there were other efforts in play, including the administration's plan to eliminate up to $20,000 in student debt for recipients of federal Pell Grants. The initiative was quickly bogged down with lawsuits. In the summer of 2023, Joe's plan to eliminate federal student loan debt for millions of Americans was struck down by a Supreme Court decision.

"You know, it's evolving," Jill said of plans to make college more affordable for Americans. "Let's say it's evolving."

SINCE THE CLINTON WHITE House tried and failed to entrust the First Lady with a major legislative initiative, First Ladies have carefully but effectively used their congressional relationships to accomplish broad policy goals. In 2002, Laura Bush testified on Capitol Hill, discussing the importance of early childhood education and traveling the country to encourage support for her husband's No Child Left Behind initiative. Michelle Obama's efforts to promote better childhood nutrition led to the bipartisan passage of the Healthy, Hunger-Free Kids Act, a 2010 law that funded free lunch programs and allowed the government to make changes to school lunches. Melania Trump, ever the outlier, was a rare sight on Capitol Hill outside of State of the Union events, and her husband did not discuss her antibullying initiative during those speeches.

Though she has told visitors to the White House that she is interested in starting a women's discussion group on Capitol Hill, Jill has been less engaged than several of her predecessors on legislative efforts. Before becoming First Lady, she had never been a Washington insider. But even if she had been, she believed that the version of Congress she had first encountered—the one that her husband still believed could show itself if he just tried hard enough to engage—was long gone.

She was no policy wonk, she wasn't an operator, and she had no interest in the intricacies of politics. ("Talk to her about delegates and her eyes glaze over," said one of her friends.) She was also jaded from years of watching politics grow tribal.

But she did know how to campaign, and she had Bernal, who, after decades in scheduling and advance, was the most talented event producer in the administration. They directed their efforts to the road.

BY THE END OF Jill's first winter in the White House, fears about the pandemic had relegated most aides to working from home, and extensive travel for the president was still out of the question. But Jill, who had enjoyed travel during her eight years as Second Lady, was anxious to leave the White House. As the public vaccination campaign continued and Democrats passed a $1.9 trillion stimulus package, the Biden East Wing began planning more travel and more events.

One early trip that I took in March 2021 with the East Wing set the tone for dozens Jill has taken since. Jill traveled to the California home district of Kevin McCarthy, then Republican House minority leader, to speak to farm workers at the Forty Acres, the headquarters of the United Farm Workers labor union, a movement led by the activist Cesar Chavez. His granddaughter Julie Chavez Rodriguez was the director of the White House Office of Intergovernmental Affairs before she left to manage Joe's reelection campaign in the spring of 2023.

On the flight to Bakersfield, Jill pored over briefing books and made last-minute edits to a speech she was planning to deliver. The speech was meant to reach people gathered at the Forty Acres to win support for a bill that could establish a path to citizenship for farm workers, many of whom are undocumented. As she read it over in her cabin, she kept tripping over one phrase—"Sí, se puede"—but her advisers urged her to keep the Spanish phrase in her remarks.

When she reached the site where Chavez had launched a hunger strike to advocate for better working conditions, she introduced herself the way she unfailingly did with people she didn't know: "Hi, I'm Jill Biden"—as if everyone within a hundred-mile radius hadn't heard one way or another that she would be in town.

The advance staff had traveled ahead of her with a roll of pink duct tape. On each trip she took in the early days, whether it was to a school or the dusty, gravelly parking lot at the Forty Acres, neon X's laid out a path in front of her so she would know where to stand and pose. During the Bakersfield event, which was essentially held in an open field, her Secret Service detail paced the perimeter trying to create a secure space. ("My boss is pissed," one young agent remarked as we surveyed the open field; it was not a preferred event scenario for the Secret Service.)

For as long as Jill has been in the spotlight, she worked hard to project a polished, gaffe-free image to the public. She seldom made a mistake. But when it was time to deliver a closing line to the farm workers, she held out her arms, raised her hands, and bungled the phrase: "Sí, se pawd-wey," she said, garbling the last word.

As she closed the folder that held her speech, the First Lady's shoulders sagged almost imperceptibly. She had said the phrase correctly two previous times when practicing. But it was the third, bungled message that conservative websites immediately pounced on. Since the Biden White House is deeply attuned to media coverage and pays close attention to whatever the First Lady and her aides say and do in public, there was some concern that West Wing aides would be noting her slip back in Washington. Several East Wing aides privately say the bungled phrase was an example of Anthony Bernal's instincts failing him; he was the one who had pushed for her to speak in Spanish. The First Lady has started taking Spanish lessons.

Back at the hotel, the First Lady and her aides reviewed the online coverage of the trip, as they often did, with glasses of wine in hand. The day was rehashed and the mistakes labored over before a group of her aides departed for an impromptu cocktail gathering on the sidewalk outside. The next morning, Jill met Bernal for breakfast, where the two of them pored over local newspapers before Jill returned to her suite to teach her NOVA class remotely. Her speech flap was no more than a blip, but it weighed on Jill, who can be hard on herself and takes a perfectionist's approach to most areas of her life.

"She doesn't like to make a mistake," Cathy Russell said. "She's careful; she doesn't want to do anything harmful. She's always trying to do her best."

There is one part of the process Jill has mastered: the sort of low-stakes media appearance that can win her a slate of flattering news coverage.

On the flight home from Bakersfield—April Fools' Day— members of the unsuspecting press pool traveling with her were treated to Dove ice cream bars by a raven-haired flight attendant. We were all wearing masks, but I remember glancing at the woman— whose striking blue eyes looked vaguely familiar and whose name tag read JASMINE—and accepting an ice cream bar before I turned back to my Kindle. By the time I looked up again, "Jasmine" had taken her wig off to reveal her loose blond curls.

"April Fools!" the First Lady said with a laugh. Even some members of her staff were confused and surprised—she'd kept the practical joke a secret. I had heard she was a prankster who, as Second Lady, once stuffed herself in an overhead bin to surprise her staff. And the morning after Mike Pence, the former vice president, had a fly land on his head during a televised debate with Kamala Harris in October 2020, Jill had climbed into her motorcade with a rubber insect affixed to her head.

When I realized Jasmine's true identity, an absurd question popped into my head: "Does this mean you travel with a wig?" I blurted out, but she was already well on her way back to the front of the plane. I never did get an answer, but one former staffer acknowledged that the First Lady, in general, seems to have access to several wigs. Of course, the wig prank made the rounds on Twitter and the news coverage of her trip.

She often does well in off-the-cuff interactions. In May 2021, when the Centers for Disease Control began a brief period of advising Americans to dispense with mask-wearing during what looked like a reassuring lull in coronavirus cases, she was the first high-ranking Biden administration official to publicly appear without a mask, disembarking bare-faced alongside Manchin in his home state of West Virginia and proclaiming, "We feel naked!" to a group of junior military officers and reporters who had gathered, along with the actress Jennifer Garner, to greet her.

Her decision to de-mask that day was not exactly impromptu: East Wing aides made calls to officials back in Washington to make sure she would not break protocol if she removed her mask. Only hours earlier, the president's advisers had been so strict about the practice of mask-wearing that they had policed private meetings, and the president only appeared without a mask in front of family members and his closest aides.

The first year of the administration was full of similar events held in service of the administration's wider priorities. Jill's was a dizzying schedule, and one that she had little intention of slowing down. The East Wing was sensitive to criticism that her work did not reflect a centralized policy effort, and aides once requested that a reporter on the East Wing beat remove the word "scattershot" from a news article detailing the First Lady's agenda.

AS JILL'S CLASSES WRAPPED up final exams that spring, she was about to embark on the most major test of Bernal's event-producing skills to date. Roughly two months into the Russian invasion of Ukraine, the East Wing put formal plans in place to send Jill to Eastern Europe.

Working with the State Department and national security officials, the East Wing policy and communications staffs floated a few options, including a trip with stops in Romania and Slovakia. As plans for the trip to Eastern Europe came into focus, Jill agreed to let her staff knit together plans, which eventually were centered around a Mother's Day theme. She would travel to Romania and Slovakia, two so-called frontline countries that were accepting the bulk of Ukrainian refugees. LaRosa told reporters that Jill's daughter, Ashley, had agreed to come along for the trip.

Ashley, who lived in Philadelphia but often stayed at the White House, had largely been living out of public view since her father took office, and especially since a right-wing organization published the contents of a diary she had kept while recovering from addiction. The Justice Department was investigating how her private journal came to be published, and the First Daughter was looking for a way to re-establish her public profile and regain control of her own story. It could also be a much-needed bonding trip for mother and daughter, who have butted heads in the past. (The mother-daughter tension between them, Jill has said, is one reason she is such an avid runner. In 1998, she ran a marathon.)

The East Wing reached out to the State Department and the National Security Council to get their approval for the trip. Clearance would also need to come from the president, who did not like his wife to be gone for more than a couple of nights at a time. (As president and First Lady, they read their briefing books and clips seated near each other in the living room of the White House residence most nights.) In the summer of 2021, Jill had nixed a planned trip to Africa, partly because Joe did not feel the trip was safe. In 2022, a second trip to the continent was pulled down, in part because Joe thought she was doing too much international travel ahead of the midterm elections. She finally ended up traveling there in February 2023.

Ahead of the Eastern Europe trip, Jill told her husband that this was something that she needed to do. And besides, she would only be gone for four nights. Though she travels often, senior aides do not look forward to the days when she is out of town, because it means they get more demands from a noticeably more demanding president. It was the same way on the 2020 campaign; Joe's mood would instantly improve at the end of a long day when he saw his wife walk into the room, particularly in the dim stretches when people were all but counting him out of the race.

On the evening of the departure, one crucial piece of the East Wing's plans was already starting to unravel: As White House officials and journalists traveling in the First Lady's motorcade sat in the driveway outside of the Executive Residence shortly before 10 P.M., the word came down from the White House that Ashley had been exposed to someone who had tested positive for the coronavirus. Her physician was recommending that she stay back out of an abundance of caution. (Two weeks later, Ashley Biden would test positive for the coronavirus and miss another international trip with her mother, this time to Central America. She eventually took a trip to France with her mother in summer 2023.) On that night, the motorcade departed and the First Lady took an overnight flight to Romania. The motorcade included a press van occupied by me, Kate Bennett of CNN, Mike Memoli of NBC News, and Tyler Pager of *The Washington Post*.

At the Mihail Kogalniceanu Air Base in Romania, Jill served a meal and delivered five gallons of ketchup for soldiers and military personnel who were on base without their preferred condiment. Almost no one who was with her in Romania knew that a high-stakes plan was about to unfold. Bernal—who approaches every event or trip as if it is "a movie," he has told people—wanted the First Lady to go farther than just Romania and Slovakia.

About ten days before the First Lady arrived in Romania, advance teams from the White House arrived in the country and in Slovakia, where she would travel onward after spending a day in Bucharest. Once those teams began reaching out to regional officials and disaster assistance teams in the area to notify them of the First Lady's coming visit, the White House received word from a third country: Ukraine. Ukrainian officials got in touch asking if it would be possible to arrange a meeting between Jill and Olena Zelenska, the wife of the Ukrainian president Volodymyr Zelenskyy. They suggested a meeting in Ukraine.

East Wing officials were intrigued by the suggestion. Joe had been to Eastern Europe since the start of the war, but neither he nor Kamala Harris had passed into Ukraine. The president had toured the

Polish border with Ukraine during his trip there a month and a half earlier. (In a sign of his influence in both the East and West Wings, Bernal was brought in to help plan the presidential trip.)

"Part of my disappointment is that I can't see it firsthand," Joe said during a stop in Rzeszów, Poland. "They will not let me." He later traveled secretly to Ukraine, in February 2023.

It is somewhat of a rite of passage for a First Lady to visit a war zone, which is defined as a hostile area where the U.S. military might serve. Melania Trump visited Iraq with her husband in 2018. Michelle Obama visited al-Udeid Air Base in Qatar in 2015 with the late-night host Conan O'Brien. Laura Bush traveled solo to Bagram Air Base in Afghanistan twice as First Lady, and made the support of Afghan women and girls a cornerstone of her messaging work.

Jill's trip to Ukraine would be more complicated than visiting an air base. Olena Zelenska had not been seen in public since February 24, the day Russian forces began invading Ukraine. Zelenskyy had publicly stated that his wife and children were assassination targets for the Russian military. Bringing an American First Lady so close to a target was a national security and diplomatic risk.

In Slovakia, the second leg of the trip, Jill traveled to the city of Košice, where she met with refugees at a bus station that had been converted to assist new arrivals to the country. There, a woman named Viktozie Kutocha clutched her daughter, Yulie, and told the First Lady that she struggled to explain to her child what had happened to their lives.

"How I can explain this to child? It's impossible," she said. "I try to keep them safe. It's my mission."

"It's senseless," the First Lady replied. She wrapped the woman and her child in a hug and lingered there with them.

From there, Jill's motorcade traveled for ninety minutes to a checkpoint village on the border of Slovakia and Ukraine where volunteers assisted fleeing Ukrainians. As she toured tents where refugees could receive medical help and food, the First Lady's staff quietly herded a group of us journalists toward a motorcade that had been reassembled on the other side of the village. We had suspected she might make the trip into Ukraine, but it was not confirmed until we saw those vehicles.

Some journalists who had traveled from Washington with the First Lady were not going to be able to cross over into Ukraine—at the last minute, the State Department had slashed the manifest of people who would be allowed in her convoy. Susan Walsh, an Associated Press photographer who was not on the approved list, dove into a vehicle full of Secret Service agents as the motorcade started rolling. The agents were not happy that a journalist was in their midst, and it was a silent car ride, but without her, there would have been few images of the newsy trip.

We did not know that Bernal had argued with the State Department to bring a full contingent of reporters into the country and had personally assured the director of the Secret Service that news of the trip would not leak before the First Lady had approached the Slovakian border on her return.

Jill was struck by her first glimpse of war-torn Ukraine. From the safety of her armored SUV, the world outside looked so normal. The sky that day was gray-blue, and the drive took her past citron-yellow canola crops toward the town of Uzhhorod. People were eating outside in cafés and standing on street corners chatting with one another. The traffic circles the motorcade zipped through were full of red tulips and dotted with blue-and-yellow Ukrainian flags. It seemed that life was continuing in this leafy European town, even as its people were living in the grip of terror.

The motorcade trundled up a narrow, tree-lined drive to the parking lot of a brick building before pulling to a stop. It was there that Zelenska quietly slipped out of a vehicle to greet her American counterpart. She was flanked by bodyguards, and her blond hair hung in a curtain, obscuring half of her heart-shaped face.

The two First Ladies embraced and then entered a school converted to assist refugees who had come from other parts of the country to Uzhhorod, a town of one hundred thousand people whose population had swollen to double its size since the beginning of the invasion. Jill had come from Slovakia, and Zelenska had traveled by armored train. The pair sat together in a nondescript conference room, bare except for a few bottled waters and a floral arrangement of peonies and roses. Jill clasped her hands at the wrists, one of which was adorned with a sock-hop-sized corsage her husband had given her for Mother's Day. (The president, who always stays updated on her movements and was monitoring cable news coverage of her visit from Washington, noted approvingly to aides that she had worn the flower.)

"I thought it was important to show the Ukrainian people that this war has to stop, and this war has been brutal," she told reporters as she sat at a table opposite Zelenska, "and that the people of the United States stand with the people of Ukraine."

Zelenska thanked Jill for making the visit.

"We understand what it takes for the U.S. First Lady to come here during a war, where the military actions are taking place every day, where the air sirens are happening every day, even today," she said. During a private meeting, the pair discussed their concerns over the war and their personal lives. At one point, Zelenska asked the First Lady how she was able to travel if she worked full-time as a teacher. Jill told her that she had just finished grading final exams and that the semester was over.

Their visit to the school was meant to be focused on children and the humanitarian work that went into housing some 160 refugees, 47 of them children, in the building, but even the most innocent interactions betrayed the strain of war: A security agent passed a handheld metal detector over a child who had entered a classroom just before the two women entered. Zelenska's main bodyguard, a hulking man with a buzz cut and a pink slash of a scar on his neck, seemed about twice the size of Jill's primary Secret Service agent.

The pair spent two hours together before departing, Jill in a motorcade and Zelenska into the security of her own armored detail. Once we were within safe distance of the border, the East Wing told us that we could notify our editors back home that Jill had made the trip. The news alerts that flashed around the world felt like a coup for the East Wing. Jill had only been in the country for two hours—less than the six hours spent on Laura Bush's first trip to Afghanistan—

but the high-stakes photo op had been flawless, thanks largely to Bernal's planning. He had pulled off the movie.

It was a digital-first installment of a textbook tactic for deploying a First Lady abroad: Not only could Jill make headlines that were in line with the administration's stance toward Ukraine at such a tense moment, but she received reams of positive news coverage and commentary for her willingness to go where her husband hadn't (yet) been able to travel.

JILL HAD ONLY BEEN back from Eastern Europe for a week when a man entered a supermarket in Buffalo and killed thirteen people in a racist attack. Then, a week after Jill returned from Latin America, an eighteen-year-old walked into Robb Elementary School in Uvalde, Texas, where he shot nineteen children and two teachers.

In Uvalde, Jill wore sunglasses and toured a makeshift memorial of flowers alongside her husband. "Do something!" a crowd screamed at the Bidens. "We will," the president said. The next month, Congress passed a bipartisan gun bill that imposed new restrictions on prospective gun buyers and poured funds into mental-health resources.

The gun bill was one of several bipartisan pieces of legislation that the Biden administration said was proof that the president's staid and steady approach to lawmaking was working. But by the summer of 2022, Joe, who had started his presidency with an approval rating above 50 percent—largely due to the passage of a coronavirus relief bill and the implementation of vaccines—was watching his popularity decline.

A botched pullout from Afghanistan had been one of the most politically damaging events of his presidency. Now American wallets were being squeezed by rising gas prices, spiked by the Russian invasion of Ukraine—a war that at first captivated attention but had turned into an ongoing and expensive slog with no end in sight. Inflation rates, the highest in decades, had taken hold, hitting household budgets in every category, from food to laundry detergent. Republicans in several state races were leading in the polls, promising to surf a "red wave" in the midterm elections, bolstered by culture-war battles. Democrats stood to lose control of both chambers of Congress, which would effectively mean the end of a productive Biden presidency.

With Joe unpopular in purple and red states, White House officials and Democratic campaigns turned to Jill, who knew the campaign trail cold. Beyond that, she took a traditional instinct of First Spouses—a tendency to be fiercely protective of her husband, his legacy, and their family—and combined it with her understanding of the media landscape to try to deliver on his goals.

After *Roe v. Wade* was overturned during the summer of 2022, the decision left open questions about whether a Supreme Court dominated by conservative justices would seek to further roll back reproductive freedoms. Democrats sensed that moderate voters would be angry enough at the fall of *Roe* to make abortion their central reason to head to the polls.

So Jill began telling a story that only a close observer would recognize as new. At a fundraiser in California that fall, Jill shared that she had helped a friend recover from an abortion in the late 1960s, years before *Roe v. Wade*. Her friend, whom she did not name, told her that she had undergone a psychological evaluation to be declared mentally unfit for parenting before a doctor agreed to administer the abortion.

"I went to see her in the hospital and then cried the whole drive home," said Jill, who was seventeen at the time. "When she was discharged from the hospital, she couldn't go back to her house, so I gathered my courage and asked my mom, 'Can she come stay with us?'"

Jill said that her mother, who died in 2008, allowed her friend to visit and that the three had kept it a secret.

After almost fifty years in politics, the Biden family has chosen several personal stories to reshare and repackage to different audiences as needed, and so, much of their private struggles has been braided into their public lives. But the abortion story was new, pulled from a private reservoir because of political necessity. In her memoir,

Jill had only made a passing mention that her mother had known when "one of the girls at school got pregnant," without adding the role she and her mother played in helping her friend recover.

As a Catholic, Joe Biden had long struggled with his public stance on supporting abortion, but in this case, Jill knew she had the freedom to share a story that was designed to make the argument that the Republican approach to curbing abortions was too extreme.

"I had to give a little bit," she said in an interview, reflecting on the political strategy behind her decision. "I mean, it was a conscious decision to tell that story—to say, 'Look, we've got to get out there and we've got to win.'"

It was a sophisticated blend of the political and the personal—driven by a desire to win—that has come to define the Biden East Wing.

Jill's presence on the trail is not just a morale boost for Democrats in close races: She is a fundraising draw who appeals to grassroots supporters, and people are more likely to donate if she asks, according to a spokeswoman who works for the Democratic National Committee. Her events, emails, text messages, and mailings have drawn millions of dollars for Democrats. In one appearance for Stacey Abrams, who was running for governor of Georgia, Jill told her audience that she knew they had already donated, but "I'm asking you to dig a little deeper." (Each had already paid at least $1,000 to attend the event.) The whole appearance took about twenty minutes, and then she was on the road to the next event, slipping out through a kitchen door with a coterie of aides.

Not every candidate Jill campaigned for in the midterms won their races. Abrams lost, and so did Val Demings, a House member who was running to replace Senator Marco Rubio of Florida. Charlie Crist, who clenched hands with Jill at city hall in Orlando, failed to unseat Ron DeSantis, the popular Republican governor of Florida and future Republican presidential candidate. But in the summer of 2023, as Jill's East Wing prepared to help Joe Biden run for the presidency for the fourth and final time, prominent Democrats still believed that she would be the president's most effective surrogate on the campaign trail as concerns swirled about his age and his ability to carry out a second term.

Celinda Lake, the veteran Democratic pollster, said that Jill is a valuable campaigner because she has the sort of public image that is rare in American politics: She's not divisive.

"She's a quiet asset in the sense that she doesn't dominate the scene, but people really like her approachability and the fact that she's continuing to teach," Lake said. "People just really think of her as in touch and relatable. In the rarefied world of top leadership and politics, that's a rare image to have."

CHAPTER TEN

"I REMEMBER EVERY SLIGHT"

SOME PEOPLE, LIKE THE BIDENS, ARE CHALLENGING TO write about because they have been in the public eye for so long that the truth of them becomes inextricably fused with assorted bits of lore. Spending time with Doug Emhoff is interesting because he still sees political life with fresh eyes.

Doug is the fifty-eight-year-old husband of Kamala Harris, the vice president. He is called the Second Gentleman, which is apparently the catchiest title anyone could come up with for the first man to hold the role of Second Spouse. In the administration's early days, he was still in such disbelief that this was his life that he would film the president's Marine One landings on the South Lawn from a balcony in the Eisenhower Executive Office Building and send the videos to his parents.

He is Brooklyn born and California bred, affable with an easy smile. It is not a stretch to picture him as a corporate entertainment attorney in his former life: He was a partner at a large law firm, DLA Piper, until he announced that he would leave before the Biden inauguration, seeking to avoid any conflict-of-interest concerns. Like many high-powered women before him, he has struggled at times with pausing his job—which paid him upward of $1.2 million a year when he walked away from it—to help Kamala, whom he married in 2014, further her political career. "I miss it every day," he tells people who ask him about giving up his legal career for life in Washington. He has since signed up to teach law at Georgetown.

"It's human," he said during an interview held in his office in July 2022. "It's a big change in our lives. It's a big change in my life."

He has been frank about how much he misses his old job—and how good he was at it—but he insists any mixed emotions he feels have given way to supporting the vice president and trying to lean into his role as best he can. He does this while simultaneously being careful to publicly acknowledge that generations of women, including Jill Biden, served in the role before he took over.

On his first official outing, he visited a farm in Washington, D.C., that serves food to a majority-Black community and is committed to delivering resources to food-insecure families. "Part of what I want to do in this role is figure out how I can help," he said that day.

Later in the year, he accompanied his wife to Paris, a visit that was meant to shore up relations with Emmanuel Macron, the French president, after a diplomatic spat over a scuttled nuclear submarine deal. The couple also used their time in France to show a more personal side of the vice president by stopping at a research lab where her mother had worked. In another stop, at E.Dehillerin, an iconic cooking store, he and the vice president engaged in a back-and-forth with reporters over his kitchen prowess, teasing out the idea that his wife is an avid cook.

"He's an apprentice," Kamala said, laughing.

"She taught me during COVID," he interjected, "out of necessity after almost burning down our apartment. Then I got a little bit better."

He is proud to be her cheerleader, helpmate, and supporter, but he is also particularly proud of the things he has been trusted to do on his own, including leading a group of administration officials on an overseas trip to the Philippines in June 2022 to attend the inauguration of Ferdinand Romualdez Marcos, Jr. A month earlier, he'd led a delegation to South Korea for the inauguration of the country's new president, Yoon Suk-yeol. He received an enthusiastic welcome as he tucked into double portions of kimbap and toured the Gwangjang Market with a celebrity chef.

"He seems like the kind of person who would go to a high-end restaurant but it was nice to see him at the market," Cha Hong-gyu, a seventy-year-old Seoulite who watched the Second Gentleman from afar, told a local paper. "I saw the good side of America in him."

In an interview with one of the country's largest newspapers, *JoongAng Ilbo*, he was asked to share his thoughts on gender equality—a loaded question in South Korea, where women are underrepresented in politics and higher education. The liberal administration of Yoon's predecessor, President Moon Jae-in, instituted gender quotas to increase the number of women in government roles and pledged to increase the number of female professors to 25 percent, up from 16 percent, by 2030. Yoon, by contrast, disparaged feminists during his campaign and claimed that men were being discriminated against. Calling gender inequality "a thing of the past," Yoon has also promised to abolish the government's gender ministry, which focuses, in part, on combating human trafficking and domestic violence.

The Second Gentleman, no stranger to questions around the issue of gender equality, used the opportunity to highlight how the gender dynamics in his own relationship were worthy not only of respect but of emulation.

"Lifting women up so that they can carry out important roles is a very manly thing," he told the *JoongAng Ilbo*. "It's also good for economic growth, to lift women up so that they can do their jobs. That is not taking away opportunities from men, but men and women growing. I also want to say that Vice President Harris lifts me up and helps me with my duties. We help each other."

In an administration where so much energy is focused on issues that feel intractable, he is the rare principal who has the freedom to look like he might be enjoying his (comparatively) low-stakes role. It is a joke among some White House reporters that he is the only man having fun in Washington.

That doesn't make him a goof or a jester, but it's hard to imagine

anyone else in the administration getting their hands dirty in a community garden in Washington, as he did in March 2022. He picked
around a garden bed until he successfully uprooted some kale, then
smiled as he looked back into the sea of waiting press cameras: "We
did it, Joe!" he said to the journalists with an impish grin, clutching a
tiny green leaf in his hand. It was a play on the infamous video of his
wife saying the same thing when Joe called to tell her the news that
they'd won the 2020 election. He tested positive for the coronavirus a
few hours later. Since he was the first member of the first or second
families to publicly report a case of the virus, the episode led to fresh
questions about White House virus-testing protocols.

Still, Doug persists, refashioning a role that only women have held
to make it his own. His office in the Eisenhower Executive Office
Building was repainted a deep shade of blue. The room is dotted with
family photos, fat-leafed plants, and a television. A wooden plaque
etched with his title—SECOND GENTLEMAN—hangs on a wall, lest
anyone forget what he is doing here.

He is part of a growing class of political spouses who have broken
barriers surrounding gender, race, and sexual orientation in politics.
Chasten Buttigieg, who is married to Pete Buttigieg, the first openly
gay confirmed cabinet secretary, is a newcomer who has invited the
Second Gentleman on walks and coffee dates. Dan Mulhern, who is
married to Jennifer Granholm, Mr. Biden's secretary of energy, who
was the first woman to be elected governor of Michigan, is another
club member.

"Men are doing what women have always done, just as women are
doing what men have always done," Mulhern said. "We're just doing
it with male egos."

In the Second Gentleman's attractive suite of offices, he has hung
photos that illustrate his journey. At the center of it, of course, is his
wife.

Kamala Harris is only the third female vice-presidential nominee
in American history, behind Geraldine Ferraro and Sarah Palin, and
only the first to make it to the White House. She is the daughter of
Shyamala Gopalan, an Indian biomedical scientist, and Donald J.

Harris, a Jamaican economist. Both immigrants, they met and fell in love while studying at the University of California at Berkeley. When they met in the 1960s, Berkeley was a hotbed of civil rights protests and marches. After their parents divorced, Kamala and her sister, Maya, were primarily raised by their mother, who taught them to prize their biracial background and honor their relationships. Accepting the nomination for the vice presidency at the Democratic National Convention in August 2020, Kamala said:

> She raised us to be proud, strong Black women and she raised us to know and be proud of our Indian heritage. She taught us to put family first—the family you're born into and the family you choose. Family is my husband, Doug, who I met on a blind date set up by my best friend.

In one of the large photos hanging in his office suite, the vice president appears to look over her husband's shoulder as he teaches a virtual class at Georgetown Law. According to their website, he leads a Wednesday-morning class called Entertainment Disputes during the fall semester and one called Introduction to Alternative Dispute Resolution in the spring.

The photograph feels like a modern, Zoom-era rendering of a Norman Rockwell painting. Instead of a man looking approvingly over a woman's shoulder, happily surveying the day's domestic work, the photo hanging in the Second Gentleman's office shows a mixed-race, female vice president smiling down at her supportive spouse, who is from another race and another faith. (Doug is Jewish, while Kamala grew up attending services at a Hindu temple and a Baptist church.)

In another photo, he shares a beer with Jill at a baseball game in Houston. The two bonded on the campaign trail when he traveled with her for a couple of weeks—the Biden campaign's version of job shadowing. He was impressed with her ability to speak and move around the stage simultaneously. He spent that time trying to study her. She spent that time trying to think of the best advice to give him, which ended up being a frank acknowledgment that there wasn't a rule book for him.

"All of the circumstances in which we took office in January of 2021 were so unique to this administration," he said—a reference to the coronavirus pandemic, but also the political violence of January 6. "So, when you add that up, all she could say is 'I honestly can't really give you any advice, other than what I've already seen of you, which is, you're best when you're yourself. Be confident, be fearless, and most of all, support your wife. That's the job.'"

Obviously and deservedly, much more attention is paid to how his wife, the first woman and person of color to hold the vice presidency, is navigating the ever-complicated dynamics that come with her role. Kamala, a former prosecutor and attorney general of California, has struggled to retain staff and has been frustrated by the items in her portfolio. She asked to take the lead on voting rights but was less enthused about taking on other issues she saw as no-wins, including examining the root causes of migration to the United States and greeting shipments of baby formula during a national shortage. (Jill ended up initially picking up the slack on the baby formula assignment.) Doug, in true political-spouse form, has groused about her portfolio to confidants.

Doug says he was always willing to sacrifice his job once the possibility of his wife becoming Joe Biden's running mate started to look more like a reality. But the pair had lengthy discussions about how their married life would change. He was startled when he saw an organizational chart that showed his name and title underneath the vice president's. On the chart, his responsibilities included the supervision of a coterie of aides and the oversight of the vice-presidential residence. He marveled that he had been assigned to a bubble on the chart that said "Family." His wife had always been the gatherer of family, the planner of dinners, and the keeper of appointments. Now a government chart suggested she offload those matters to her spouse.

"The vice president and I had a lot of conversations about how we were going to, you know, maintain a normal marriage in this milieu of me stepping away from my partnership with the firm and being there to really openly and publicly support her as her husband," he said, referring to his wife by her title.

Some of those discussions were uncomfortable for him. It helped that he and Kamala were—and continue to be—busy.

"We really didn't have almost any time to think about any of these issues personally, because we had so much to do," he said. "I was with some of my friends last night, and they said, 'How are you feeling? How's it going?' And I don't have time to think about that stuff."

He is more focused on making sure the vice president is successful. During spates of unflattering news coverage, Kamala's aides would try to keep the worst clippings out of her daily briefing materials. Inevitably, one of those aides said, Doug would flag his wife and her staff and produce the offending news clipping. He might not have as much experience in this world as other political spouses, but the instinct to screen for the worst material about his partner and run it up the food chain is another classic of the political-spouse genre—especially in the time of Google alerts. Melania Trump closely watched coverage of her family and was vigilant about searching for the Trump name on Google and Twitter. But the tradition predates the internet: Louisa Adams, the British-born First Lady who spent much of her time ensconced in the White House, was well known for scouring newspaper clippings and reporting the coverage back to her husband. There is no such thing as a political spouse who is deeply uninterested in how their family is written about or discussed in the news media. Doug is no exception.

The Second Spouse is the vice president's loyal protector, and, after spending years observing Jill, he has learned from one of the fiercest.

ON JANUARY 19, 2022, the day before President Biden's first anniversary in office, dozens of masked reporters filed into the East Room and crammed into seats under the cut-glass chandeliers. They had gathered to participate in what had become one of the rarest rituals of the Biden presidency: a news conference.

It had been nearly a year since the president had taken solo questions from reporters in such an event at the White House, and reporters had been clamoring for months for the opportunity to press him on matters ranging from the Biden administration's handling of the ongoing coronavirus pandemic to the increasingly likely possibility that Vladimir Putin of Russia might invade Ukraine.

The president's aides had prepared him for the better part of a week, briefing him on a wide range of issues that might come up in a news conference packed with journalists. They could prepare the president for questions on Russia, on the economy, and on Build Back Better. They could send the president out with sharpened blades against Republicans, who had been opposed to the administration's ambitious plans for social spending and just about everything else suggested by Biden.

"What are Republicans for?" he asked at one point, answering a reporter's question about his stalled political agenda with a question of his own. "What are they for? Name me one thing that they are for."

What Biden's aides could not do was protect the president from himself. He is a famously long-winded politician who will continue talking until he is physically directed away. (I was on Air Force One during the only off-the-record session he has ever conducted with a group of reporters aboard the aircraft, on a flight from Seattle to Washington, D.C., and the discussion, which went longer than thirty minutes, only ended because the plane hit severe turbulence.) Critics who attribute his long-windedness to his advancing age seem to be willfully ignorant of the nearly fifty years of interviews, stump speeches, and news conferences that provide evidence to the contrary. Joe Biden has always been a talker, and as stringently press-avoidant as the apparatus around him is, he does not shy away from journalists when he is facing questioning. In these moments, he risks being backed into a corner, and that is when he tends to make mistakes.

That afternoon was no different. Biden delivered a two-hour news conference, a defiant performance in which he defended his administration's choices on handling everything from the coronavirus pandemic to voting-rights issues. He made several factual errors, including when he exaggerated the number of Americans receiving vaccinations each week (he overshot the figure by at least a million); oversold a bipartisan infrastructure bill's ability to remove the country's lead pipes; and claimed that child poverty had continued to decline, even though the child tax credit negotiated in the American Rescue Plan had expired a month earlier. Content to go down the line of waiting journalists, Biden continued taking questions, calling on reporter after reporter. Eventually, a dark-haired man stepped forward and took the microphone.

"Thank you very much for this honor," James Rosen, a reporter with the conservative website Newsmax, said. "I'd like to—I'd like to raise a delicate subject but with utmost respect for your life accomplishments and the high office you hold: A poll released, this morning, by Politico/Morning Consult found 49 percent of registered voters disagreeing with the statement 'Joe Biden is mentally fit.'"

Rosen, a former Fox News reporter, has circulated baseless theories about election fraud in the 2020 election. That day, he was there to circulate in a nationally televised news conference another favorite theory of the far right: that the president was not in control of his mental faculties. "Why do you suppose such large segments of the American electorate have come to harbor such profound concerns about your cognitive fitness?"

It was the kind of question that was kryptonite to the people closest to the president, and the Biden team decided long ago that the best way to deal with questions like those were to avoid situations where the president may encounter them. When he finally did confront such a question, Biden's instinct was to shrug it off.

"I have no idea," Biden replied to Rosen. Perhaps now more determined than ever to continue, Biden went on to take several more questions before pulling up his sleeve and looking at his watch. It was nearly 6 P.M.

"With all due respect, I'm going to see you next conference, okay?"

Biden said, before grabbing his briefing book and walking toward the Executive Residence.

He was trailed by a small group that included Ron Klain, Joe's first chief of staff; Kate Bedingfield, his communications director; and Jen Psaki, Joe's first White House press secretary. The trio were some of the most trusted aides in the Biden White House, but all for different reasons.

Of all the president's aides, Klain was the best at keeping the meander-prone Biden on track. Bedingfield was known among the president's aides—and among the Washington press corps—as one of the most ferociously protective Biden faithfuls in a West Wing packed with them. Psaki was different.

A former State Department spokeswoman and White House communications director under President Barack Obama, Psaki was affable and battle-trained and had an easy command of the many issues pelting the White House daily. She had not hitched her career to the Bidens, coming on during the presidential transition rather than during the fledgling days of the campaign, and she was clear-eyed about the president. This made her a valuable rarity in the upper ranks. Jill had been present when Joe was interviewing Psaki for the job, which was a clear signal to Psaki that the White House press secretary would be representing both Bidens.

After the news conference, that group gathered with Joe in the Treaty Room, the president's study in the Executive Residence. Months earlier, the Treaty Room had been the backdrop for the president's announcement that the United States would be pulling out of Afghanistan. It is one of the most somber rooms in the White House, a place where powerful men have stewed under the glow of lamplight.

As dinnertime approached, the group discussed the president's decision to bring up Republicans. Suddenly, they saw another person in the doorway: Jill. She had watched the news conference, and the look on her face told everyone in the room—from the president on down—that they had some explaining to do.

"Why didn't anyone stop that?" she demanded.

Everyone stayed silent, looking at one another, and then at her, and back to one another. That included the most powerful man in the world. Her husband essentially played along, not offering an answer, even though aides had slipped him a card suggesting he end the press conference.

"Where were you guys?" she asked the group again. "Where was the person who was going to end the press conference?"

This dressing-down, delivered to some of the most senior members of the Biden administration after the marathon presidential news conference, illustrated the degree to which she is her husband's fiercest protector.

Jill often stays out of the fray of day-to-day operations in the West Wing, but watching her husband embark on a rambling, two-hour news conference without guardrails was not the sort of thing that a political spouse with her experience was going to abide. The Biden operation had been designed, over the course of many decades, to be risk averse and protective of the family. Leaving Joe in an open-ended news conference, in Jill's mind, was not protecting him. So she was fine, that day, to leapfrog West Wing hierarchy and demand an answer from the press secretary, chief of staff, and communications director.

The role of White House press secretary is one of the toughest jobs in Washington for a reason, and so, understanding that the president's most invested confidante was demanding an answer, it was Psaki who finally made the decision to speak. "You're absolutely right. It was our responsibility," she told the First Lady. Psaki would recall to others that it was among the most stressful days of her tenure. Jeff Zients, who replaced Klain after two years in the job, has told associates he understands how important it is to keep the First Lady happy. They speak about once a week, often about personnel matters, according to people familiar with their discussions.

There is little doubt among those who have been around the couple that between the two of them, she is the one who is not to be crossed. It is a fact well known throughout the Biden White House.

"The best place to work is with Dr. B., because no one could ever fire you," said one person who knows her well, commenting on the stature she holds within the administration and the fierceness with which she protects those close to her, including people who work for her.

At the same time, that person said, "You would not want to have Dr. B. unhappy with you for something."

When Joe has a difficult decision to make, he often turns to Jill as his "gut check" and as his closest confidante, according to several people who know them both. Infrequently, she weighs in on policy—*The New York Times* reported that she was initially uncomfortable with the idea of widespread student-loan forgiveness, but ultimately supported her husband's doomed decision to move forward with an initiative forgiving up to $20,000 in federally held loans.

She is not in every policy discussion, but she is automatically involved in nearly every high-level staff decision and most political conversations. And there is little doubt among those who know her that Jill Biden's highest priority is shielding her husband and family from danger. She does not work out of the West Wing and is not a frequent presence there. She is rarely, if ever, in policy-related meetings but is nearly always alongside her husband at political meetings in the White House residence or at the family home in Delaware. She is watchful but not obsessed with her husband's day-to-day movements; she had aides remove the television from her East Wing office about a month into the presidency. But one of the best ways to describe her is with her own words: She is the family's self-appointed grudge holder. "I remember every slight committed against the people that I love," she wrote in her memoir. "I can forgive, sure—but I don't believe in rewarding bad behavior."

JILL WAS NOT BORN into the Biden family, but over time, she grew to become its defiant backbone. Nowhere is this more apparent than in her embrace of her last surviving son, Hunter.

Biden allies describe Joe's sons as two forks in a river, or a yin and a yang, two parts that made a whole. Beau was the idealistic one, with dreams of public service. Hunter is academically gifted and artistic, but he also inherited his father's hothead tendencies—his Irishness.

Later in his life, Beau, reflecting on his childhood, praised Jill to his friends, telling one of them that she always "showed up" for him and his brother, Hunter, when they were young—even after a disagreement, even if things were still tense.

"I think when you have things thrown at you like she did, the last person who can be tentative or unsure of themselves or waver is the mom," said her friend Catherine Stevens. "Another way to put it is: You don't have the luxury of 'What about me?'"

Jill and Hunter have a close relationship, according to people who know them, but the nature of their bond was different. Hunter was attached to his aunt Valerie and uncle Jimmy, who had stepped in to help raise the boys—all living under one roof, for a time—before Jill came into the picture. In his memoir, Hunter recalled sometimes feeling left out of the jokes Beau and Jill would tell, sometimes at his expense, though he ultimately praised her for "doing a great job, especially with everyone watching."

As adults, Beau pursued politics, while Hunter felt pressure to make money; both had grown up in a great man's shadow, as one family friend anonymously put it, "and the one who had an easier time with it died."

The details of the extent of Hunter's addiction problems, which spiraled after Beau's death, were made public when the contents of a laptop he had left at a repair shop were publicly disseminated by conservative websites ahead of the 2020 election. Tabloid reporters quickly published graphic photos that depicted him using drugs. They also published the contents of some of his private text messages and emails.

In the messages, Hunter appeared to disparage several family members, including Jill. In texts to his uncle Jimmy, Hunter called Jill "vindictive" and a "moron." But in texts to Joe, Hunter would be apologetic, asking for Jill's forgiveness and expressing his love for her. When Hunter became the subject of a federal investigation into his

tax filings, national newspapers followed suit, examining correspondence from the laptop that detailed Hunter's business dealings in Europe and Asia while his father served as vice president. In June 2023,
Hunter struck a deal with the Justice Department to plead guilty to
two misdemeanor tax charges and accept terms that would allow him
to avoid prosecution on a separate gun charge, though the saga began
anew when the deal quickly unraveled.

Hunter most explosively clashed with Jill when she helped lead a
family effort to get him clean. In 2018, as Hunter was seeking out
crack in dirty hotel rooms along the East Coast, Jill called him and
invited him for dinner at the family home in Delaware. It turned out
to be an intervention. As he entered the home and looked around at
his family and daughters and former addiction counselors, he became
angry that she had deceived him. He escaped to California, where he
continued to use. It was not a treatment program that pulled Hunter
back from the abyss, but a blind date with Melissa Cohen, a South
African woman he met for dinner at the Sunset Marquis in May 2019.

"You have the exact same eyes as my brother," was the first thing
he said to her.

Shortly after meeting Melissa, he told her he loved her, but also
disclosed he was a crack addict.

"Not anymore," she replied. "You're finished with that."

They married six days after meeting.

The Bidens are relieved to have their surviving son back from the
wilderness of addiction and focused on his sobriety, but they are concerned for his emotional health as he remains the target of Republican investigations and torrents of criticism in conservative media,
according to people who know the family. So, Joe and Jill have made
grand gestures, in public and in private, to show him that they love
him.

At the White House, Jill has asked chefs to make birthday cakes
for Hunter. She has made sure that Hunter and his family are included in family-related events like the White House Easter Egg
Roll. During his recovery, Hunter embraced painting, and a piece of

his artwork hangs in her East Wing office. Once, Jill planned to secretly visit a New York gallery that featured Hunter's artwork but
abruptly canceled when reporters were tipped off.

The Bidens have included Hunter on official trips, including Joe's
family-heritage trip to Ireland in 2023 where he slept on a cot in his
father's hotel room, and traveled with him aboard Marine One. They
have ensured that he is on the guest list at state dinners. And Hunter's
youngest child, blond-haired Beau, is often seen bopping across the
South Lawn with his grandparents.

According to several accounts from people close to the family, the
topic of Hunter is so sensitive—and Hunter remains in such a fragile
state—that only Joe and Jill's closest advisers can talk to them about
their last surviving son. Maintaing loyalty toward Hunter is more
important than almost anything else, and it was tested in June 2023,
when Hunter settled a child-support case with Lunden Roberts, a
woman he'd fathered a child with in 2018. Throughout the years, allies
of Roberts had spoken to the news media about Hunter's failure to
acknowledge the little girl, and about the unwillingness of her paternal grandparents to include her in the family. Those allies pointed out
that only six of the grandchildren had Christmas stockings hanging
on the First Family's fireplace mantel during the holidays. And they
claimed that the little girl had not been given Secret Service protection, even though the Bidens arranged security details for other family members. (A Secret Service official confirmed to me that this was
true.)

After the case was settled, Roberts told me that she would like for
the president to acknowledge his granddaughter.

"She's very proud of who her grandfather is and who her dad is,"
Roberts said. "That is something that I would never allow her to think
otherwise."

This interview with Lunden Roberts ran in *The New York Times*
after I spent several weeks reporting a story on the child-support case.
It was one of the hardest assignments of my career because, as I told
my editors, the little girl at the center of the case—who is aware that

her father was Hunter Biden and that her grandfather is the president—is innocent and had asked for none of this.

I had reservations about bringing further attention to a situation that was toxic and increasingly politicized, with both Democrat and Republican operatives working to sling dirt at both families. After weeks of resisting, my editors told me that I would not have to write a story I was uncomfortable with, but that they did want me to report.

So I quietly took a trip to Arkansas and slowly reached out to members of the Roberts family, one by one, knocking on doors and making cold calls. Batesville, where the Roberts family lives and has a gun-manufacturing business, is bucolic and verdant when you take a drive past the main roads. While I was knocking around Batesville, Hunter Biden was preparing to travel to Little Rock to provide a deposition in the child-support case. During that visit, the two parents met face-to-face for the first time in years, and hammered out a settlement in time to avoid trial.

What I found in rural Arkansas was a close clan that wanted the world to know that the little girl, whose name is Navy, is loved, and will be loved, regardless of whether she is ever embraced by the Bidens.

"She is awesome and needs for nothing and never will. I told them a long time ago that I may not be the POTUS but I am the one that will take a bullet for her," her maternal grandfather, Rob Roberts, told me on my second day in Arkansas. He also said that his granddaughter loved to play with her three cousins, racing four-wheelers and spending time with her relatives at family cookouts. Eventually, she would learn to hunt turkey and gator, just like her mother did when she was young.

"The kid is brilliant and witty, and carries on a conversation at an adult level," he said. "She knows everything. Full of crap like a Christmas goose."

I returned to Washington and wrote a story about what it meant to have the Biden birthright. The story brought national attention to a real contradiction within the Biden political brand. In this case, associates of the family told me, Hunter was calling the shots, and Joe and Jill were abiding by his wishes by staying quiet. Their devotion to keeping Hunter safe, people close to them said, was worth enduring the onslaught of criticism from both Republicans and Democrats.

This decision had consequences. There were several aides inside the White House who were distressed by the choice not to acknowledge Navy—as one senior aide, who grew emotional as we spoke, put it to me: They had believed in Joe, and had fought so hard for him to win the presidency because of the strength of his character. But, this person said, they simply could not defend his choice to ignore his granddaughter. The Biden family brand, built and nurtured over the past fifty years, is loyalty and empathy, but in this case, the Bidens were clear that their loyalty was with Hunter and not a little girl in Arkansas, even if she, too, had Biden blood.

Lunden Roberts did not return my calls until hours before the story ran. She called from a blocked number. The voice on the other end of the phone was syrupy and Southern, but she was not afraid of me, and she was not afraid to defend herself or her choices. (She said that, contrary to a slew of tabloid reports, she was not stripping when she met Hunter, but she did not say how they met. Hunter has written that he does not remember the encounter during which he fathered Navy.) People in Hunter Biden's orbit, she knew, had suggested to reporters that she had spent the bulk of her daughter's child-support funds—upwards of $750,000 before a new settlement was reached—on luxury items. That, she said, was what made her angry enough to finally return my calls.

"When it comes to that and making it seem as if I'm a bad mom," Roberts said, "people can call me whatever they want, but they can't call me that."

Navy Joan Roberts will not grow up with the Biden surname— "we worked it out amongst ourselves," Roberts said of that decision— and it is unclear how much of a relationship she will have with the paternal side of her family. Roberts hopes that Navy will eventually build a relationship with Hunter, who has embarked on a career as a painter, by selecting pieces of art from him, a provision of the child-support agreement. There is no guarantee Hunter will do this in person.

After my story, Maureen Dowd, the longtime columnist for *The New York Times*, wrote a column that pulled no punches and spoke directly to the president: "With Hunter, his father can seem paralyzed about the right thing to do. But the president can't defend Hunter on all his other messes and draw the line at accepting one little girl. You can't punish her for something she had no choice about."

Twenty days after Maureen's column, with national attention on the case hitting a fever pitch, the Bidens released a statement to the friendly *People* magazine on a Friday evening: "Our son Hunter and Navy's mother, Lunden, are working together to foster a relationship that is in the best interests of their daughter, preserving her privacy as much as possible going forward. This is not a political issue, it's a family matter. Jill and I only want what is best for all of our grandchildren, including Navy."

At the end of the day, Biden allies point out, Hunter is a private citizen, and warn that scrutinizing his personal life could establish an uncomfortable precedent for whoever seeks higher office—and their relatives—going forward. And it is not at all uncommon for presidential families to have a relative whose behavior draws unflattering attention. Billy Carter, the younger brother of President Jimmy Carter, drew a string of headlines in the 1970s for making anti-Semitic remarks, for urinating on the runway of an airport in Atlanta—he was a steady drinker—and for taking paid speaking engagements. "If people are crazy enough to pay money to hear me speak, I'm crazy enough to do it," he once said. The business and political dealings of Tony and Hugh Rodham, Hillary Clinton's brothers, became constant grist for conservative media, and Roger Clinton was pardoned by his brother, President Bill Clinton, for a drug-trafficking conviction.

The Biden White House has said Hunter will not receive a pardon from his father, but beyond that, neither the president nor his aides will say much about Hunter's various legal and personal problems on the record. Behind the scenes, the worry among Biden allies is that Hunter's sobriety and mental health are so precarious that saying or doing the wrong thing could result in Joe losing his last surviving son.

Jill has said the best thing she can do is keep Hunter close.

"I'm his mom," she said. "I mean, I have to support him and love him, and, you know, I'm constantly talking to him, sending him texts: 'How you doing?' Because it's tough. They've already really been hard on him."

She has had difficulty forgiving people she believes have attacked her relatives or left them vulnerable, including Senator Lindsey Graham of South Carolina, their former family friend. In an interview, Graham praised Jill as an "accomplished" and sometimes "underestimated" confidante of the president.

"I hate for any family to go through the stress they have with Hunter," Mr. Graham said. "But it comes with the territory. They take a wrecking ball to the Trump family, so they set those things in motion."

He added that he didn't feel he was on bad terms with the Biden family, instead owing the tension to "contention within our country.

"And yeah," he added, "I'm focused on keeping my party together."

Jill is also said to have an icy relationship with Hunter's ex-wife, Kathleen Buhle, according to multiple people familiar with that relationship. In March 2017, the *New York Post* reported that Hunter had separated from Kathleen and started a relationship with Beau's widow, Hallie. Relations with Joe and Jill got frostier when Kathleen refused to let Hunter see his children while he sought treatment for addiction. The Bidens were incensed that Hunter was kept from seeing his children—and, in turn, that Joe was prevented from seeing his grandchildren.

Buhle did not respond to a request for comment.

"I'm convinced that depriving someone for a month or more at a time of the most important relationships in his or her life—in my case, my three daughters—is too often a critical failure in how addicts are treated," Hunter wrote in his memoir. Kathleen filed for divorce in 2017, and the details, which included alleged drug use and infidelity, were leaked to the media. Kathleen, who grew up on the South Side of Chicago, is close friends with Michelle Obama, whose daughter Sasha grew up attending Sidwell Friends School and playing soccer and basketball with Kathleen and Hunter's daughter Maisy. At soccer games, observers recalled the Bidens standing on one side of the field. Kathleen stood on the other. Years later, the two sides reached a détente to celebrate Naomi's White House wedding. But Kathleen's allies have privately pointed out that she was relegated to the background while Jill posed for a *Vogue* cover with Naomi.

Jill's defense of her family has cropped up in ways that have felt unexpected to people who have witnessed her reactions. A person who attended a White House function during the winter of 2022 was surprised at the First Lady's emotional response when she overheard someone praise the legacy of President George W. Bush.

"He sent my son to war," Jill replied angrily. "He sent my son to war."

Beau Biden had enlisted in the Delaware Army National Guard in 2003 and was deployed to Iraq in 2008. Jill was so upset by Bush's reelection in 2004 that she pushed Joe to run for the presidency in 2008.

"Jill's a dove," one aide said, using a moniker that describes someone who is against war. In 2012, Jill wrote a children's book, called *Don't Forget, God Bless Our Troops*, from the perspective of Beau's daughter, Natalie.

"My experience through my son's deployment made me realize how important it is for all Americans to get a glimpse inside the life of a military family and to understand what it means when a family member is deployed," she wrote in the book's introduction.

Jill has spent much of her career as a political spouse supporting military families. Her stoicism as a wife and military parent was tested in August 2021, when the Biden administration's disastrous drawdown of American forces from Afghanistan resulted in the deaths of thirteen American marines and more than one hundred Afghan civilians who were killed by a terrorist's bomb.

At the end of the month, the Bidens traveled to Dover Air Force

Base to oversee the dignified transfer of the soldiers' remains, and Joe, seeking to bond over stories of losing a loved one, told several Gold Star parents that he, too, had lost a son. As president, he invokes Beau's memory often. In the wake of the attack, I interviewed Mark Schmitz, the father of Lance Cpl. Jared Schmitz, a twenty-year-old marine who had been killed, who said that he was upset when the president seemed more interested in speaking not about the son he lost but about the death of Beau. In a planning call ahead of the president's trip to Dover, several senior aides were advised to tell Joe not to bring up Beau to the grieving families, but the message was either ignored or never received, according to a person involved in the planning.

"I respect anybody that lost somebody," Mr. Schmitz said, "but it wasn't an appropriate time."

The criticism after the drawdown stung Jill.

"I love him, and it's hurtful," she said when I interviewed her, looking directly back at me. "I do feel the sting of it. I wouldn't be a good partner if I didn't."

ON OCCASION, JILL'S FEELINGS about people she believes have wronged her husband have become a matter of public record. Several Biden aides said that she was the primary holdout on the choice of Kamala Harris as her husband's running mate after Kamala attacked him during a Democratic primary debate in June 2019.

In that debate, Kamala took aim at Biden's past interest in negotiating with senators who had been segregationists—weeks before the debate, he had waxed wistfully about the "civility" he had found in previous iterations of the Senate—and his opposition to integrating schools using busing in the 1970s. In response, Kamala assailed Joe on personal terms.

"And there was a little girl in California who was part of the second class to integrate her public schools, and she was bused to school every day," she said. "And that little girl was me." Kamala's official Twitter account quickly sent out a picture of a young Kamala Harris wearing hoop earrings and pigtails. "That little girl was me," the caption reiterated.

The performance gave her a bump in the polls and put the Biden campaign on its heels. The moment served as the catalyst for a multi-week apology tour that saw Joe atoning for his past comments and showcasing his track record on civil rights.

"Every candidate's record will (and should) be scrutinized in this race. It's a competition to become president of the United States," Ian Sams, who served as the Harris campaign's press secretary before joining the Biden administration, tweeted at the time. "There are no free passes."

The debate bump was not enough to sustain Kamala, who has historically had a difficult time retaining staff and has an equally difficult time maintaining a sense of direction. Within six months, Kamala, lacking money and suffering from a staff exodus, would be out of the race. Two months after she pulled out of the race, Black Democrats in South Carolina helped a limping Biden campaign to its feet.

When it came time for the campaign to vet running mates, Jill was not keen on having the woman who had implied that her husband had racist sympathies aboard the ticket. As Jonathan Martin and Alex Burns wrote in their book, *This Will Not Pass: Trump, Biden, and the Battle for America's Future,* she didn't understand why Harris was the chosen one. "There are millions of people in the United States," she said. "Why do we have to choose the one who attacked Joe?"

But the opinions of the other poohbahs in the inner circle, including Ron Klain, won out. Klain has had his own struggles with returning to Jill's good graces. He'd raised eyebrows within the family when he signed on to Hillary Clinton's presidential campaign in 2015, without waiting to see if Joe would declare a run for the presidency. Klain knew he had run afoul of the Biden loyalty test.

"It's been a little hard for me to play such a role in the Biden demise—and I am definitely dead to them," Klain wrote to John Podesta, Clinton's campaign chairman, in an October 2015 email that was later published by WikiLeaks. Once again, Joe's selection of Klain was done with his ever-watchful wife keeping track of past violations, and when Klain came back on board, it was the result of a substantial amount of inner-circle lobbying; "Do you know how much diplomacy I had to do to get our lady on board with this?" one aide recalled of the discussions about Jill grudgingly accepting Klain back into the fold.

In this case and others, Jill and Joe have relaxed their rigid loyalty rules when an operative's strategic value outweighs their past infractions.

The most high-profile example of this, of course, is the vice president. When Biden world was assessing Kamala as Joe's running mate, Klain and others reasoned that she was the politically smart choice. It would make Biden look like he was above the attacks and interested in placing the country's future ahead of his own pride. According to a close Biden adviser, Jill eventually came around, even though she had first favored and promoted the idea of choosing Susan Rice, who went on to become Joe's top domestic policy adviser.

"She obviously wanted to protect her husband," a person close to her said about her thought process around these decisions. "She's always going to pause and say, 'Are you *sure* we're making the right decision?'"

In the end, Jill told her husband that Kamala was the best person for the vice-presidential nomination.

"When I talked to Jill, I realized Jill gave exactly the same advice Beau would've given," the adviser said, adding that "she did not let her personal feelings get in the way" of choosing a running mate who could help her husband win. Still, Jill has never denied a report that she used an expletive to describe Kamala's decision to criticize her husband on the night of the debate.

"With what he cares about, what he fights for, what he's committed to, you get up there and call him a racist without basis?" she was reported as saying to a group of supporters as she reflected on the debate-stage flap a week after it happened. "Go fuck yourself," she said, according to an account by the journalist Edward-Isaac Dovere.

Jill has said that everyone involved has "moved on" from the incident. According to aides, Kamala is liked by the president, though Joe was quoted in Chris Whipple's book about the Biden presidency as saying his vice president was "a work in progress." She has never made it into Joe's closest circle of advisers, an inner sanctum that is as much Jill's domain as his.

Everyone may have moved on from the campaign flap, but Jill has not gone out of her way to support the vice president. In March 2022, Jill traveled to California for the funeral of Richard Blum, the husband of Senator Dianne Feinstein, and added a fundraiser to her schedule. In a private home in the wealthy Pacific Heights neighborhood of San Francisco, she told around two dozen guests about how hard her husband was working and how demanding the Russian invasion of Ukraine had been.

"The phone never stops ringing, all night long," she told the group. "And Joe is on his feet trying to help solve this crisis."

According to two people at the event, one of the hosts praised Kamala to the First Lady, telling her that the selection was politically and personally meaningful to the people of San Francisco. The people in the room, the cohost said, were proud of Kamala and hoped that she was serving the Bidens well.

Attendees noticed the awkward pause that followed. Jill did not respond and instead brought up another topic completely.

"What about Ketanji?" Jill said brightly, steering the conversation away from the vice president and toward her husband's selection of Ketanji Brown Jackson as his first Supreme Court nominee.

Her intention was to steer the conversation away from a well-publicized rift that had happened years before. Still, the reaction puzzled people in the room who heard it.

It did not surprise people who know her well.

"She's an Italian," one friend said with a shrug, by way of explanation. "She's all about loyalty."

"THEY WANT YOU
TO BE STRONG"

As the Bidens looked toward their final campaign, there were no longer questions about whether Jill wanted her husband to run. She began enthusiastically telling their allies before he did.

In December 2022, the Bidens welcomed Emmanuel Macron, the president of France, and his wife, Brigitte, to the White House for a state visit. Over a selection of American cheeses and wines at a state dinner, Jill and the French president discussed how exhausting it was to be on the campaign trail. After she told him that a strict exercise regimen kept her in campaign-ready shape, Macron interjected: Did this mean she was ready for her husband to run again in 2024? "Absolutely," she replied. The Bidens then joined the Macrons in a playful toast to the reelection. It was a jovial moment, but the fact that they were willing to disclose their plans to a foreign leader—and a gossipy one at that—showed that the Bidens were taking the idea seriously. Throughout the fall and winter, Joe repeatedly said that he planned to run, but observers still doubted whether the oldest president in American history would really be up for another campaign, this time without the coronavirus-era provisions that restricted his travel and kept him away from people.

On a tour of Africa in February 2023, Jill was impatient when she was asked, yet again, if her husband planned to run. "How many times does he have to say it for you to believe it?" she asked Darlene Superville.

On a tour of Ireland to visit his distant relatives weeks later, in early April, Joe participated in an event that looked a lot like a soft launch of an election bid. In Ballina, a town where his ancestors lived, he drew on a life story that was rooted in resilience and hope. In another appearance in front of Irish lawmakers, he presented his age—the fact that he would be eighty-six at the end of a second term, should he win—as an asset and not a hindrance.

"I'm at the end of my career, not the beginning," the eighty-year-old president said, adding that with his age came "a little bit of wisdom. I come to the job with more experience than any president in American history. It doesn't make me better or worse, but it gives me few excuses."

Then he returned to the United States and filmed a campaign ad.

On April 25, 2023, Joe Biden announced his final campaign for reelection with a video, just like he'd done before. This time, though, Jill and her work as First Lady were featured heavily throughout. For decades, she had been seen as the swing vote toward another race or sitting it out, but she was more supportive than ever this time. Still, she knows how much energy the presidency has taken out of her husband.

"It has to be his decision," she said in Rehoboth.

"I saw Joe as VP and how tough that was. But when I see what he does, when I see the table as you get off that elevator and I see a pile like this every single night with briefing books," she said, placing her two hands apart for emphasis, "and I see him reading and writing, it's a lot."

Though the midterm elections went better for Democrats than almost anyone expected, Americans of all political stripes began publicly expressing concern about Joe's age. He tripped more than once while climbing the stairs of Air Force One. In June 2023, he tripped and fell while delivering a commencement address at the Air Force Academy. Conservative websites and television channels questioned his capacity to lead every time he flubbed a speech, which, for a politician as gaffe-prone as Joe was in his earlier years, was often. With widespread pessimism about the state of the economy and about the leadership of both the Republican and Democratic parties, it seemed deeply unclear whether voters would give the Bidens four more years to deliver on a promise to promote unity over division, extoll the virtues of democracy over rising authoritarianism around the globe, or course-correct nagging inflation that has driven scores of working-class Americans further into debt. Younger, more progressive Democrats assailed the Biden administration for failing to deliver on a range of promises to voters who trusted Joe when he said he would serve as a "bridge" to a new generation of politicians. They were angry over what they see as empty words about protecting the environment, easing student-loan debt, protecting voting rights, and codifying the provisions of *Roe v. Wade* into law. And even their allies believed the Bidens had a liability—and a blind spot—when it came to their son Hunter, who has been a reliable target for conservatives.

By summer 2023, the field of Republican nominees had widened, but at the center of it was Donald Trump, who lost his bid for re-election in 2020. He was facing dozens of felony charges for hoarding boxes of classified documents after leaving the White House, and withholding them from investigators. A month earlier, a jury in New York found that he'd sexually abused and defamed the writer E. Jean Carroll, who'd accused him of attacking her in a department-store dressing room. In another case, he pleaded not guilty to fraud charges related to the hush money paid to Stormy Daniels. He was again indicted in his push to overturn the 2020 election results, and may face more charges before this book goes to print. With each charge, his base only circled around him even tighter. Other potential Republican candidates, including Governor Ron DeSantis of Florida, were hungry to promote a brand of culture-war politics, but Trump remained the favorite.

Amid the concern over Joe's age and his lack of popularity, the Bidens were still in the fight, with a hard-won awareness of how quickly fortunes can change.

What would a second-term Jill look like? Her aides and friends say she would likely keep up a vigorous travel schedule, with no immediate plans to retire from teaching, and that she would continue serving as her husband's protector and confidante.

Whatever happens, Jill's role itself is poised to continue undergoing a major transformation in an era where Americans are increasingly partisan and American politicians are more willing than ever to challenge institutions. If Joe wins in 2024, at age eighty-two, there is a non-zero chance that circumstances could quickly change and Kamala Harris could be called to serve out the end of a second term. This would give America the first East Wing led by a man.

If Donald Trump continues his campaign and wins the election, Melania Trump could continue her anything-goes approach for another four years. Perhaps she would be a First Lady based in Palm Beach. She has spent her post–White House time lying low and has adopted the curious habit of selling the digital trinkets known as NFTs. According to people close to the Trumps, Melania is focused on getting her son into college. She has declined requests from her husband to make appearances on the campaign trail, though Trump campaign officials say that this may change as the campaign heats up. In a rare interview in May 2023, she told Fox News that she would "prioritize the well-being and development of children" if she reprised the role. But people who know her say she is happy keeping to herself behind the walled gates of Mar-a-Lago or ensconced in Trump Tower.

As the Obamas taught us, there could be a lightning-in-a-bottle candidate whom we do not yet see, whose partner or spouse would continue changing the role in unexpected ways.

But what is clear now, as of the summer of 2023, is that the Bidens have no intention of giving America a glimpse of what lies beyond their tenure, despite promising to be a bridge to the future. After so many years trying to make it to the White House, their case for reelection is based on the idea that they still have more to do, and that they want to be president and First Lady for all Americans, whether they voted for Joe Biden or not.

—

ON THE DAY JOE announced his run, Jill posted a photo on Insta-gram. Dressed in a pale-blue pantsuit, the First Lady was holding two sensible workbags and standing in front of a brick building at North-ern Virginia Community College: "Just like four years ago—I'm off to teach and Joe's launched his (reelection) campaign," she wrote. "Let's finish the job!"

If she has another term, she is likely to continue changing the role in ways we might not see or understand until after she is gone. Each First Lady's decisions have inevitably made it easier on whoever comes next. The next First Spouse will have a blueprint for keeping a career, should they choose, and they will know that maintaining a cool head in the face of gendered criticism helps the storm pass quickly. They can choose to focus on being a parent and learn that establishing firm boundaries at the outset can buy them the time they need to take on more if they choose. They might try to lead alongside their spouse, and if they do, they'll have an idea of what their ambi-tion might cost them. They might even choose to disappear from the public eye for weeks at a time and wear pieces of clothing with cryptic messages scrawled on the back. There's a long menu of options. It all depends on the price they want to pay.

When I first started this book, Jill Biden was a mystery to me. I couldn't quite understand how someone would voluntarily step into a family that had been so broken by tragedy. And I could not under-stand how someone could have the patience to be at the side of a man who spent decades pursuing the nation's highest office and failing. What her friends and family say is true: She is much steelier than she appears, and her love for her husband and their family is a significant part of what drives her. But she is also disciplined about compart-mentalizing her emotions to protect herself and others. It is a skill she learned from her own mother and brought to a complicated family when she met the widower senator from Delaware.

There was a moment I saw her in Ukraine when she was shaken but dry-eyed as she listened to the stories of women who had fled the war with their children. She was solemn as she played with children, some of whom looked stricken. On the way back to Slovakia, I asked her how she had managed to get through the day without growing emotional. I remember the interaction because she looked at me and seemed slightly puzzled by the question. The answer was obvious to her. The sight of a weeping American First Lady wouldn't have done a room full of traumatized women and children any good.

During our interview in Rehoboth, I asked her to revisit that moment. I wanted to know what prepared her for the sort of life she has lived, which has required her to pull a broken family together, campaign for the presidency several times, and now, as First Lady, serve not only as mom in chief during a pandemic but as an emissary to a war-torn country whose women and children are suffering.

"Because you have to," she replied. "They want you to be strong. Because a lot of times they can't. And I understand that. Because I've been in situations where I haven't been strong. But if they can look at their First Lady as someone who is strong and can help them through a struggle, whether it's depression, whether they're suffering from an illness, whether their child has been shot at a school, you have to be strong."

Suddenly, she brought up her mother, Bonny Jean.

"Our mother was really strong, really strong," she said. "And we all felt, all five girls felt, that our mother was really strong, and admired her for that."

She paused: "I think I've had to take over that role in my own family."

Understated, as usual.

ACKNOWLEDGMENTS

IT TRULY DOES TAKE A VILLAGE, AND I'M SO LUCKY TO HAVE been supported by friends, family, colleagues, and readers like you along the way.

Thank you to Matt Latimer of Javelin for seeing a project with potential and thinking of me, and to Libby Burton, my editor at Crown, for seeing me through a project that grew more ambitious and complicated as I worked on it. I am thankful that the two of you were with me on this journey. Thank you to Crown's Gillian Blake, for pushing us to make this book the best it could be. I'm so appreciative that Aubrey Martinson and Cierra Hinckson kept me appropriately wrangled throughout the process. And I owe much to the production editor Mark Birkey and copy editor Mimi Lipson, who reviewed this manuscript closely and had sharp suggestions for refining the writing.

Thank you to the talented Ben Wiseman for an incredible, that's-the-one cover design, and to Barbara Bachman for designing a beautiful and clean book. I am indebted to Sarah Feightner, the book's production manager, and her talented team for helping get this project into shape. Thank you to Chantelle Walker and Penny Simon and the rest of the wonderful marketing and publicity team.

Thank you to Elisabeth Bumiller, our fearless leader in the Washington bureau of *The New York Times*, for bringing me to the bureau and for giving me the opportunity of a lifetime. Every time I pulled up a beautifully written story about the Bush White House while researching this book, there was never any need to look at the byline: It was always Elisabeth. I owe so much to her and to Cliff Levy for hiring me at the *Times*.

Thanks to Dean Baquet, Phil Corbett, and others at *The New York Times* who agreed to let me pursue this project. And a hearty thanks to Elizabeth Kennedy and Bill Hamilton, two White House editors who have challenged me and pushed me and made me better.

I learn something new every day from my Biden-beat colleagues, past and present, who make it look easy: Peter Baker, Zolan Kanno-Youngs, Mike Shear, Jim Tankerseley, and David Sanger. I am honored every day to work alongside all of you. And special thanks to Steve Eder, an investigative reporter for the *Times*, who understood how the Freedom of Information Act could help the public learn more about the reasons Joe Biden ran for the presidency, and the reasons Jill Biden put her own career on hold to support him.

Thank you to Matt Cullen, a dynamo who assisted with research, and Justine Makieli, a talented *New York Times* editor and mother of two who somehow found the time to fact-check this book. Thank you to the sublimely talented Erin Schaff for taking my author photo. Thank you to Carlos Lozada for reading a few pages and sharing your thoughts.

I am indebted to two friends I made on the Trump White House beat: Annie Karni and Maggie Haberman. You two are incredible journalists. You have taught me so much about reporting, but, more important, I have turned to you during some tough real-life moments, and you have both always had my back. I am a better mother and a better friend because of both of you.

I'm grateful to have leaned on several other lionhearted friends during this process: T. J. Ortenzi, Dan Zak, Erica Green, and Olivia Nuzzi, whom I admire for their intelligence, creativity, resilience, and good humor. I was fortified by my friendships with Abi Wood, Ellen Nyquist, Amanda Segni, Amanda Zamora, Kat Braun, Kellen Henry, Mary Squillace, and Diane Rusignola. All of you were part of my brain trust, and I am blessed to have all of you in my life. Thank you to Melania Kim, an avid reader who always provided feedback and encouragement when I needed it most.

Thanks to Kate Bennett, a hilarious and gifted reporter who covered the First Family better than any of us, for her insights and reporting, which I referenced frequently as I wrote. And a shout-out to several beat colleagues: Jen Jacobs, Jeff Mason, Darlene Superville, Tyler Pager, Mike Memoli, Jada Yuan, and Emily Goodin, who have been good-humored and gracious as we've traveled the world together. It has been my experience that reporters who cover both wings of the White House are always ferociously sourced and write the kind of stories people want to read. Infinitely true with this talented group!

I also took inspiration from Darlene, Kate, and several other First Lady biographers, including Kate Andersen Brower, Susan Page, Karen Tumulty, and Ann Gerhart. I don't know how you all did it, but I'm so glad that you did. Thank you to the Key West Literary Seminar, an amazing organization that provided me with two crucial weeks in my favorite place in the world, so I could emerge with a better understanding of where I wanted to go with this book.

I owe much to my family, especially Andrew Rogers, my brother, who has been my biggest supporter for as long as I can remember. He is the writer in the family and the bravest person I know, so I trusted him when he told me I could do this project. Thanks to my sister-in-law, Emma Gryce, for the advice and thoughtful conversations. And thanks to Trevor Miller, my youngest brother, for his love and good cheer.

My mom, Lori Holewczynski, brought me into this world and nurtured my creativity. Richard Rogers, my dad, taught me all the lessons worth knowing, and I hear him in my laughter. My stepmom, Manette Zeitler, and her sisters—Michele, Madelyn, Marjorie, and Melanie—deserve all the credit for raising me to be a reader and writer, along with my grandparents, Jim and Beverly Rogers and Philip and Beverly Zeitler. My grandmothers made sure I had an education and made it possible for me to see the world, and this book is for them.

A special thanks to Maria Paz Hernandez, who took care of our daughter, Lily, so I could get this book done, and who has treated my family with love and respect for the past three years. I could not have done this without her. Thank you to my wonderful in-laws, Mike and Susan Chinoransky, for the love, acceptance, and grace they have shown me over the years, and for always reading my stories. I'm lucky to be a part of your family.

And I would not have made it to the beginning or the end of this project without the support and love and hard work of my husband, John Chinoransky. Thank you for loving me and Lily so completely and for making our life together a haven. I love you.

PHOTOGRAPH CREDITS

(INSERT)

Page 1, top: Courtesy Thomas of Stiltz
Page 1, middle: Courtesy of the Stevens Family
Page 1, bottom: George Widman/Associated Press
Page 2, top: Jerome Delay/AFP via Getty Images
Page 2, middle: Joe Raedle/Getty Images
Page 2, bottom: Patrick T. Fallon/Bloomberg via Getty Images
Page 3, top: Chip Somodevilla/Getty Images
Page 3, bottom: Jim Watson/AFP via Getty Images
Page 4, top: Courtesy of the author
Page 4, bottom: Erin Schaff/Pool/AFP via Getty Images
Page 5, top: Courtesy of the author
Page 5, middle: Nathan Posner/Anadolu Agency via Getty Images
Page 5, bottom: Nicholas Kamm/AFP via Getty Images
Page 6, top: Courtesy of the author
Page 6, bottom: Courtesy of the author
Page 7, top: Maureen Keating/Library of Congress
Page 7, bottom: SSG Randy Yackiel 55th Signal Company/
        Combat Camera
Page 8, top: Library of Congress
Page 8, middle: Carol M. Highsmith/Library of Congress
Page 8, bottom: Rob Crandall/Pool via CNP/Getty Images

NOTES

THIS BOOK IS BASED ON MORE THAN 125 ORIGINAL INTER-
views with White House officials, former aides, friends, lawmakers,
one Second Gentleman, and two First Ladies. I obtained contempo-
raneous emails, text messages, and correspondence, and I relied on my
original reporting for *The New York Times,* in which I chronicled the
Trump and Biden presidencies in real time.

Many of the interviews were conducted on background to preserve relationships or because the subject was not authorized to speak
publicly.

Most of Jill Biden's official speeches and remarks have been distributed through official White House channels. I also used Twitter,
Instagram, and White House YouTube accounts to gather public
comments from current and former First Ladies, as well as White
House archives and related resources.

There are several excellent books on First Ladies that provided me
with important insights into the lives of the women I wrote about,
and a few memoirs in which I could hear from the First Ladies in
their own words. Below are notes on sources from my own reporting,
and from places other than my own reporting.

INTRODUCTION

x   **$8 million book deal:** Steve Eder and Katie Glueck, "Joe Biden's Tax Returns Show More Than $15 Million in Income After 2016," *New York Times,* July 9, 2019.

x   **$2.7 million home:** Michela Tindera, "How Covid Helped Boost the Value of Joe Biden's Beach House by $700,000," *Forbes,* March 15, 2021.

xi   **"Grab onto the stair railing":** Author interview.

xi   **"counterfeit love":** Jill Biden, *Where the Light Enters: Building a Family, Discovering Myself* (New York: Flatiron Books, 2020), 41.

xii   **"Dad, we think we should marry Jill":** @DrBiden on Instagram, April 26, 2019.

xii   **Commander, the family's German shepherd:** Zolan Kanno-Youngs. "Bidens' Dog Has Bitten Several Secret Service Agents, Emails Show," *New York Times,* July 25, 2023.

xii   **bit at least one Secret Service agent:** Kate Bennett, "Biden's German Shepherd Has Aggressive Incident and Is Sent Back to Delaware," CNN, March 10, 2021.

xii   **None were found:** Glenn Thrush, Michael D. Shear, and Maggie Haberman, "F.B.I. Search of Biden Beach House Finds No Classified Documents," *New York Times,* February 1, 2023.

xiii   **onetime child actor:** Anthony R. Bernal, Imdb.com.

xiii   **"an oenophile of the first degree":** Michael D. Shear, Katie Rogers, and Annie Karni, "Beneath Joe Biden's Folksy Demeanor, a Short Fuse and an Obsession with Details," *New York Times,* May 14, 2021.

xv   **"I don't think there's really much difference":** Author interview.

xvi   **"She's just grounded in her friends":** Author interview.

xvi   **"The one area":** Author interview.

xvi   **"She gets after it":** Lauren Egan and Eli Stokols, "Jill Biden's SoulCycle Routine Will Make You Feel Bad," *Politico,* June 14, 2023.

xvii   **"It's not really a job":** Author interview.

xvii   **over fifty women:** The First Ladies: Biographies and Portraits, The White House Historical Association.

xviii   **breakfast tacos:** Patrick Svitek, "Jill Biden Apologizes for Calling Latino Community 'Unique as the Breakfast Tacos' in San Antonio," July 12, 2022.

xix   *Suspicion, or Persecuted Innocence:* Louisa Adams First Spouse $10 Gold Coin First Lady, 1825–1829, United States Mint website.

xix   *Jacqueline Kennedy: The White House Years:* Metmuseum.org.

xix   **the *Mona Lisa:*** Lisa Fayne Cohen, "How First Lady Jackie Kennedy Pulled Off the Mona Lisa's Historic U.S. Visit," *Galerie,* February 28, 2018.

xxiii   **"Until relatively recently":** Author interview.

xxiii   **"We really reminded people":** Author interview.

CHAPTER ONE: MERMAIDS

4   **"Wellesley teaches":** Fox Butterfield, "At Wellesley, a Furor over Barbara Bush," *New York Times,* May 4, 1990.

4 **the term "womanist"**: "A Brief History of Civil Rights in the United States: The Womanist Movement," Research Guides, Howard University School of Law website.

5 **"I don't think you can"**: Author interview.

5 **"I think these young women"**: Butterfield, "At Wellesley, a Furor."

5 **"Now, I know your first choice"**: "Mrs. Bush's Commencement Address to the Wellesley College Class of 1990," Wellesley College website.

6 **"You have to decide now"**: Ibid.

6 **three major networks**: Steve Hendrix, "The Day Barbara Bush Wowed Wellesley's Feminist Protesters with a Graduation Speech," *Washington Post*, April 18, 2018.

6 **"At the end of your life"**: Ibid.

6 **"Somewhere out in this audience"**: Ibid.

7 **A JOB WELLESLEY DONE**: Eleanor Clift, "A Job Wellesley Done," *Newsweek*, June 10, 1990.

7 **"You can see the winds of change"**: Author interview.

7 **Some struggled with addiction**: Myra MacPherson and Donnie Radcliffe, "Betty Ford Says That She Is Addicted to Alcohol," *Washington Post*, April 22, 1978.

7 **"state prisoner"**: "Letter, Martha Washington to Fanny Bassett Washington, October 23, 1789," Collections, George Washington's Mount Vernon website.

8 **Roosevelt's expansion**: "The Evolving Modern Presidency," Brookings website.

8 **"encroach on my husband's"**: Maurine Hoffman Beasley, *Eleanor Roosevelt and the Media: A Public Quest for Self-Fulfillment* (Champaign: University of Illinois Press, 1987), 46.

8 **"the president's eyes, ears, and legs"**: "Eleanor Roosevelt Biography," Franklin D. Roosevelt Presidential Library and Museum website.

8 **"I hate to do it"**: Lorena A. Hickok, *Eleanor Roosevelt: Reluctant First Lady* (New York: Dodd, Mead & Company, 1962), 1.

9 **researchers have found**: "What Makes a Good President?," American Psychological Association website.

9 **a survey of historians**: Women and Leadership, chapter 2 of "What Makes a Good Leader, and Does Gender Matter?," Pew Research Center website, January 14, 2015.

9 **previewed in the press release**: "Eleanor Roosevelt Retains Top Spot as America's Best First Lady," Siena College, February 15, 2014.

10 **"Each one's had her own adjustment period"**: Katie Rogers, "Reluctant First Lady? Melania Trump Wouldn't Be the First to Claim That Title," *New York Times*, February 18, 2017.

12 **"to take care of the President"**: "Jacqueline Lee Bouvier Kennedy," White House.gov.

12 **"if you bungle raising your children"**: Ibid.

12 **the name of a racehorse**: Author interview.

12 **"My conclusion: Stay in"**: Julia Sweig, *Lady Bird Johnson: Hiding in Plain Sight* (New York: Random House, 2021), xx.

13 **"Even people who can recall the Nixon presidency"**: Rogers, "Reluctant First Lady?"

14 **"No! Oh, no—heavens, no"**: Enid Nemy, "Betty Ford, Former First Lady, Dies at 93," *New York Times,* July 8, 2011.

14 **"I do not believe"**: Sarah Fling, "Betty Ford: Activist First Lady," White House Historical Association website, November 5, 2019.

14 **"Steel Magnolia"**: Wayne King, "Rosalynn Carter, a Tough, Tireless Campaigner, Displays Same Driving Quality as Her Husband," *New York Times,* October 18, 1976.

16 **"I'm not a psychologist"**: Karen Tumulty, *The Triumph of Nancy Reagan* (New York: Simon & Schuster, 2021), 16.

17 **"I've been very lucky"**: Ibid.

17 **"But the rewards are so great"**: Ibid., 203.

18 **"Nothing can happen to my Ronnie"**: Lou Cannon, "Nancy Reagan, an Influential and Protective First Lady, Dies at 94," *New York Times,* March 6, 2016.

18 **pack the president's schedule**: Gerald M. Boyd, "Reagan Caught in Feud Between Wife and Aide," *New York Times,* February 21, 1987.

19 **"In spite of everything I've learned"**: Tumulty, *The Triumph of Nancy Reagan,* 499.

19 **"She really hated us"**: Susan Page, *The Matriarch: Barbara Bush and the Making of an American Dynasty* (New York: Twelve, 2019), 72.

19 **"You can hug and pick up AIDS babies"**: Jonathan Capehart, "Barbara Bush, a Baby and Breaking a Shameful Silence on AIDS," *Washington Post,* April 18, 2018.

20 **"Well, the controversy ends here"**: "Mrs. Bush's Commencement Address, 1990."

CHAPTER TWO: AMBITION

21 **"I'm a working woman"**: Author interview.

21 **"I am an English teacher at NOVA"**: email from Jill Biden to colleagues, Freedom of Information Act request, *New York Times.*

22 **"It's my profession"**: "Real Running Mates," *Los Angeles Times Special,* July 29, 1987.

22 **"Forget the small thrill of being Dr. Jill"**: Joseph Epstein, "Is There a Doctor in the White House? Not If You Need an M.D.," *Wall Street Journal,* December 11, 2020.

22 **In the 2008 presidential race**: Joseph E. Uscinski and Lilly J. Goren, "What's in a Name? Coverage of Senator Hillary Clinton During the 2008 Democratic Primary," *Political Research Quarterly* 64, no. 4 (December 2011), 884–96.

22 **"So what?"**: Morgan Gstalter, "Tucker Carlson Responds to Guest Correcting Pronunciation of Kamala Harris's Name: 'So What?,'" *The Hill,* August 12, 2020.

22 **"lotus flower"**: Amiri Nash, "Say Kamala Harris' Name Correctly—Names Are a Form of Power to Black Americans," *Brown Political Review,* February 19, 2021.

22 **Tucker shocked the media world:** Jeremy W. Peters, Katie Robertson, and Michael M. Grynbaum, "Tucker Carlson, a Source of Repeated Controversies, Is Out at Fox News," *New York Times,* April 24, 2023.

23 **"It was really the tone of it":** Virginia Chamlee, "'Such a Surprise': Jill Biden Talks Controversial 'Wall Street Journal' Op-Ed about Her 'Dr.' Title," *People,* December 18, 2020.

23 **"This story would never":** @DouglasEmhoff on Twitter, December 12, 2020.

23 **"What was at the root":** Eleanor Herman, *Off with Her Head: Three Thousand Years of Demonizing Women in Power* (New York: William Morrow, 2022), 283.

23 **"mistaken for housewives":** @Page88 on Twitter, December 12, 2020.

24 **seemed wary of the scar tissue:** Soledad O'Brien, "One-on-One with Michelle Obama," CNN, February 1, 2008.

24 **"Even though I considered it in passing":** Author interview.

25 **Hillary strode over:** Aaron Parsley, "The Clintons Look Young and Giddy in Throwback Photo Hillary Shares on Valentine's Day," *People,* February 14, 2022.

25 **so-called segregation academy:** Amy Chozick, "How Hillary Clinton Went Undercover to Examine Race in Education," *New York Times,* December 27, 2015.

26 **"I don't believe you change hearts":** Maggie Haberman, "Hillary Clinton, Pressed on Race, Issues Her Own Challenge," *New York Times,* August 19, 2015.

26 **"You cannot make my life up":** Michael Collins, "'You Cannot Make Up My Life': Hillary Clinton's Ties to Impeachment Inquiries Against Three Presidents," *USA Today,* October 26, 2019.

27 **"It was up to her":** Amy Chozick, "Stress Over Family Finances Propelled Hillary Clinton into Corporate World," *New York Times,* August 10, 2016.

27 **$1,000 in cattle futures:** Seth C. Anderson, John D. Jackson, and Jeffrey W. Steagall, "A Note on Odds in the Cattle Futures Market," *Journal of Economics and Finance* 18 (September 1994), 357–65.

27 **struck a deal with Jim McDougal:** Stephen Engelberg with Jason Deparle, "Clintons' Whitewater Investment: Details of a Land Deal That Soured," *New York Times,* February 7, 1994.

28 **a woman named Gennifer Flowers:** Susan Dominus, "Gennifer Flowers, Donald Trump and the Making of the Sex-Scandal Culture," *New York Times Magazine,* September 26, 2016.

28 **"Wait a minute":** Virginia Chamlee, "'Not Sittin' Here as Some Little Woman': Looking Back at Hillary and Bill Clinton's '60 Minutes' Interview," *People,* October 27, 2021.

28 **"I'm not sittin' here":** Ibid.

29 **"buy one, get one free":** Peter W. Stevenson, "'Buy One, Get One Free': Bill Clinton's Turn as His Wife's Presidential Bonus," *Washington Post,* January 5, 2016.

29 **"It wasn't a shallow kind of thing":** Author interview.

29 **"If the wife comes through":** Maureen Dowd, "Campaign Trail; From Nixon, Predictions on the Presidential Race," *New York Times,* February 6, 1992.

30 "You know, I suppose I could have stayed home": Michael Kruse, "The TV Interview That Haunts Hillary Clinton," *Politico,* September 23, 2016.

30 "While Bill talked about social change": Hillary Clinton, *Living History* (New York: Scribner, 2004), 110.

30 "I found an incredible opportunity": Author interview.

32 "We all accommodated his pronouncements": Ibid., 12.

32 Sister Frigidaire: Dan Zak, "Always Running, Always Prepared: Hillary Clinton as a High School Politician," *Washington Post,* October 17, 2016.

32 "I simply could not imagine": Hillary Clinton, *Living History,* 21.

33 "right down to my cowgirl outfit": Ibid.

33 "returned to campus wearing a black armband": Ibid., 33.

34 "We don't need any more women at Harvard": Ibid., 38.

34 Hillary wrote that she suggested to Adams: Ibid.

35 "coercive protest": Ibid.

35 "We're not in the positions yet": Frances Stead Sellers and Marilyn W. Thompson, "Hillary Clinton's Breakout Moment at Wellesley College," *Washington Post,* August 14, 2016.

35 "Courtesy is not one of the stronger virtues": Ibid.

35 *Life* magazine featured her: "The Class of '69," *Life,* June 20, 1969.

35 During a photo session: Ben Cosgrove, "Hillary Clinton's First National Splash," Life.com.

36 "I am grateful that Hillary": William J. Clinton, "Remarks and an Exchange with Reporters on Health Care Reform," The American Presidency Project at U.C. Santa Barbara website, January 25, 1993.

36 In October 1993: Robert Pear, "Congress Is Given Clinton Proposal for Health Care," *New York Times,* October 28, 1993.

37 "This will be an opportunity": Ibid.

37 By the summer, Vince Foster: Stephen Labaton, "A Report on His Suicide Portrays a Deeply Troubled Vince Foster," *New York Times,* October 11, 1997.

37 $52 million: Lorraine Adams, "$52 Million Starr Probe Costliest Ever," *Washington Post,* April 1, 2000.

38 convicted of bank fraud: Susan Schmidt, "James McDougal Dies While Awaiting Parole," *Washington Post,* March 9, 1998.

38 farmers doused an effigy of Hillary: "Kentuckians Burn First Lady in Effigy," *Washington Post,* August 29, 1994.

38 "I don't know how they got so close": Author interview.

38 "I regret very much": Erin C. J. Robertson, "When Dems Lost in the 1994 Midterms, Hillary Clinton Took the Blame #TBT," *Washington Post,* November 6, 2014.

39 "The issue is that Hillary really pushed": Author interview.

39 "If I had known that being a First Lady": Author interview.

39 "a dream for me": Ibid.

40 "I started doing things": Ibid.

40 Hillary traveled to Beijing: "Hillary Rodham Clinton: Remarks to the U.N. 4th World Conference on Women Plenary Session," AmericanRhetoric.com.

40 **"radical feminist" agenda:** Amy Chozick, "Hillary Clinton's Beijing Speech on Women Resonates 20 Years Later," *New York Times,* September 5, 2015.

40 **"Human rights are women's rights":** Ibid.

40 **"Not only would this serve":** Ibid.

40 **"It was a call-in show":** Author interview.

41 **a woman approached her:** Todd S. Purdum, "The First Lady's Newest Role: Newspaper Columnist," *New York Times,* July 24, 1995.

41 **" 'You sure look like Hillary Clinton' ":** Hillary Clinton, Talking It Over, July 23, 1995.

41 **"As time evolved":** Author interview.

42 **"Hillary Clinton is a woman":** Karen Tumulty, "How Hillary Clinton Helped Create What She Later Called the 'Vast Right-Wing Conspiracy,'" *Washington Post,* September 3, 2016.

42 **"vast right-wing conspiracy":** Ibid.

42 **"inappropriate intimacy":** Hillary Clinton, *Living History,* 466.

43 **"the most devastating, shocking and hurtful":** Ibid.

43 **"Gingrich had a big role":** Author interview.

43 **She left office with approval ratings:** Wendy W. Simmons, "Eight Dramatic Years Ending on a Positive Note for Hillary Clinton," Gallup, January 3, 2001.

43 **"Americans are fundamentally fair":** Hillary Clinton, *Living History,* 477.

44 **"When the Taliban":** Author interview.

44 **"God's green earth":** Ibid.

44 **"a classic sort of example":** Author interview.

CHAPTER THREE: TRADITION

45 **The listening session:** Mike Allen, "Inside Biden's Private Chat with Historians," *Axios,* March 25, 2021.

46 **"I'm no FDR":** Ibid.

48 **"A year plus":** Author interview.

49 **"What interests me":** Recording obtained by author.

51 **"The meeting that I was in":** Author interview.

52 **"Well, not really":** Author interview.

53 **"a spring reborn":** "First Inaugural Address of William J. Clinton; January 20, 1993," Yale Law School website.

53 **"an angel still rides":** "Full Text of President George W. Bush's Inaugural Speech," ABC News.

53 **"made for this moment":** "Inaugural Address by President Barack Obama," ObamaWhiteHouse.archives.gov.

53 **"This American carnage stops right here":** "Full text: 2017 Donald Trump Inauguration Speech Transcript," *Politico.*

53 **"We shall write":** Aaron Blake, "4 Takeaways from Joe Biden's Inaugural Address," *Washington Post,* January 20, 2021.

54 **"I wouldn't call it a dynasty":** Page, *The Matriarch,* 306.

55 **rebuffed by Donald Trump:** James Barragán, "Texas Attorney General Ken

Paxton Easily Defeats George P. Bush in GOP Primary Runoff," *Texas Tribune*, May 24, 2022.

55 **only achieving a 25 percent:** George Lardner, Jr., and Lois Romano, "At Height of Vietnam, Bush Picks Guard," *Washington Post*, July 28, 1999.

56 **annual medical exam:** Andrew Glass, "George W. Bush Suspended from Texas Air National Guard, Aug. 1, 1972," *Politico*, August 1, 2013.

56 **"One of my first recollections":** Ibid.

56 **he was arrested:** "Bush Acknowledges 1976 DUI Charge," CNN, November 2, 2000.

56 **would later recall 1974:** Jonathan Weisman, "Bush Says He's Been Drug-Free 25 Years," *Baltimore Sun*, August 20, 1999.

57 **would sit and read:** Kristine Hansen, "Laura Bush's Childhood Home in Midland, Texas Goes Up for Sale," *Chron*, May 16, 2017.

57 **"Any sort of pretensions":** "Laura Bush, from West Texas to the White House," NPR, May 6, 2010.

57 **"It was the first time that I had prayed to God":** Laura Bush, *Spoken from the Heart* (New York: Scribner, 2010), Kindle location 1047.

58 **"she is an empathetic person":** Ann Gerhart, "First Ladies Influence Image," C-SPAN, February 8, 2014.

58 **drive-in theater:** A. L. Bardach, "Behind Laura Bush's Car Crash," *Daily Beast*, July 14, 2017.

58 **"You just never know":** Ann Gerhart, *The Perfect Wife: The Life and Choices of Laura Bush* (New York: Simon & Schuster, 2005), 34.

59 **"when he did that":** Ibid., 35.

59 **"a lovely creature":** Ibid., 48.

59 **"Audrey Hepburn walking into the Animal House":** Ibid., 57.

59 **"I read, I smoke, and I admire":** Ibid., 51.

60 **Laura was the one:** Mimi Swartz, "The Good Wife," *Texas Monthly*, November 2004.

60 **"It wasn't like other couples":** Gerhart, *The Perfect Wife*, 50.

60 **"they hate to be 'interpreted'":** Author interview.

60 **"I promise you":** Jill Biden, *Where the Light Enters*, 68.

61 **"'Honey, you'll be the kickoff speaker'":** Frank Bruni, "For Laura Bush, a Direction She Never Wished to Go In," *New York Times*, July 31, 2000.

61 **"This is a guy who's got problems":** Gerhart, *The Perfect Wife*, 74.

61 **"It's either Jim Beam or me":** Laura Bush, *Spoken from the Heart*, Kindle location 1856.

61 **fortieth-birthday weekend:** Laura Bush, *Spoken from the Heart*, Kindle location 1857.

61 **"Our marriage was enduring":** Ibid.

62 **"My motivation was":** Nicholas D. Kristof, "For Bush, Thrill Was in Father's Chase," *New York Times*, August 29, 2000.

62 **a $5,000-a-month:** Ibid.

62 **"I'm a married man":** Ibid.

63 **compassionate brand of conservatism:** Alison Mitchell, "Bush Draws Campaign Theme from More Than 'the Heart,'" *New York Times*, June 12, 2000.

63 **a historic increase in executions:** Jim Yardley, "Bush and the Death Penalty; Texas' Busy Death Chamber Helps Define Bush's Tenure," *New York Times*, January 7, 2000.

63 **"'if I'm going to be a public figure'":** Gerhart, *The Perfect Wife*, 92.

63 **"She's a Republican by marriage":** Author interview.

63 **"I think she was good":** Author interview.

64 **"I have a lifelong passion":** Elaine Sciolino, "Laura Bush Sees Everything in Its Place, Including Herself," *New York Times*, January 15, 2001.

66 **"parents need to reassure their children":** Laura Bush, *Spoken from the Heart*, Kindle location 3140.

66 **"From the way he spoke":** Ibid.

66 **2,977 people:** "9/11: The Steel of American Resolve," National Archives, GeorgeWBushLibrary.gov.

66 **soared to 86 percent:** "Bush and Public Opinion: Reviewing the Bush Years and the Public's Final Verdict," Pew Research Center website, December 12, 2008.

66 **approval ratings cratered:** Hannah Hartig and Carroll Doherty, "Two Decades Later, the Enduring Legacy of 9/11," Pew Research Center website, September 2, 2021.

67 **"Civilized people":** David Stout, "Mrs. Bush Cites Women's Plight Under Taliban," *New York Times*, November 18, 2001.

67 **"perhaps a reaction":** Lauren Wright, *On Behalf of the President: Presidential Spouses and White House Communications Strategy Today.*

68 **"$8 million advance":** Elisabeth Bumiller, "Laura Bush's View of Life After 9-11," *New York Times*, November 9, 2001.

68 **"I'm also working out":** Ibid.

68 **"Everybody knew":** Author interview.

68 **"all families":** Elisabeth Bumiller, "The Egg Roll (Again!) Becomes a Stage for Controversy," *New York Times*, April 10, 2006.

69 **"Sure, of course, everyone does":** Ibid.

69 **"First ladies are stereotyped":** Krissah Thompson, "Laura Bush's Latest Role: Booster of Her Husband's Legacy," *Washington Post*, September 9, 2014.

70 **"I'd been studying First Ladies":** Author interview.

70 **approval rating among American adults:** Jeffrey M. Jones, "Laura Bush Leaves White House as Popular Figure," Gallup, January 14, 2009.

70 **"universal human rights":** "Statement by President George W. Bush and Mrs. Laura Bush on Afghanistan," Bush Center website, December 22, 2022.

70 **"I used to say to her":** Author interview.

CHAPTER FOUR: EXPECTATION

72 **Jill was not the political "infant":** Richard Ben Cramer, *What It Takes: The Way to the White House* (New York: Vintage, 1993), 556.

73 **"The boys actually knew"**: Joe Biden, *Promises to Keep*, 119.

73 **"Honey, don't listen to anyone"**: Cramer, *What It Takes*, 618.

74 **all curated by her longtime stylist**: André-Naquian Wheeler, "Meet the Stylist Behind Michelle Obama's Bottega Moment," *Vogue*, November 23, 2022.

74 **twisted into tree braids**: @kitchentalkwithnjeri on Instagram, December 23, 2022.

74 **a question she detests**: "Michelle Obama: Being Kind to Myself Is a Challenge," BBC, November 15, 2022.

75 **She wanted to say no**: Michelle Obama, *The Light We Carry: Overcoming in Uncertain Times* (New York: Crown, 2022), 62.

75 **"I didn't want to live with"**: Ibid.

76 **"weird" before she met him**: Jodi Kantor and Jeff Zeleny, "Michelle Obama Adds New Role to Balancing Act," *New York Times*, May 15, 2007.

76 **"I'd have to think"**: Susan Saulny, "Michelle Obama Thrives in Campaign Trenches," *New York Times*, February 14, 2008.

76 **"I didn't come to politics"**: Michelle Obama, *Michelle Obama in Her Own Words*, edited by Lisa Rogak (New York: PublicAffairs, 2009), 115.

76 **"For the first time"**: Tom Kertscher, "David Clarke Says Michelle Obama Said She Was Proud of U.S. Only After Barack Obama Became President," PolitiFact, February 23, 2017.

76 **"Obama's baby mama"**: "Fox News Calls Michelle Obama 'Baby Mama,'" CBS News, June 13, 2008.

76 **a speech criticizing "whitey"**: Ta-Nehisi Coates, "The Michelle Obama 'Whitey' Video," *The Atlantic*, May 25, 2008.

76 **"something that George Jefferson"**: Michael Powell and Jodi Kantor, "After Attacks, Michelle Obama Looks for a New Introduction," *New York Times*, June 18, 2008.

77 **$656 million**: "Candidate Summary, 2008 Cycle," OpenSecrets.org.

77 **"careful and slightly anxious preparation"**: Michelle Obama, *The Light We Carry*, 247.

77 **"the affirming embrace of a father's love"**: "Transcript: Michelle Obama's Convention Speech," NPR, August 25, 2008.

77 **"eighteen million cracks in the glass ceiling"**: Ibid.

77 **53 percent of the popular vote**: Michael Nelson, "Barack Obama: Campaigns and Elections," University of Virginia, Miller Center website.

78 **"No, ma'am"**: Emily Stewart, "Watch John McCain Defend Barack Obama Against a Racist Voter in 2008," *Vox*, September 1, 2018.

78 **$273,618 a year**: D'Angelo Gore, "Michelle Obama's Salary," FactCheck.org, May 17, 2009.

78 **"It is something of an irony"**: Rachel L. Swarns, "From Home and Away, Advice for a First Lady," *New York Times*, November 23, 2008.

78 **Michelle is still explaining**: Kristine Parks, "Michelle Obama Claims She Was Criticized by Feminists for Prioritizing Motherhood in White House," Fox News, December 22, 2022.

78 **"I have to control what I can'"**: Candice Ortiz, "Michelle Obama Recalls

Backlash to Her Prioritizing Being 'Mom-in-Chief' at White House: 'I Got Criticized by Feminists for That,'" Mediaite.com, December 21, 2022.

78 **she considered delaying:** Jodi Kantor, *The Obamas* (New York: Back Bay Books, 2012), 16.

79 **Melvinia Shields McGruder:** Rachel L. Swarns and Jodi Kantor, "In First Lady's Roots, a Complex Path from Slavery," *New York Times*, October 7, 2009.

80 **"How come you talk like a white girl?":** Michelle Obama, *Becoming* (New York: Crown, 2018), 40.

80 **"a kind of equal-opportunity nirvana":** Ibid., 54.

81 **"it was safe to be smart":** Ibid., 58.

81 **"The fanfare was fun":** Ibid., 64.

81 **enrolled in the fall of 1981:** Michael Powell and Jodi Kantor, "Michelle Obama Is Ready for Her Close-up," *New York Times*, June 18, 2008.

81 **"If you're young and black":** Powell and Kantor, "After Attacks, Michelle Obama Looks for a New Introduction."

81 **"The path I have chosen":** Ibid.

82 **"To me, he was sort of like a unicorn":** Michelle Obama, *Becoming*, 112.

83 **"As Sasha and Malia grew":** Ibid., 203.

84 **"You actually pulled this off?":** Jodi Kantor, *The Obamas*, 15.

84 **"The political committees wanted her":** Author interview.

84 **"She had these big sunglasses":** Ibid.

84 **"She was fiercely protective":** Author interview.

85 **A visit to CVS:** Lisa Respers France, "Ellen DeGeneres Goes Shopping with FLOTUS," CNN, September 15, 2016.

85 **launch day:** Sheryl Gay Stolberg, "Childhood Obesity Battle Is Taken Up by First Lady," *New York Times*, February 9, 2010.

86 **"solving our obesity challenge":** Ibid.

87 **"Don't tell me that's not a serious person":** Author interview.

87 **"It made me wonder":** "Remarks by the First Lady at Tuskegee University Commencement Address," ObamaWhiteHouse.archives.gov, May 9, 2015.

87 **"And at the end of the day":** Ibid.

88 **"When they go low, we go high":** Sunlen Serfaty and Eric Bradner, "Michelle Obama: 'When They Go Low, We Go High,'" CNN, July 26, 2016.

88 **"I can't believe":** "Remarks by the First Lady at Hillary for America Campaign Event in Manchester, NH," ObamaWhiteHouse.archives.gov, October 13, 2016.

88 **"You know I hate politics":** "Michelle Obama's Full Remarks at the Democratic National Convention," Reuters, August 18, 2020.

89 **"Maybe more than I ever had":** Michelle Obama, *The Light We Carry*, 36.

CHAPTER FIVE: RELUCTANCE

90 **the family would be fine:** Scott Stump, "Joe Biden's Grandchildren Open Up About Their Bond with Obama's Daughters," Today.com, January 20, 2021.

90 **"We were in the in-between":** Author interview.

91 **"In some ways she was a less excited political spouse"**: Author interview.

91 **"Things were happening"**: Author interview.

91 **"I would rail against injustice"**: Author interview.

92 **"I would be very traditional"**: Joyce Wadler, "A Model as First Lady? Think Traditional," *New York Times*, December 1, 1999.

93 **"I want to do something great"**: Mary Jordan, *The Art of Her Deal: The Untold Story of Melania Trump* (New York: Simon & Schuster, 2020), 77.

93 **She was a homebody**: Ibid.

93 **"He wanted my number"**: Alex Kuczynski, "Melania Trump's American Dream," *Harper's Bazaar*, January 6, 2016.

94 **"If I couldn't do that"**: Jordan, *The Art of Her Deal*, 120.

94 **"Melania Knauss: cleared for takeoff!"**: GQ Staff, "Melania Trump—the First Lady in Our Nude Photo Shoot," GQ-magazine.co.uk, November 8, 2016.

94 **he had been "bombarded"**: Alex Ritman, "GQ Editor Recalls Donald Trump Wife's Controversial Nude Photo Shoot," *Hollywood Reporter*, March 25, 2016.

94 **"I'm going to do everything I can"**: GQ Staff, "Melania Trump."

94 **"I will put all my effort into it"**: Ibid.

95 **"I don't want to have to go home"**: Donald and Melania Trump, *Larry King Live*, May 17, 2005.

95 **"We are very equal in the relationship"**: Ibid.

95 **"He's 'Donald' to her"**: Katie Rogers, Julie Hirschfeld Davis, and Maggie Haberman, "Melania Trump, a Mysterious First Lady, Weathers a Chaotic White House," *New York Times*, August 17, 2018.

95 **"Why doesn't he show his birth certificate?"**: Michael Barbaro, "Donald Trump Clung to 'Birther' Lie for Years, and Still Isn't Apologetic," *New York Times*, September 16, 2016.

96 **Trump claimed on NBC**: Alexander Mooney, "Trump Sends Investigators to Hawaii to Look into Obama," April 7, 2011.

96 **"It's not only Donald"**: Lily Herman, "Melania Trump Supported Her Husband's Racist Birtherism Claims on TV," *Teen Vogue*, January 23, 2017.

96 **On April 27, 2011**: Dan Pfeiffer, "President Obama's Long Form Birth Certificate," ObamaWhiteHouse.archives.gov.

97 **"We must protect our borders"**: *New York Times* reporters, "Donald Trump's Inaugural Speech, Annotated," *New York Times*, January 20, 2017.

98 **"her family and her home"**: Author interview.

98 **"I didn't want to look back in ten years"**: Michael Scherer, "The Donald Has Landed. Deal with It," *Time*, August 20, 2015.

98 **Melania disassembled the draft**: Maggie Haberman and Michael Barbaro, "How Melania Trump's Speech Veered Off Course and Caused an Uproar," *New York Times*, July 19, 2016.

99 **"This was my mistake"**: Jason Horowitz, "Behind Melania Trump's Cribbed Lines, an Ex-Ballerina Who Loved Writing," *New York Times*, July 20, 2016.

99 **"You know, I'm automatically attracted"**: "Transcript: Donald Trump's Taped Comments About Women," *New York Times*, October 8, 2016.

99 **"The words my husband used"**: "Melania Trump Says Husband's Words Are

'Unacceptable' and Don't Represent Man She Knows," ABC News, October 8, 2016.

99   **"People think and talk about me"**: Eric Bradner, "Melania Trump: Donald Trump Was 'Egged On' into 'Boy Talk,'" CNN, October 18, 2016.

99   **"boy talk"**: Ibid.

100 **"a fantastic First Lady"**: NewsToday NT, "Trump on Melania: 'I Think She's Gonna Be a Fantastic First Lady,'" YouTube, February 16, 2017.

101 **"I think she felt important and empowered"**: Author interview.

101 **Melania renegotiated the particulars**: Jordan, *The Art of Her Deal*, 34.

102 **"She's so private"**: Author interview.

102 **filed a defamation lawsuit**: Cory Shaffer, "Ex-Trump Staffer Max Miller Files Defamation Lawsuit Against Stephanie Grisham over Abuse Allegations," Cleveland.com, October 5, 2021.

104 **"Our country encourages freedom of speech"**: @FLOTUS45 on Twitter, August 12, 2017

104 **the basketball star LeBron James**: Amanda Holpuch and Ben Jacobs, "Melania Trump Praises LeBron James in Statement After Husband Insults Him," *The Guardian*, August 4, 2018.

105 **another plagiarism scandal**: Katie Rogers, "As Melania Trump Faces Plagiarism Claims, Her Staff Lashes Out at News Media," *New York Times*, May 8, 2018.

105 **"At its launch"**: Author interview.

105 **"The Fake News Media has been so unfair"**: @realDonaldTrump on Twitter, June 6, 2018.

105 **"She wasn't dying or anything like that"**: Author interview.

105 **She also traveled separately**: Katie Rogers and Maggie Haberman, "Melania Trump, Out of Sight Since Report of Husband's Infidelity, to Attend State of the Union," *New York Times*, January 29, 2018.

106 **"I think she was pissed"**: Author interview.

106 **"a real example"**: Author interview.

106 **"My wife feels very strongly about it"**: Kate Bennett, "Melania Trump Helped Convince President to Address Family Separations," CNN, June 20, 2018.

107 **her attorney Michael Wildes**: Mary Jordan, "Questions Linger About How Melania Trump, a Slovenian Model, Scored 'the Einstein Visa,'" *Washington Post*, March 1, 2018.

107 **H-1B visa:** "H-1B Program," U.S. Department of Labor website.

107 **Viktor and Amalija Knavs**: Annie Correal and Emily Cochrane, "Melania Trump's Parents Become U.S. Citizens, Using 'Chain Migration' Trump Hates," *New York Times*, August 9, 2018.

108 **"Some people come in"**: @realDonaldTrump on Twitter, November 1, 2017.

108 **I REALLY DON'T CARE, DO U?**: Katie Rogers, "Melania Trump Wore a Jacket Saying 'I Really Don't Care' on Her Way to Texas Shelters," *New York Times*, June 21, 2018.

108 **"You know, I often asking myself"**: David Choi, "Melania Trump Says the Message on Her Controversial 'I Really Don't Care. Do U?' Jacket Was Meant

for 'the Left-Wing Media Who Are Criticizing Me,'" Insider.com, October 12, 2018.

109 **"most bullied person in the world"**: Katie Rogers, "Melania Trump Talks About Being 'the Most Bullied Person' in the World," *New York Times*, October 11, 2018.

109 **"She wasn't a big-picture woman"**: Author interview.

109 **pith helmet**: Katie Rogers, "Melania Trump Raises Eyebrows in Africa with Another White Hat," *New York Times*, October 5, 2018.

109 **"I wish people would focus on what I do"**: Katie Rogers, "On Africa Trip, First Lady Reveals a Trump-like Side," *New York Times*, October 7, 2018.

110 **"an elegant limestone exterior"**: Author interview.

111 **"I think it is challenging"**: Ibid.

111 **"Yesterday, POTUS (and FLOTUS)"**: Author-obtained correspondence.

112 **"The fact that the Trumps"**: Author interview.

113 **"I'm working my ass off"**: Caroline Kelly, "Secretly Recorded Tapes Show Melania Trump's Frustration at Criticism for Family Separation Policy and Her Bashing of Christmas Decorations," CNN, October 2, 2020.

114 **"I think she felt very independent and strong"**: Author interview.

115 **"pretty checked out and exhausted"**: Author interview.

116 **"Something *bad* happened"**: Ibid.

116 **whether she would still have access to security**: Author interview.

116 **"What I saw was a war scene"**: Luke Broadwater, "'Trump Was at the Center': Jan. 6 Hearing Lays Out Case in Vivid Detail," *New York Times*, June 9, 2022.

116 **"All she cared about"**: Author interview.

117 **when Donald asked Max Miller**: Stephanie Grisham, *I'll Take Your Questions Now: What I Saw at the Trump White House* (New York: Harper, 2021), 305.

117 **"The work of the moment"**: Remarks to the Nation by President-Elect Joe Biden in Wilmington, Delaware, The American Presidency Project, January 6, 2021.

117 **"We shall nobly save"**: Ibid.

118 **"GA, Dr B!"**: Author intervew.

118 **"I hardly ever see Jill unsettled"**: Author interview.

119 **"I can remember just thinking"**: Author interview.

119 **"some kind of mix"**: David S. Hilzenrath and Steven Mufson, "Keeper of the Flame," *Washington Post*, May 9, 1993.

120 **"There was a protocol breach"**: Annie Karni and Katie Rogers, "Can Someone Please Open the Door?" *New York Times*, January 21, 2021.

121 **the Bidens guard their privacy**: Katie Rogers, "In Delaware, Biden Indulges One of His Oldest Habits: Commuting," *New York Times*, June 4, 2021.

122 **"It was the culmination"**: Jordan Williams, "Jill Biden Thanks 'Service Members, First Responders, Civil Servants' in First Video Statement," *The Hill*, January 21, 2021.

122 **more gracious than he'd expected**: Maggie Haberman, Katie Benner, and Glenn Thrush, "The Final Days of the Trump White House: Chaos and Scattered Papers," *New York Times*, August 20, 2022.

122 **never forgive Trump:** Michelle Obama, *Becoming* (New York: Crown, 2018), 353.

123 **"typical good-luck letter":** Author interview.

123 **"I do a lot of correspondence:"** Ibid.

CHAPTER SIX: "THE PROFESSOR MUST TEACH"

126 **"a blessing from God":** Maggie Haberman and Katie Thomas, "Trump Calls His Illness 'a Blessing from God,'" *New York Times,* October 7, 2020.

126 **"He's in his damn basement again":** Aaron Sharockman, "Biden Isn't in the Basement, but the Trump Campaign Keeps Saying So," PolitiFact, October 4, 2020.

127 **"We're rounding the turn":** "Debate Transcript: Trump, Biden Final Presidential Debate Moderated by Kristen Welker," *USA Today,* October 23, 2020.

127 **"220,000 Americans dead":** Ibid.

127 **"Joey, no one is better than you":** @JoeBiden on Twitter, April 15, 2020.

127 **"I learned so much":** American Institute for Stuttering, "VP Joe Biden Delivers Heartfelt Speech on Stuttering at AIS Gala," YouTube, June 6, 2016.

128 **"People don't think about":** Author interview.

129 **"Through it all":** "Joe Biden and Dr. Jill Biden Speak Live from Luzerne County, Pennsylvania," YouTube, October 24, 2020.

129 **"You know, people":** Author interview.

130 **"He said, 'Barack called'":** Rita Braver, "Jill Biden: Second Lady of the Land," CBS News, December 13, 2009.

130 **"second banana":** Glenn Thrush, "Obama and Biden's Relationship Looks Rosy. It Wasn't Always That Simple," *New York Times,* August 16, 2019.

130 **"Turning down the nominee of your party":** Hunter Biden, *Beautiful Things* (New York: Gallery Books, 2021), 89.

130 **"We would love it":** Julie Bosman, "'Amtrak Joe' No More," *New York Times,* November 21, 2008.

131 **"He would write about":** Email from Jill Biden to colleagues, Freedom of Information Act request, *New York Times.*

131 **McClellan is beloved at NOVA:** "McClellan, Jimmie Rex," Living Legends of Alexandria website, 2012.

131 **"I told Joe when we were elected":** Symone Sanders interview with Jill Biden, MSNBC, May 7, 2022.

132 **"She would sit there":** Author interview.

132 **gave her first name as Nooria:** Author interview.

132 **"I didn't have insurance":** Lauren Lumpkin, "Most People Know Her as Jill Biden. But to Some She Is Dr. B, the Compassionate and Challenging Educator Who Went the Extra Mile," *Washington Post,* January 12, 2021.

132 **"Why . . . is my English professor":** Ibid.

133 **"tough grader":** Katie Rogers, "A First for a First Lady: Jill Biden Will Balance Her Career and East Wing Duties," *New York Times,* January 20, 2021.

133 **"She's their teacher":** Author interview.

133   **"My students are really nonplussed"**: Katie Rogers, "Jill Biden Is Chasing the President's Most Elusive Campaign Promise: Unity," *New York Times*, September 19, 2021.

133   **"I am getting pressure"**: Katie Glueck and Steve Eder, "Why Jill Biden Is Taking Time Off to Help Her Husband Get a Job," *New York Times*, February 1, 2020.

133   **"I'd like to talk to Joe first"**: Ibid.

134   **"I hope so"**: Rita Braver, *CBS News Sunday Morning*, "Dr. Biden on Family, Teaching, Loss and Levity," YouTube, August 9, 2020.

135   **"Baby," Joe said**: Author interview.

135   **$81,000 salary**: Asher Notheis, "Jill Biden Paid $80k+ for Her Fulltime Professor Job at Community College," *The College Fix*, August 16, 2021.

135   **"third rail" discussion topic**: Author interview.

135   **"The professor MUST teach"**: Email from Anthony Bernal to NOVA officials, Freedom of Information Act request, *New York Times*.

136   **"I took the training, but it is hard stuff"**: Email from Jill Biden to colleagues, Freedom of Information Act request, *New York Times*.

137   **"If we win, I'm gonna keep teaching"**: Author interview.

CHAPTER SEVEN: "THE KIND OF WOMAN I'D LIKE TO MEET"

138   **a guy named Bill Stevenson**: Author interview.

138   **"a look-at-me car"**: Ibid.

138   **she was friends with Stiltz**: Jill Biden, *Where the Light Enters*, 45.

138   **"staggeringly beautiful"**: Author interview.

139   **"That's the kind of woman I'd like to meet"**: Joe Biden, *Promises to Keep: On Life and Politics* (New York: Random House, 2008), 100.

140   **"beautiful millionaire"**: Kitty Kelley, "Death and the All-American Boy," *Washingtonian*, June 1, 1974.

140   **"She looks better than a Playboy bunny"**: Ibid.

140   **"I do indeed want to get married again"**: Ibid.

140   **"I know I could have easily made the White House"**: Ibid.

140   **"Um, this is Joe Biden?"**: Joe Biden, *Promises to Keep*, 100.

140   **"When I called back"**: Ibid.

141   **"Look, Frankie"**: Jill Biden, *Where the Light Enters*, 45.

141   **"I know her"**: Ibid.

141   **"My God, what have I gotten myself into?"**: Ibid., 46.

142   **she is a diehard fan**: Michael D. Shear and Katie Rogers, "Self-Proclaimed 'Philly Girl' Jill Biden Is Ready to Cheer on the Eagles," *New York Times*, February 10, 2023.

142   **"not shy"**: Author interview.

142   **"A couple of times it got a little rowdy"**: Ibid.

143   **"Shangri-la"**: Ibid.

143   **"As the oldest of five girls"**: Author interview.

143   **"They weren't quite the Montagues and Capulets"**: Ibid.

144 "star-crossed lovers": Ibid., 5.

144 inscrutable smile: @Flotus on Instagram, June 19, 2022.

144 her mother was nineteen: Author interview.

144 "ribbons of pasta": "Remarks Prepared for First Lady Jill Biden Honoring the 2022 National Student Poets and the 10th Anniversary of the Student Poets Program," WhiteHouse.gov, September 27, 2022.

145 "Ma wasn't a warm woman": Jill Biden, *Where the Light Enters*, 6.

145 "My mother's mother realized": Julie Pace and Darlene Superville, *Jill: A Biography of the First Lady* (New York: Little, Brown and Company, 2022), 11.

145 Mae, listed "rowdy-dow": "Mabel Frances Godfrey," Ancestry.com.

145 "She smiled and smiled and was a villain still": Ibid.

146 "I had to give a couple of students": Author interview.

146 "warped Ellis Island interpretation": Jill Biden, "My Family's Love Story," Forbes.com, December 20, 2018.

147 "In the sixties and seventies": Author interview.

147 "We dated the lifeguards": Pace and Superville, *Jill*, 8.

147 "I had to make money": Author interview.

147 "I looked at her": Author interview.

148 "destined for each other": Jill Biden, *Where the Light Enters*, 37.

149 "It was surreal": Ibid., 32.

149 Donald Scott Mackenzie: Ibid., 34.

150 "I didn't know Jill": Author interview.

150 "We got married in '70": "Jill Biden Denies Ex-Husband's Claim She Had Affair with Joe Biden Before They Split," *Inside Edition*, September 21, 2020.

151 "She hates him": Author interview.

151 "I think she thinks she was left behind": Author interview.

151 "She's a target": Ibid.

152 Carrying just eighty-nine dollars: Joe Biden, *Promises to Keep*, 27.

152 "When she turned toward me": Ibid., 28.

153 "You know, we're going to get married": Ibid., 31.

153 "I guess the only time": Al Cartwright, "Biden Wanted Wife to Organize Capital Office," *News Journal*, December 22, 1972.

153 "Once I had Neilia with me": Joe Biden, *Promises to Keep*, 33.

153 "I took mental notes": Valerie Biden Owens, *Growing Up Biden* (New York: Gallery Books, 2021), 66.

154 "'She's beautiful, Sue'": Abby Weiss, "The One," *Daily Orange*, February 2022.

155 "Hi! I'm Neilia Biden": Bill Frank, "When Everyone in Delaware Wept," *Morning News*, December 27, 1972.

155 "Biden is 29": Al Cartwright, "They All Thought They Could Beat Cale Boggs," *News Journal*, March 29, 1972.

155 "Cale Boggs' generation": *News Journal*, October 27, 1972.

155 "To Cale Boggs": Ibid.

156 "There were only two people": Cartwright, "Biden Wanted Wife to Organize Capital Office."

156 **"I don't know the Kennedys"**: "Neilia Biden Had It All, and Then . . . ," *News Journal,* December 19, 1972.

156 **"We have very few"**: Curtis Wilkie, "In Triumph or Tragedy, Chutzpah Is Biden's Thing," *News Journal,* January 3, 1973.

156 **"She was just a dynamo"**: Patricia Talorico, "Meet the Brains Behind Biden's First Victory," *News Journal,* November 10, 2020.

156 **"it's too perfect"**: Richard Ben Cramer, *What It Takes: The Way to the White House* (New York: Vintage, 1993).

157 **the Chevy spun for 150 feet**: Cartwright, "Biden Wanted Wife to Organize Capital Office."

157 **Their brother Jimmy called Valerie**: Ibid.

157 **he was given sedatives**: Ibid.

157 **"I would never have"**: Kelley, "Death and the All-American Boy."

158 **"She had an easy, natural beauty"**: Jill Biden, *Where the Light Enters,* 39.

158 **"Here they were"**: Ibid.

158 **"They were letting me in"**: "The Choice 2020: Trump vs. Biden," *Frontline,* PBS, September 22, 2020.

159 **"I had to be 100 percent"**: Jill Biden, *Where the Light Enters,* 64.

159 **"I've been as patient as I know"**: Ibid., 66.

159 **"Son Told Joe to Marry Jill"**: Al Cartwright, "Son Told Joe to Marry Jill," *News Journal,* July 17, 1977.

160 **"We've been dating"**: Ibid.

160 **"entitled to a little privacy"**: Ibid.

160 **"I thought the fact that"**: Al Cartwright, "Delaware," *News Journal,* July 24, 1977.

160 **"were like puppies"**: Jill Biden, *Where the Light Enters,* 53.

161 **"She is such an unusual human"**: Author interview.

CHAPTER EIGHT: "A FORCE TO BE RECKONED WITH"

162 **"I wanted a degree"**: Author interview.

163 **low enrollment**: Andréa Miller and Antonio Prado, "Remembering Claymont High: First White Public School in Delaware to Admit Black Students," *USA Today,* October 21, 2008.

163 **"I don't think Jill"**: Author interview.

163 **"I just cannot let this go by"**: Pace and Superville, *Jill,* 52.

164 **"were the first couple"**: Cindy McCain, *Stronger: Courage, Hope, and Humor in My Life with John McCain* (New York: Forum Books, 2021), 15.

164 **"red bandana clenched in his teeth"**: Robert Timberg, *The Nightingale's Song* (New York: Free Press, 1996), 266.

164 **"I started looking"**: Joe Biden, *Promises to Keep,* 149.

164 **"gut politician"**: Matt Flegenheimer, "Biden's First Run for President Was a Calamity. Some Missteps Still Resonate," *New York Times,* June 3, 2019.

165 **"Jill turns to him"**: Author interview.

165 **"We got a call, Jill"**: Jill Biden, *Where the Light Enters,* 119.

166 "as if he were slowly becoming an old family portrait": Ibid., 120.

166 "We have to get him to the hospital now": Ibid., 119.

166 "Wait a minute!": Ibid., 124.

166 "She's right": Ibid., 124.

167 "He looked me in the eye": Michael Daly, "Surgeon Who Saved Biden's Life Recalls Fateful Prediction," *Daily Beast,* November 8, 2020.

167 "At that point, it was all over": Author interview.

167 "She has a very good sense": Author interview.

167 "I'd rather be at home making love": Jeff Dufour, "Making Love in the White House Is Even Better," *The Hill,* June 27, 2006.

168 "You mean the one I've had": Author interview.

168 "You see these boots?" Author interview.

168 "a couple of times": Author interview.

169 "very fine people on both sides": Angie Drobnic Holan, "In Context: Donald Trump's 'Very Fine People on Both Sides' Remarks (Transcript)," PolitiFact, April 26, 2019.

169 Hunter had become "unmoored": Author interview.

170 "an accounting of the vulnerabilities": Author interview.

170 "She's in a different place": Author interview.

171 "brightest of a thousand points": "Major Moments of President George Bush's Funeral," *New York Times,* December 5, 2018.

171 " 'Joe, you have to decide' ": Author interview.

171 "He doesn't give up, as you know": Ibid.

171 "She very much believed": Katie Rogers, "Jill Biden Is Chasing the President's Most Elusive Campaign Promise: Unity," *New York Times,* September 19, 2021.

171 "That meant she had a seat": Author interview.

172 "Yes, it's happened to me": Morgan Gstalter, "Jill Biden: Joe Will Need to Be a 'Better Judge' When It Comes to Comforting People," *The Hill,* April 30, 2019.

172 "I cannot be satisfied": Sheryl Gay Stolberg and Carl Hulse, "Joe Biden Expresses Regret to Anita Hill, but She Says 'I'm Sorry' Is Not Enough," *New York Times,* April 25, 2019.

173 "He apologized": Danielle Kurtzleben, "Jill Biden Says 'It's Time to Move On' from Anita Hill Controversy," NPR, May 7, 2019.

173 "You can't change the candidate": Author interview.

173 "Your candidate might be better": Katie Glueck, "Jill Biden, Stressing Trump Matchup, Makes a Blunt Case for Her Husband," *New York Times,* August 19, 2019.

174 "More of this!!": Author interview.

174 "Whenever I was angry": Author interview.

174 "I've just been so busy": Email from Jill Biden to colleagues, Freedom of Information Act request, *New York Times.*

175 "How can I convince you?": Holly Bailey, "Jill Biden Tries to Close the Deal for Her Husband, One Tiny Iowa Town at a Time," *Washington Post,* January 16, 2020.

175 "You can take the girl out of Philly": @DrBiden on Twitter, February 10, 2020.

175 **"The people of South Carolina"**: CBS News, "'The People of South Carolina Gave Us Wings,' Jill Biden Says After Joe's South Carolina Victory," YouTube, February 29, 2020.

176 **"It was a rough few weeks"**: Author interview.

176 **"Let dairy die!"**: Jonathan Allen and Amie Parnes, *Lucky: How Joe Biden Barely Won the Presidency* (New York: Crown, 2021), 240.

176 **"We're okay"**: Bloomberg Quicktake, "Jill Biden Moves to Block Protesters from Her Husband During Super Tuesday Rally," YouTube, March 4, 2020.

176 **"Let's be clear"**: Allen and Parnes, *Lucky*, 240.

177 **"Goddamn it"**: Author interview.

177 **"Going high means"**: "Michelle Obama's Full Remarks at the Democratic National Convention," Reuters, August 18, 2020.

178 **"When I taught English"**: "Dr. Jill Biden 2020 DNC Speech Transcript," Rev.com, August 18, 2020.

178 **"You know, motherhood"**: Ibid.

179 **"Hey, everyone"**: Ibid.

179 **"Tonight, Jill Biden"**: @LindseyGrahamSC on Twitter, August 18, 2020.

179 **"Her nickname"**: Author interview.

CHAPTER NINE: "A QUIET ASSET"

182 **"work marriage"**: Author interview.

183 **"'Oh my god, I love you'"**: Author interview.

183 **"trash talker"**: Author interview.

183 **a report on the news website *Politico***: Alex Thompson and Tina Sfondeles, "Jill's Enforcer Has a Mean Streak," *Politico*, August 2, 2021.

184 **"If you're ever working"**: Alexander Kacala, "Biden Promises Appointees He Will Fire Them 'On the Spot' If They Disrespect Others," Today.com, January 20, 2021.

184 **"Anthony's loyalty"**: Thompson and Sfondeles, "Jill's Enforcer."

184 **"It is my job"**: Author interview.

185 **"Her life's ambition"**: Author interview.

185 **"This opportunity came about"**: @Flotus on Twitter, July 27, 2021

186 **Jill was on the road within weeks**: Katie Rogers and Erica L. Green, "Biden Administration Steps Up Push for School Reopenings," *New York Times*, March 3, 2021.

187 **"Jill was a community college professor"**: "Remarks as Prepared for Delivery by President Biden—Address to a Joint Session of Congress," WhiteHouse.gov, April 28, 2021.

187 **the estimated $88 billion**: Aatish Bhatia, Francesca Paris, and Margot Sanger-Katz, "See Everything the White House Wanted, and Everything It Got," *New York Times*, October 20, 2022.

187 **"told me the same old story"**: Author interview.

188 **"'Joe, tough,'"**: Author interview.

189 **"You know, it's evolving"**: Author interview.

190 "Talk to her about delegates": Author interview.

191 "Sí, se pawd-wey": Nur Ibrahim, "Did Jill Biden Mispronounce the Spanish Phrase 'Si Se Puede'?," Snopes.com, April 2, 2021

192 "She doesn't like to make a mistake": Author interview.

193 "We feel naked!": Katie Rogers and Nicholas Fandos, "Removing Masks Becomes the First Bipartisan Activity of Biden's Washington," *New York Times*, May 13, 2021.

194 how her private journal: Michael S. Schmidt and Adam Goldman, "Ashley Biden's Diary Was Shown at Trump Fund-Raiser. Weeks Later, Project Veritas Called Her," *New York Times*, March 20, 2022.

196 "Part of my disappointment": "Remarks by President Biden and President Andrzej Duda of Poland in Briefing on the Humanitarian Efforts for Ukraine," WhiteHouse.gov, March 25, 2022.

198 "I thought it was important": Katie Rogers, "Jill Biden's Secret Ukraine Trip," *New York Times*, May 8, 2022.

198 "We understand what it takes": Ibid.

199 a crowd screamed: Abby Livingston, "'Do something!' Biden Is Urged as He Leaves Uvalde Church," *Texas Tribune*, May 9, 2022.

200 "I went to see her in the hospital": Katie Rogers, "Jill Biden, Rebuking 'Extremist Republicans,' Discusses Friend's Abortion," October 7, 2022.

201 "one of the girls at school": Jill Biden, *Where the Light Enters*, 28.

201 "I had to give a little bit": Author interview.

201 people are more likely to donate: Katie Rogers, "Democrats in Tight Races Turn to Jill Biden on the Campaign Trail," *New York Times*, October 16, 2022.

201 "I'm asking you to dig a little deeper": Ibid.

202 "She's a quiet asset": Author interview.

CHAPTER TEN: "I REMEMBER EVERY SLIGHT"

204 "It's human": Author interview.

204 "Part of what I want": Virginia Chamlee, "Doug Emhoff Makes Trip to Highlight Food Insecurity in First Outing as First-Ever Second Gentleman," *People*, January 28, 2021.

204 "He's an apprentice": Asma Khalid, "Doug Emhoff Is America's First Second Gentleman. In Paris, He Showed What That Means," NPR, November 14, 2021.

205 "He seems like the kind of person": Chun Su-jin, "U.S. 'Second Gentleman' Gets a Kick out of Seoul," *Korea JoongAng Daily*, May 11, 2022.

205 disparaged feminists: Haeryun Kang, "How South Korea's 'Anti-Feminist' Election Fueled a Gender War," *Washington Post*, March 12, 2022.

205 "Lifting women up": Chun Su-jin, "U.S. 'Second Gentleman.'"

206 "We did it, Joe!": @EugeneDaniels on Twitter, March 15, 2022.

206 "Men are doing what women have always done": Author interview.

207 Both immigrants: Ellen Barry, "How Kamala Harris's Immigrant Parents Found a Home, and Each Other, in a Black Study Group," *New York Times*, September 13, 2020

207 "She raised us to be proud": "Transcript: Kamala Harris' DNC Speech," CNN, August 20, 2020.

208 "All of the circumstances": Author interview.

208 "The vice president and I": Author interview.

210 "What are Republicans for?": Michael D. Shear, "Biden Says He Will Pursue a Scaled-Back Agenda as He Defends His First Year in Office," *New York Times,* January 19, 2022.

211 He made several factual errors: Jessica McDonald, Robert Farley, et al., "Fact-Checking Biden's Press Conference," FactCheck.org, January 20, 2022.

211 "Thank you very much for this honor": "Remarks by President Biden in Press Conference," WhiteHouse.gov, January 19, 2022.

214 student-loan forgiveness: Michael D. Shear, Jim Tankersley, and Zolan Kanno-Youngs, "Biden Gave In to Pressure on Student Debt Relief After Months of Doubt," *New York Times,* August 26, 2022.

214 "I remember every slight": Jill Biden, *Where the Light Enters,* 25.

215 "I think when you have things thrown at you": Author interview.

215 feeling left out of the jokes: Hunter Biden, *Beautiful Things,* 60.

215 "doing a great job": Ibid.

215 "the one who had an easier time with it": Author interview.

215 appeared to disparage several family members: Lea Veloso, "Hunter Biden Allegedly Called Stepmom Jill a 'Vindictive Moron' in Newly Uncovered Texts," Yahoo.com, July 9, 2022.

215 subject of a federal investigation: Adam Entous, Michael S. Schmidt, and Katie Benner, "Hunter Biden's Tangled Tale Comes Front and Center," *New York Times,* January 11, 2023.

216 Hunter's business dealings: Katie Benner, Kenneth P. Vogel, and Michael S. Schmidt, "Hunter Biden Paid Tax Bill, but Broad Federal Investigation Continues," *New York Times,* March 16, 2022.

216 Hunter struck a deal: Glenn Thrush and Michael S. Schmidt, "Competing Accounts of Justice Dept.'s Handling of Hunter Biden Case," June 27, 2023.

216 Jill called him: Ibid.

216 "You have the exact same eyes": Hunter Biden, "Hunter Biden: 'I Come from a Family Forged by Tragedies,'" *Sydney Morning Herald,* May 7, 2021.

216 "Not anymore": Ibid., 233.

217 Hunter settled a child-support case: Katie Rogers, "Hunter Biden's Daughter and a Tale of Two Families," *New York Times,* July 1, 2023.

221 "I'm his mom": Author interview.

221 the *New York Post* reported: Emily Smith, "Beau Biden's Widow Having Affair with His Married Brother," *New York Post,* March 1, 2017.

221 "I'm convinced that depriving someone": Hunter Biden, *Beautiful Things,* 107.

221 Kathleen filed for divorce: Emily Smith and Julia Marsh, "Inside Hunter and Kathleen Biden's Divorce," March 2, 2017.

222 upset by Bush's reelection: Kathryn Q. Seelye, "Jill Biden Heads Toward Life in the Spotlight," *New York Times,* August 24, 2008.

222 "Jill's a dove": Author interview.

222 **"my son's deployment"**: Dr. Jill Biden and Raúl Colón, *Don't Forget, God Bless Our Troops* (New York: Simon & Schuster/Paula Wiseman Books, 2012).

223 **he invokes Beau's memory often**: Katie Rogers, "In Invoking Beau, Biden Broaches a Loss That's Guided His Presidency," *New York Times*, September 4, 2021.

223 **"I respect anybody that lost somebody"**: Ibid.

223 **"I love him"**: Author interview.

223 **about the "civility"**: Andrew Prokop, "Joe Biden's Controversial Comments About Segregationists and Wealthy Donors, Explained," *Vox*, June 19, 2019.

223 **"a little girl in California"**: Dylan Matthews, Dara Lind, Li Zhou, German Lopez, and David Roberts, "4 Winners and 3 Losers from the Second Night of the Democratic Debates," *Vox*, June 28, 2019.

223 **picture of a young Kamala Harris**: @KamalaHarris on Twitter, June 27, 2019.

224 **"Every candidate's record"**: @IanSams on Twitter, July 6, 2019.

224 **Within six months**: Jonathan Martin, Astead W. Herndon, and Alexander Burns, "How Kamala Harris's Campaign Unraveled," *New York Times*, November 29, 2019.

224 **"There are millions of people"**: Jonathan Martin and Alexander Burns, *This Will Not Pass: Trump, Biden, and the Battle for America's Future* (New York: Simon & Schuster, 2022), 55.

224 **"It's been a little hard"**: Andrew C. McCarthy, "Podesta Leaks: Ron Klain's 'Role in the Biden Demise,'" *National Review*, October 12, 2016.

225 **"Do you know how much diplomacy"**: Author interview.

225 **"When I talked to Jill"**: Author interview.

225 **"Go fuck yourself"**: Edward-Isaac Dovere, "The Inside Story of the Biden-Harris Debate Blowup," *Politico*, May 19, 2021.

225 **"moved on"**: Talia Lakritz, "Jill Biden Says She and Kamala Harris Have 'Moved On,'" Insider.com, May 23, 2021.

226 **"a work in progress"**: Chris Whipple, *The Fight of His Life: Inside the Joe Biden White House* (New York: Scribner, 2023), 128.

226 **"She's an Italian"**: Author interview.

EPILOGUE: "THEY WANT YOU TO BE STRONG"

232 **"Because you have to"**: Author interview.

232 **"Our mother was really strong"**: Author interview.

INDEX

A B O U T   T H E   A U T H O R

KATIE ROGERS is a White House correspondent for *The New York Times*, where she has worked since 2014. She has traveled the world covering two presidential administrations, writing extensively about domestic policy, foreign policy, and the complicated dynamics of first families. A native Hoosier, Katie lives in Washington, D.C., with her husband and daughter. This is her first book.

ABOUT THE TYPE

This book was set in Caslon, a typeface first designed in 1722 by William Caslon (1692–1766). Its widespread use by most English printers in the early eighteenth century soon supplanted the Dutch typefaces that had formerly prevailed. The roman is considered a "workhorse" typeface due to its pleasant, open appearance, while the italic is exceedingly decorative.